X²³
INNOCENCE LOST

Story by Craig Kyle
Writers: Craig Kyle & Christopher Yost
Pencils: Billy Tan
Inks: Jon Sibal
Colors: Brian Haberlin
Letters: Chris Eliopoulos &
Virtual Calligraphy's Cory Petit
Assistant Editor: Cory Sedlmeier
Editor: Axel Alonso

X-23 created by Craig Kyle

Collection Editor: Jennifer Grünwald
Assistant Editor: Michael Short
Senior Editor, Special Projects: Jeff Youngquist
Vice President of Sales: David Gabriel
Production: Jerry Kalinowski
Book Designer: Dayle Chesler
Vice President of Creative: Tom Marvelli

Editor in Chief: Joe Quesada
Publisher: Dan Buckley

1

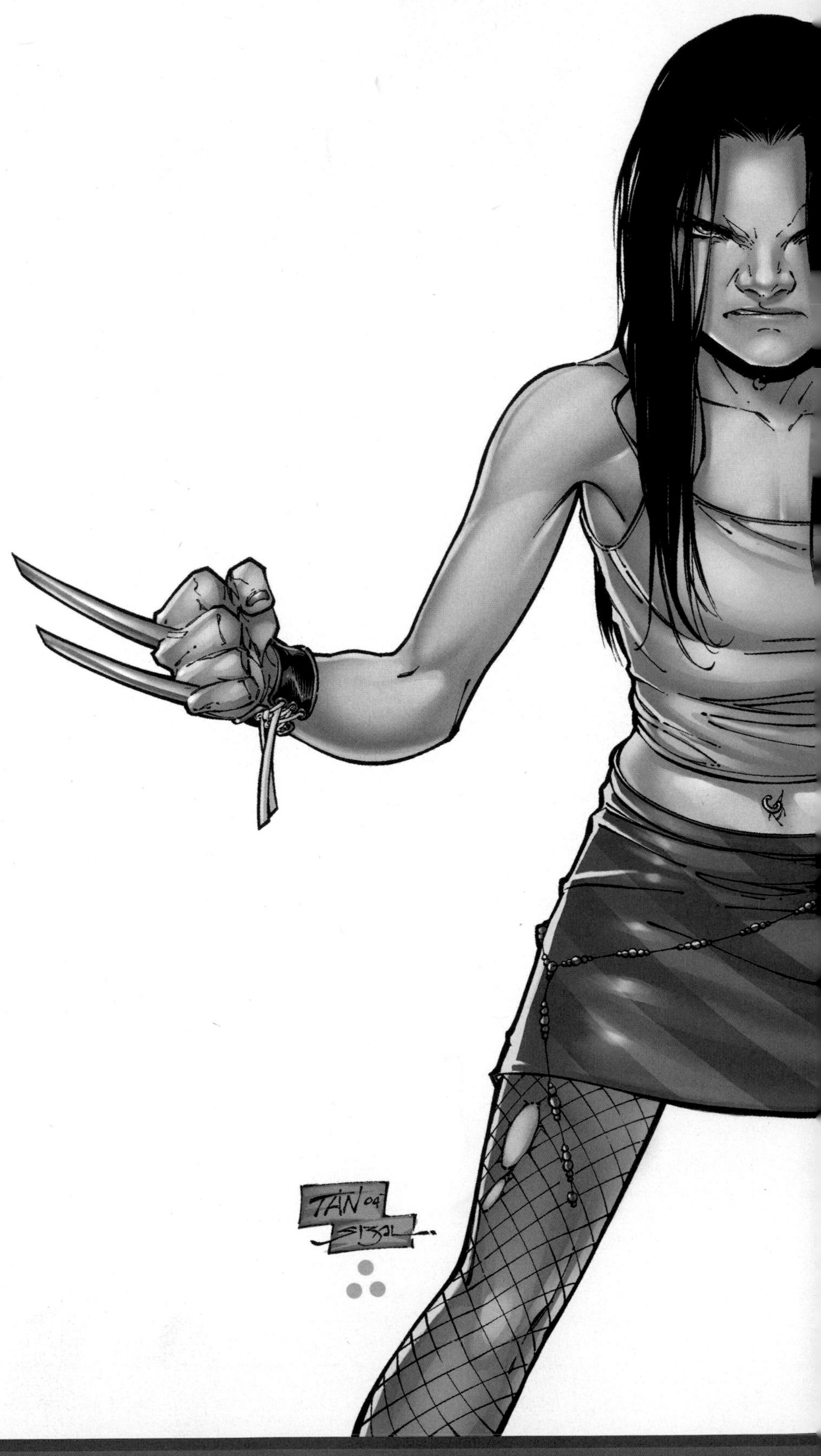

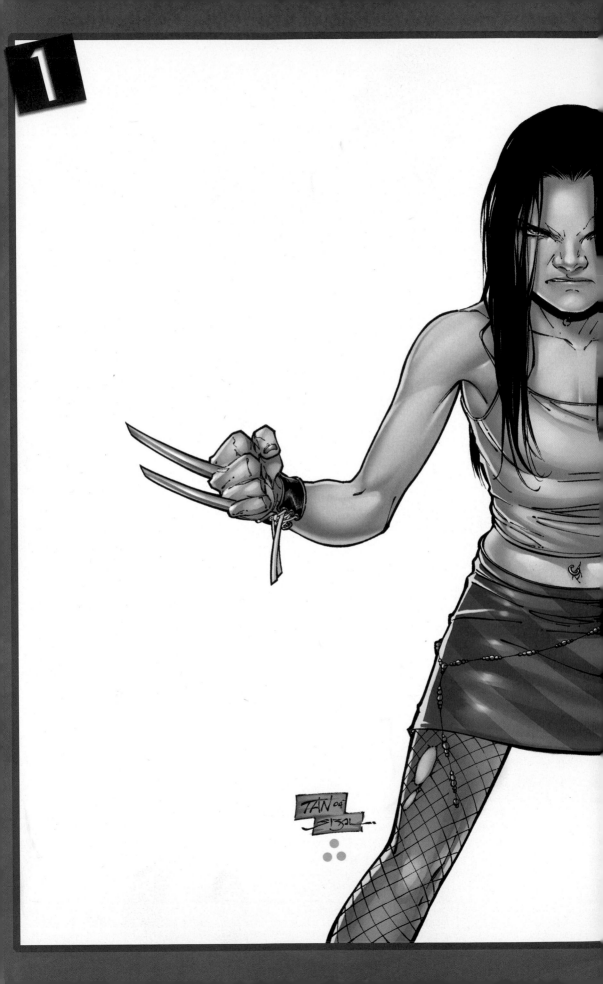

X23

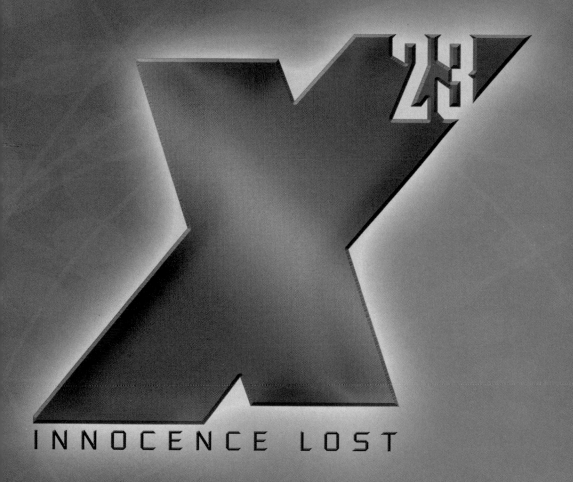

INNOCENCE LOST

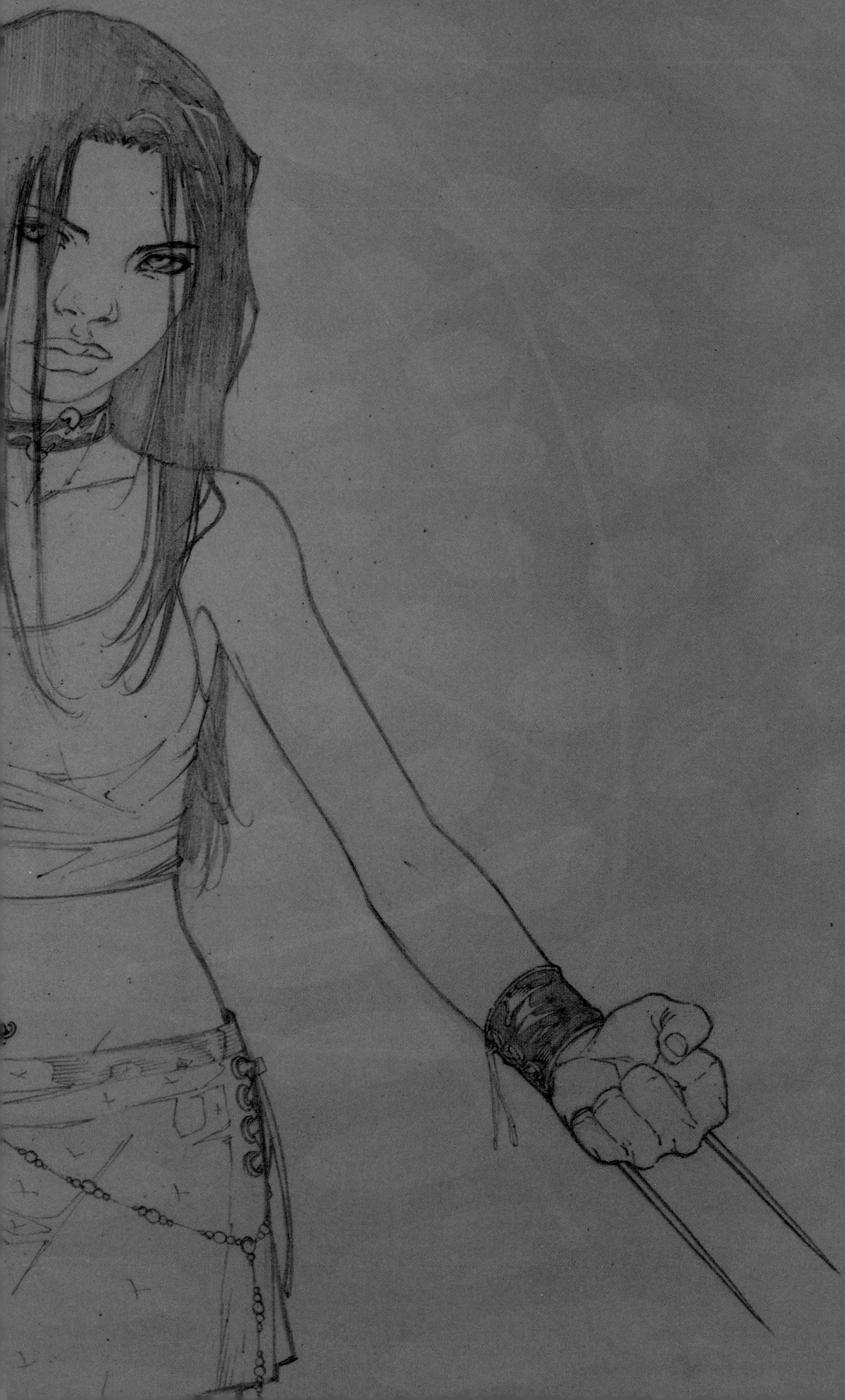

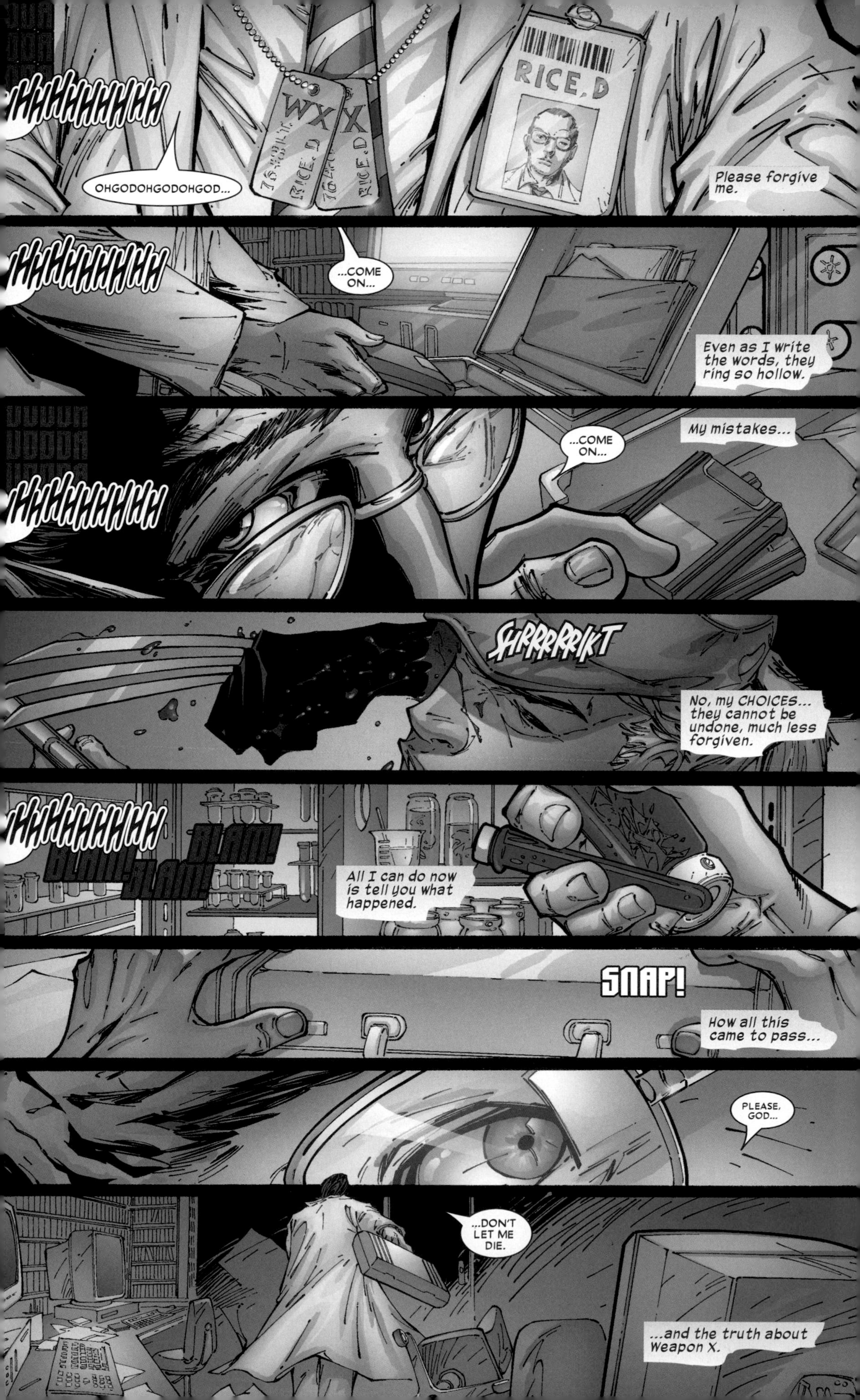
RICE, D
OHGODOHGODOHGOD...
Please forgive me.
...COME ON...
Even as I write the words, they ring so hollow.
My mistakes...
...COME ON...
SHRRRRRIKT
No, my CHOICES... they cannot be undone, much less forgiven.
BLAM! BLAM! BLAM!
All I can do now is tell you what happened.
SNAP!
How all this came to pass...
PLEASE, GOD...
...DON'T LET ME DIE.
...and the truth about Weapon X.

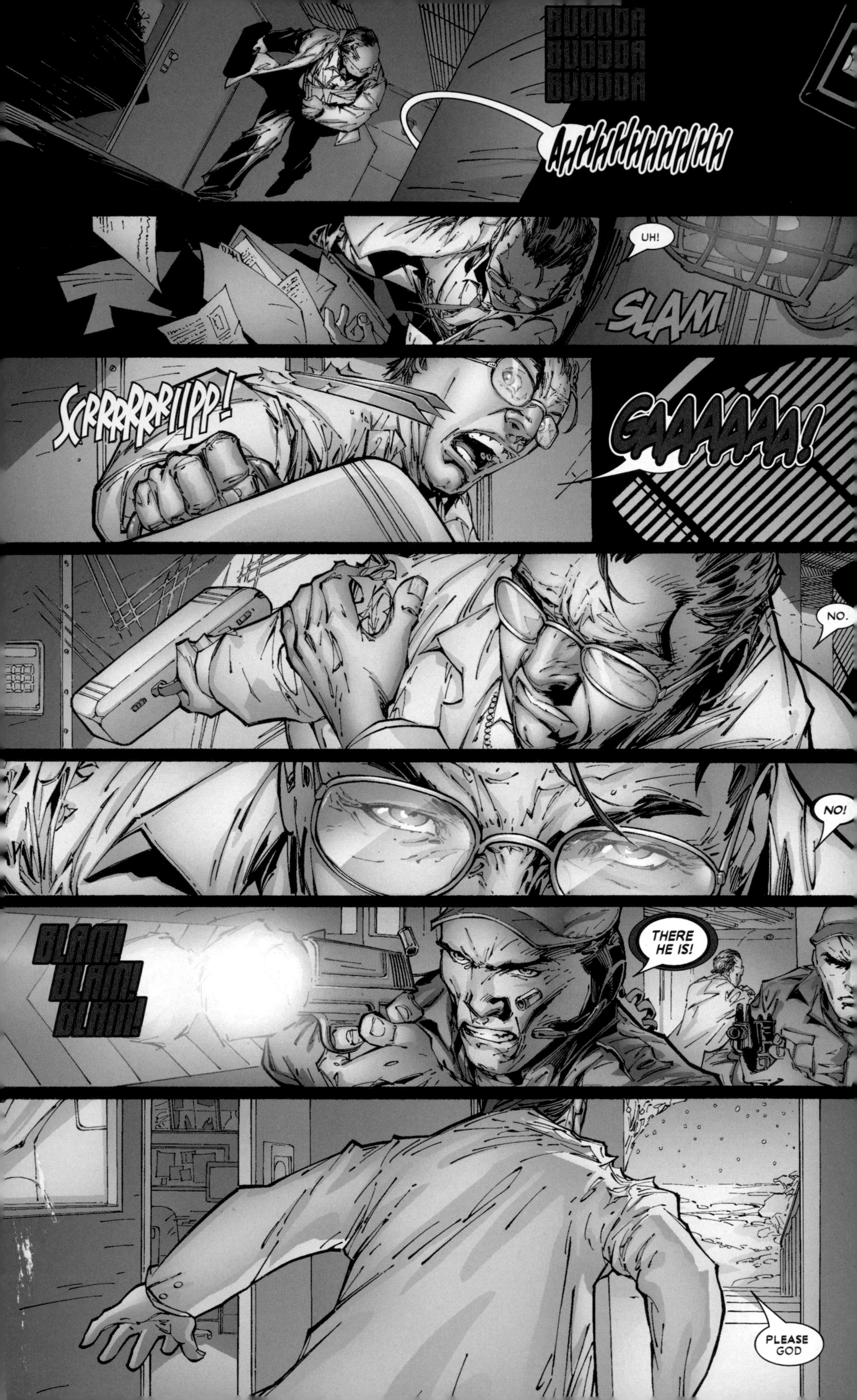
BUDDDA BUDDDA BUDDDA
AHHHHHHHHHHH
UH!
SLAM
SCRRRRRRIIPP!
GAAAAAA!
NO.
NO!
BLAM! BLAM! BLAM!
THERE HE IS!
PLEASE GOD

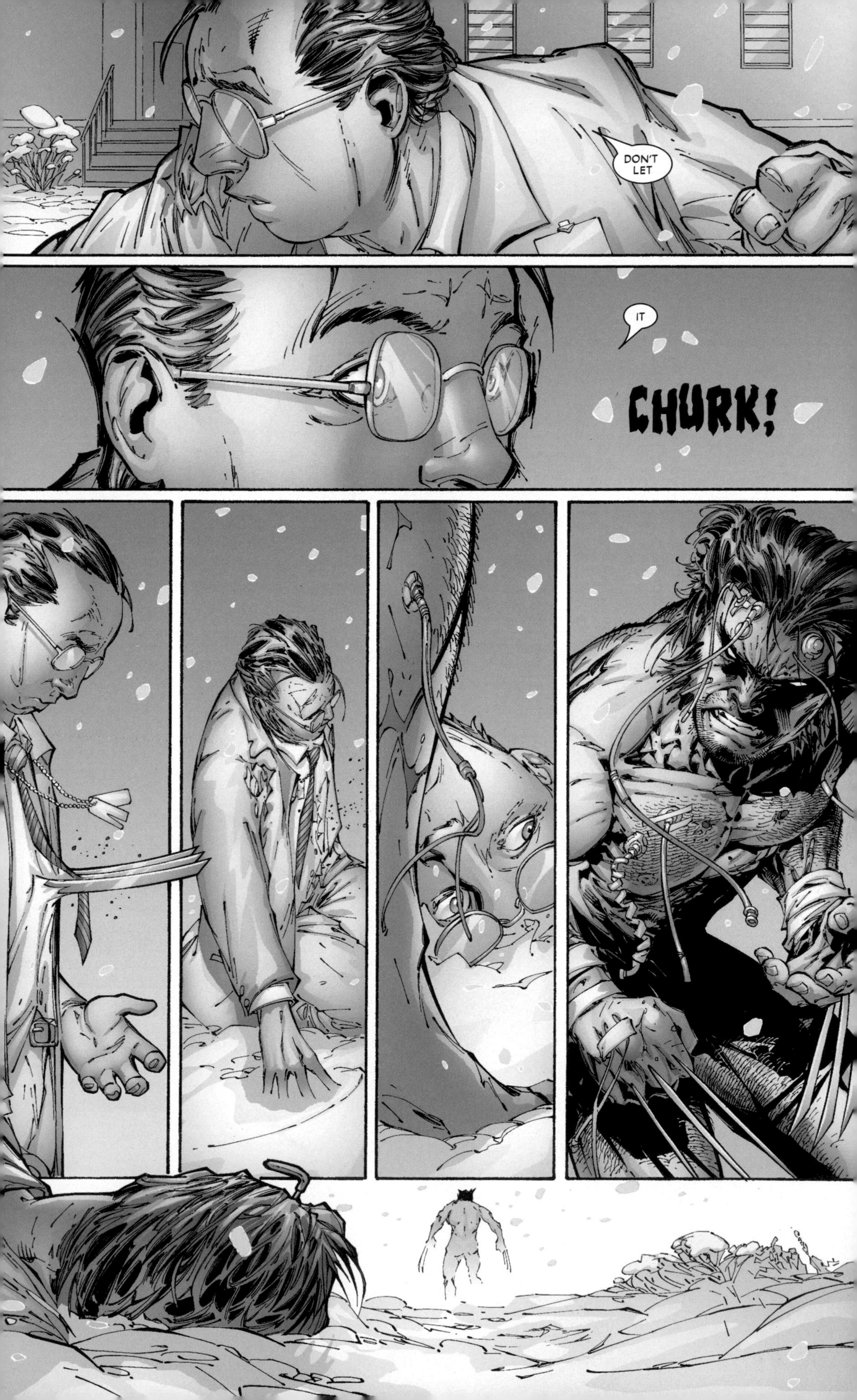
DON'T LET
IT
CHURK!

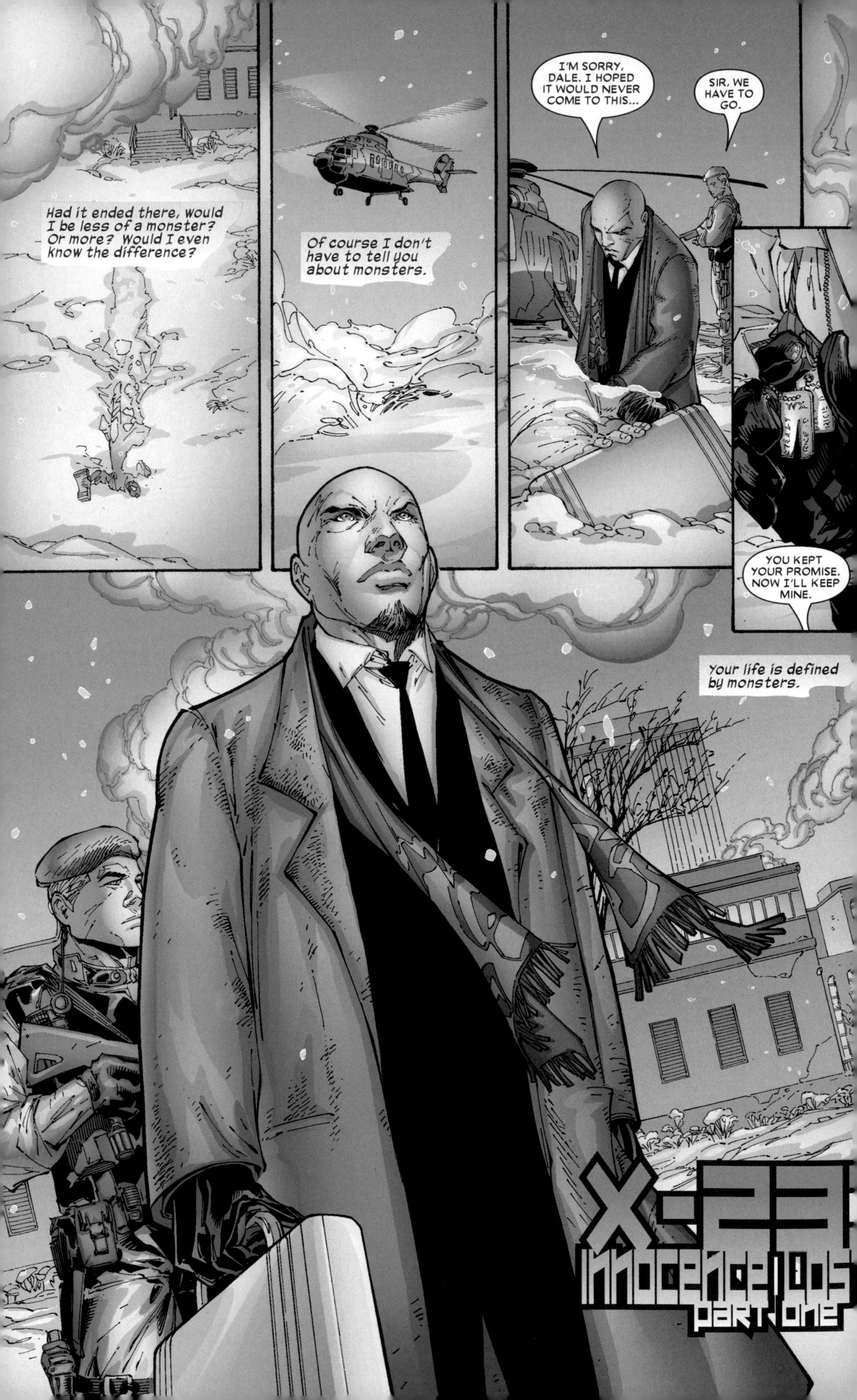

Had it ended there, would I be less of a monster? Or more? Would I even know the difference?
Of course I don't have to tell you about monsters.
I'M SORRY, DALE. I HOPED IT WOULD NEVER COME TO THIS...
SIR, WE HAVE TO GO.
YOU KEPT YOUR PROMISE. NOW I'LL KEEP MINE.
Your life is defined by monsters.
X-23
INNOCENCE LOST
PART ONE

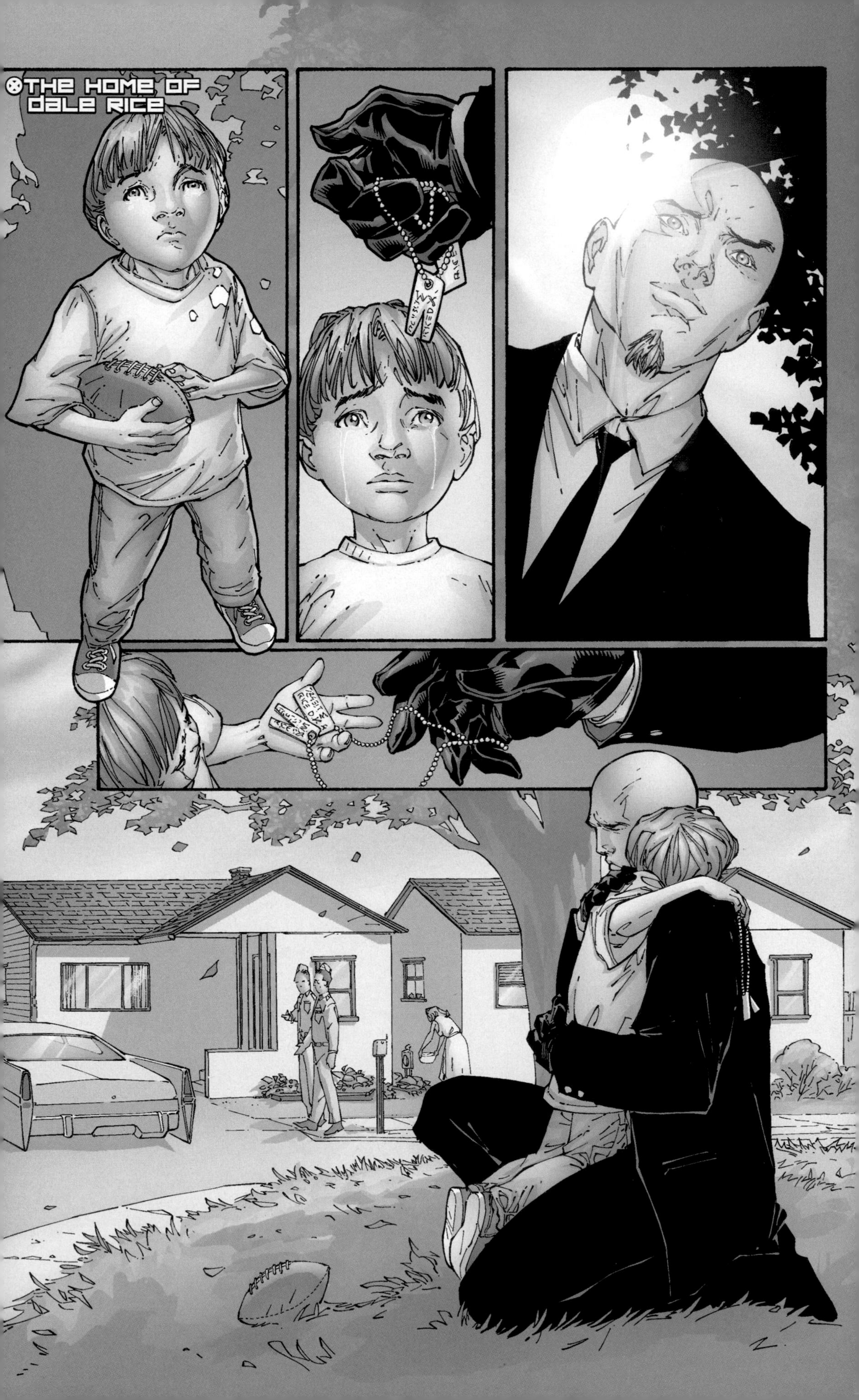
THE HOME OF DALE RICE

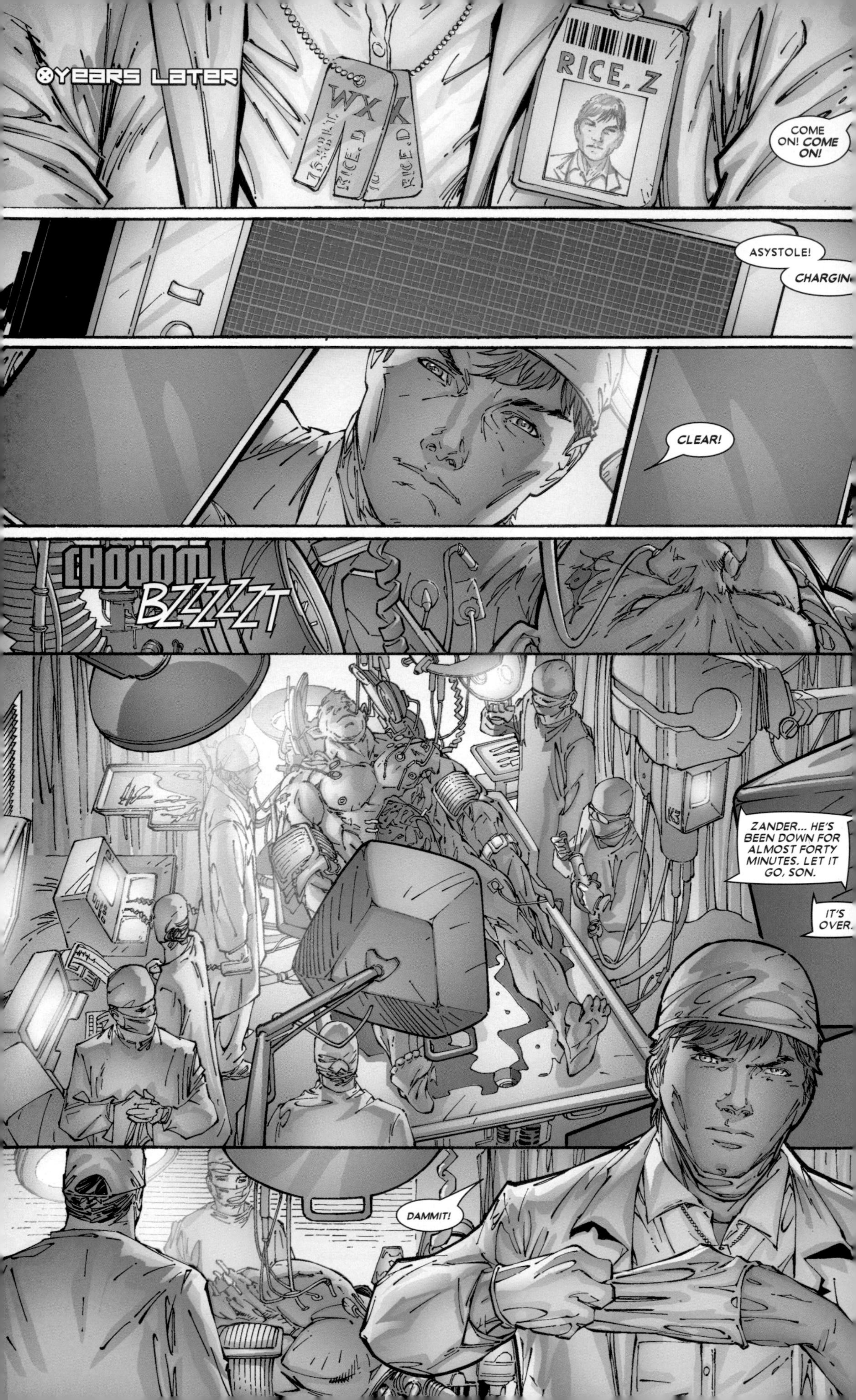
YEARS LATER
WXK
RICE, D
RICE, Z
COME ON! COME ON!
ASYSTOLE!
CHARGING
CLEAR!
CHOOOM
BZZZZZT
ZANDER... HE'S BEEN DOWN FOR ALMOST FORTY MINUTES. LET IT GO, SON.
IT'S OVER.
DAMMIT!

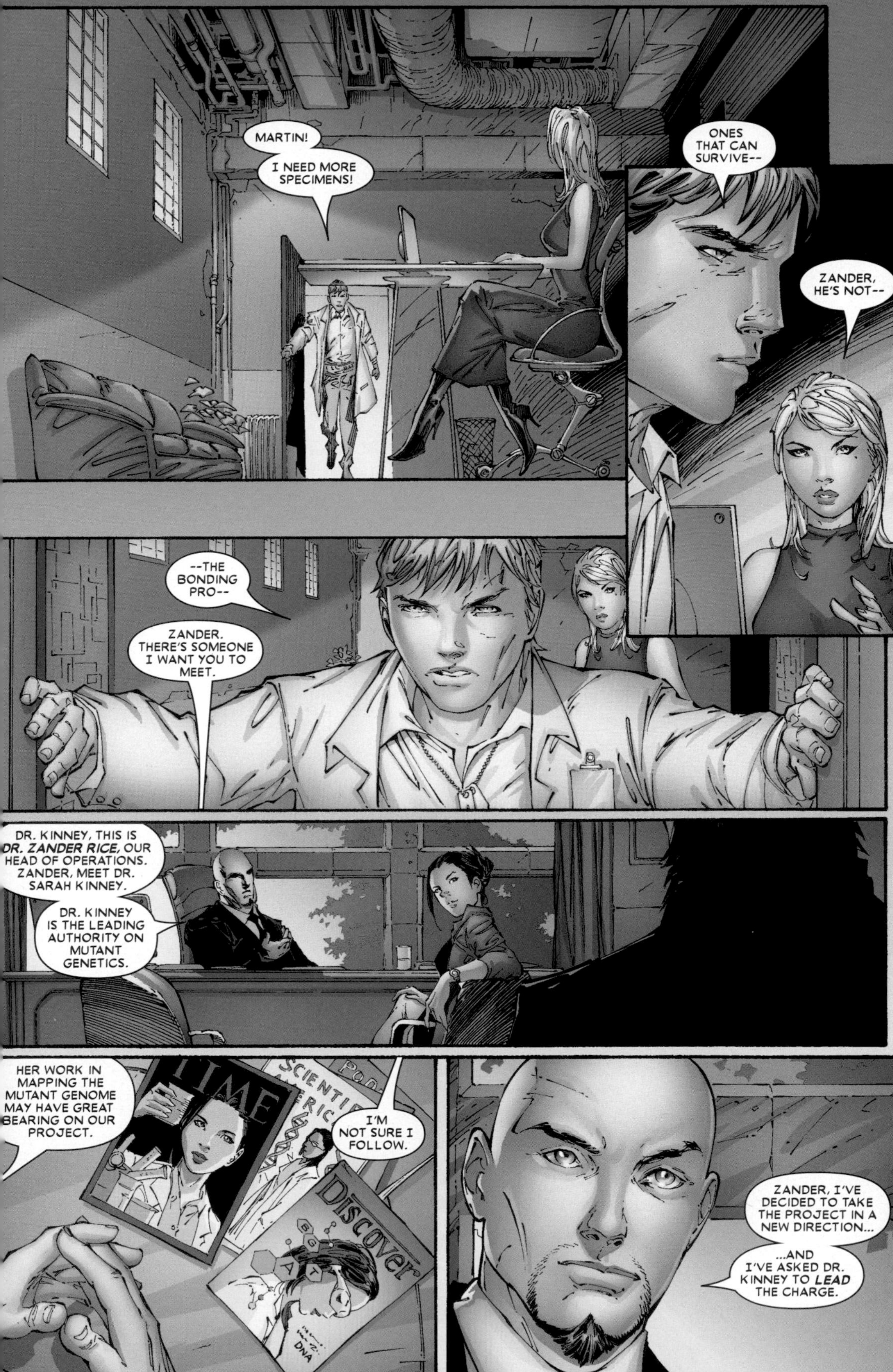
MARTIN!
I NEED MORE SPECIMENS!
ONES THAT CAN SURVIVE--
ZANDER, HE'S NOT--
--THE BONDING PRO--
ZANDER. THERE'S SOMEONE I WANT YOU TO MEET.
DR. KINNEY, THIS IS DR. ZANDER RICE, OUR HEAD OF OPERATIONS. ZANDER, MEET DR. SARAH KINNEY.
DR. KINNEY IS THE LEADING AUTHORITY ON MUTANT GENETICS.
TIME
SCIENTIFIC AMERICAN
Discover
DNA
HER WORK IN MAPPING THE MUTANT GENOME MAY HAVE GREAT BEARING ON OUR PROJECT.
I'M NOT SURE I FOLLOW.
ZANDER, I'VE DECIDED TO TAKE THE PROJECT IN A NEW DIRECTION...
...AND I'VE ASKED DR. KINNEY TO LEAD THE CHARGE.

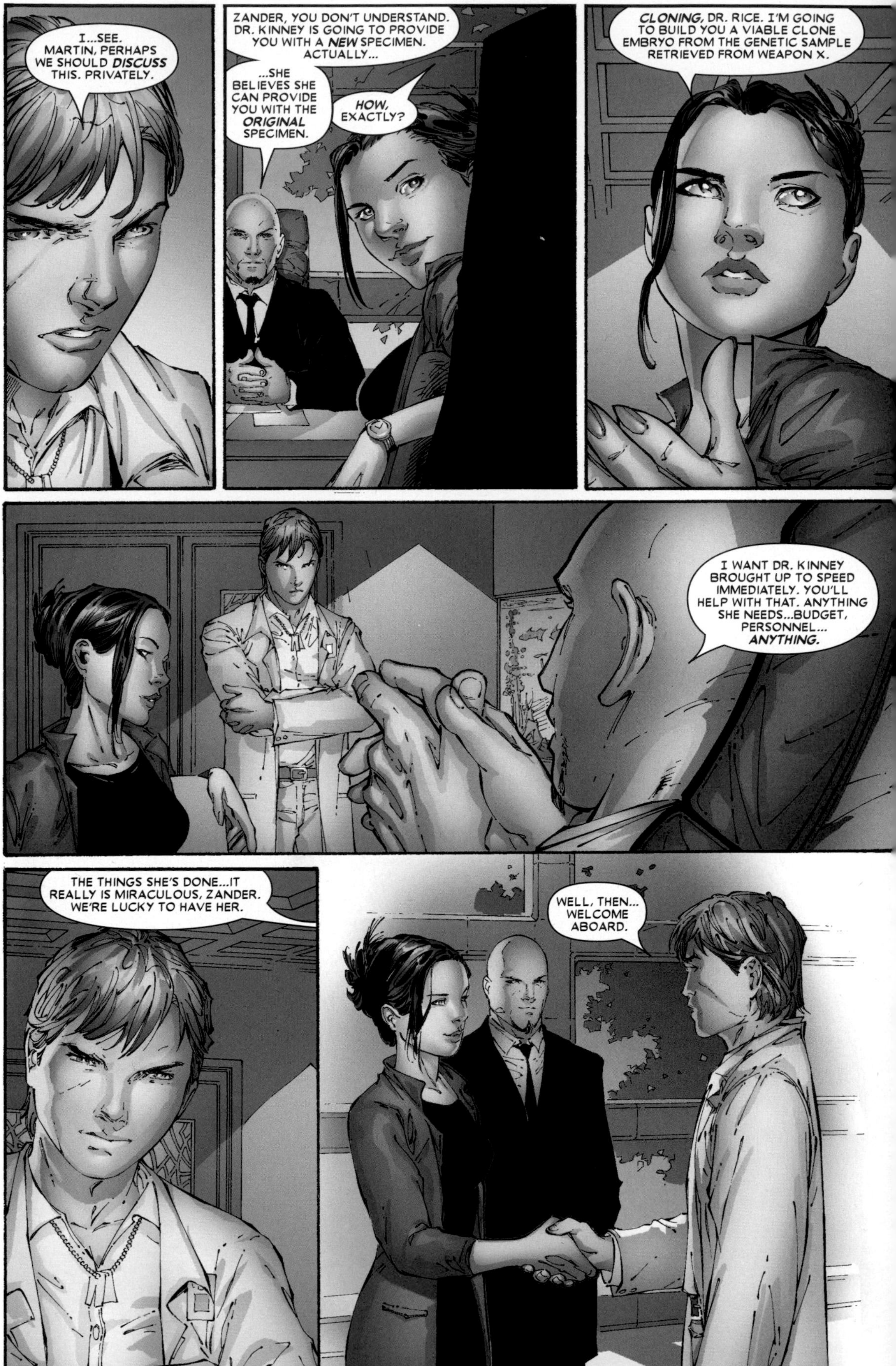
I...SEE. MARTIN, PERHAPS WE SHOULD DISCUSS THIS. PRIVATELY.
ZANDER, YOU DON'T UNDERSTAND. DR. KINNEY IS GOING TO PROVIDE YOU WITH A NEW SPECIMEN. ACTUALLY...
...SHE BELIEVES SHE CAN PROVIDE YOU WITH THE ORIGINAL SPECIMEN.
HOW, EXACTLY?
CLONING, DR. RICE. I'M GOING TO BUILD YOU A VIABLE CLONE EMBRYO FROM THE GENETIC SAMPLE RETRIEVED FROM WEAPON X.
I WANT DR. KINNEY BROUGHT UP TO SPEED IMMEDIATELY. YOU'LL HELP WITH THAT. ANYTHING SHE NEEDS...BUDGET, PERSONNEL... ANYTHING.
THE THINGS SHE'S DONE...IT REALLY IS MIRACULOUS, ZANDER. WE'RE LUCKY TO HAVE HER.
WELL, THEN... WELCOME ABOARD.

"UNLIMITED RESOURCES AND NO POLITICAL OR LEGAL RESTRAINTS ON YOUR WORK. *THAT'S* WHAT WE HAVE TO OFFER, DR. KINNEY..."

...HOWEVER, THERE ARE *SACRIFICES* INVOLVED. WE'VE ALL MADE THEM. PHYSICALLY, YOU'D BE TOTALLY CUT OFF FROM THE OUTSIDE WORLD, ALTHOUGH YOU CAN STILL RECEIVE MAIL AND PHONE CALLS THROUGH OUR ROUTING SYSTEM. AND OF COURSE YOU'D BE COMMITTED FOR THE LIFE OF THE PROJECT.

I ALSO NEED TO KNOW IF YOU CAN LIVE WITH THE MORAL IMPLICATIONS OF WHAT YOU'D BE DOING HERE.

NO GOVERNMENT INTERFERENCE. REMIND ME TO NEVER ASK HOW YOU MANAGE THAT.

"MORAL IMPLICATIONS? AND HERE I THOUGHT WE WERE TALKING ABOUT *SCIENCE.*"

POLICE REPORT.

OFFICERS WERE CALLED IN REPONSE TO AN ANONYMOUS TIP REGARDING SUSPECTED CHILD ABUSE. WHEN QUESTIONED, THE ALLEGED VICTIM - SARAH KINNEY (AGE 9) WAS NON RESPONSIVE. NO APPARENT PHYSICAL SIGNS OF ABUSE PRESENT. AND SUBSEQUENT QUESTIONING OF ALLEGED VICTIM'S FATHER - RON KINNEY - AND MOTHER - LESLIE KINNEY - AS WELL AS FEMALE SIBLING DEBORAH KINNEY ALL DENIED ANY ALLEGATIONS OF ABUSE OCCURING IN HOME. AFTER SUSTAINED QUESTIONING, ALLEGED VICTIM WOULD NOT CONFIRM ANY ABUSE OCCURRED. PER PROCEDURE, WITHOUT SUBSTANTIVE EVIDENCE, REFERRED CASE TO DEPARTMENT OF CHILD AND FAMILY SERVICES...

"DR. SUTTER, I APPRECIATE YOUR CONCERN, BUT I'D WORRY MORE ABOUT YOUR MAN RICE CONSIDERING HIS WARM RECEPTION IN YOUR OFFICE."

"SHARING CONTROL WON'T BE EASY FOR HIM. HE'LL NEED TIME TO ADJUST. YOU HAVE TO UNDERSTAND...THE PROJECT WOULDN'T *EXIST* WITHOUT ZANDER'S FATHER."

"HE RETRIEVED THE SAMPLE YOU'LL BE WORKING WITH. AT THE COST OF HIS LIFE."

OLICE REPOR

ALLED IN REPONSE TO
GARDING SUSPECTE
TIONED, THE ALLEGE
) WAS NONRESPONS
IGNS OF ABUSE PRE
TIONING OF

WE ALL MAKE SACRIFICES.

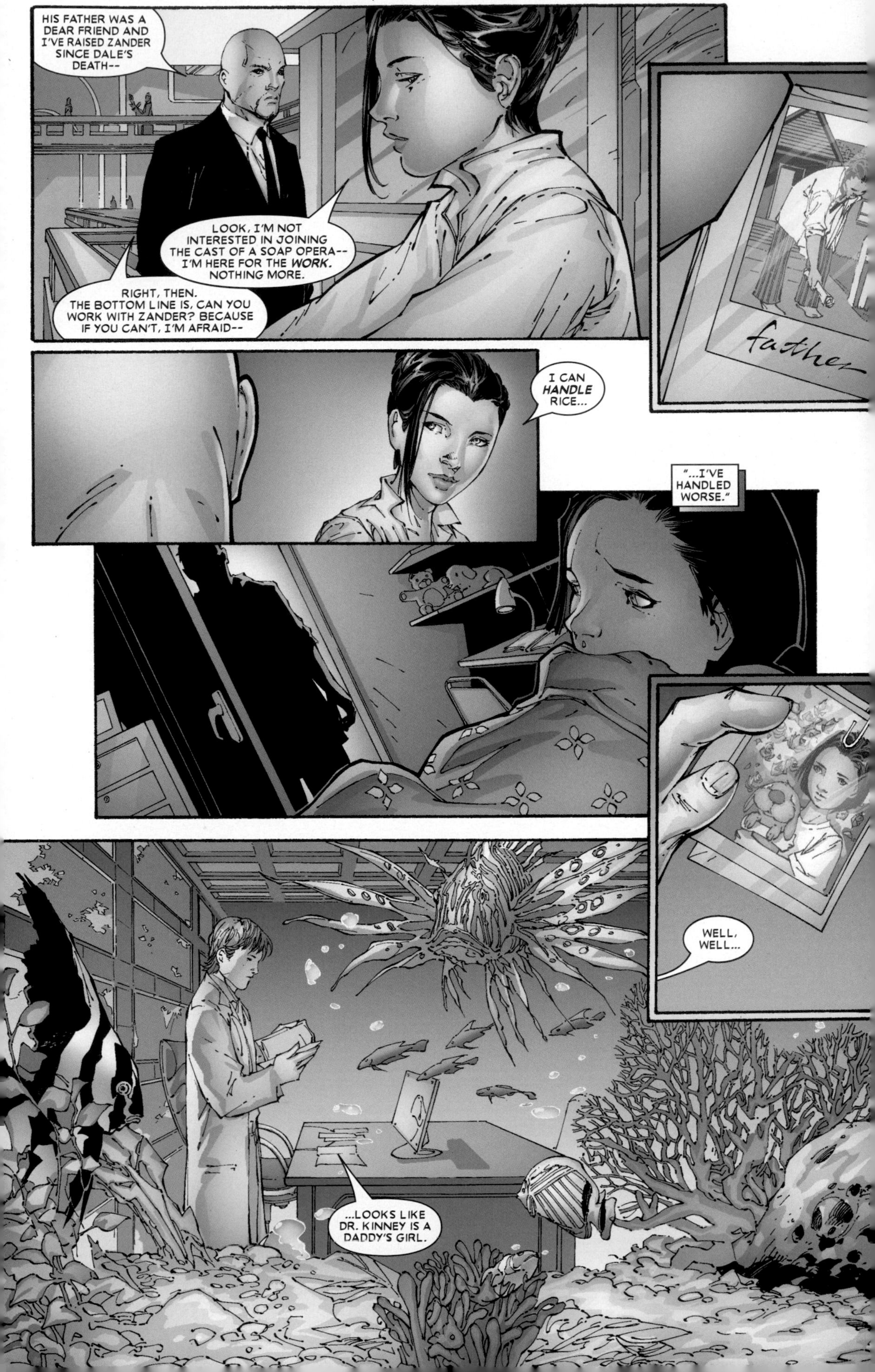
HIS FATHER WAS A DEAR FRIEND AND I'VE RAISED ZANDER SINCE DALE'S DEATH--
LOOK, I'M NOT INTERESTED IN JOINING THE CAST OF A SOAP OPERA-- I'M HERE FOR THE WORK. NOTHING MORE.
RIGHT, THEN. THE BOTTOM LINE IS, CAN YOU WORK WITH ZANDER? BECAUSE IF YOU CAN'T, I'M AFRAID--
father
I CAN HANDLE RICE...
"...I'VE HANDLED WORSE."
WELL, WELL...
...LOOKS LIKE DR. KINNEY IS A DADDY'S GIRL.

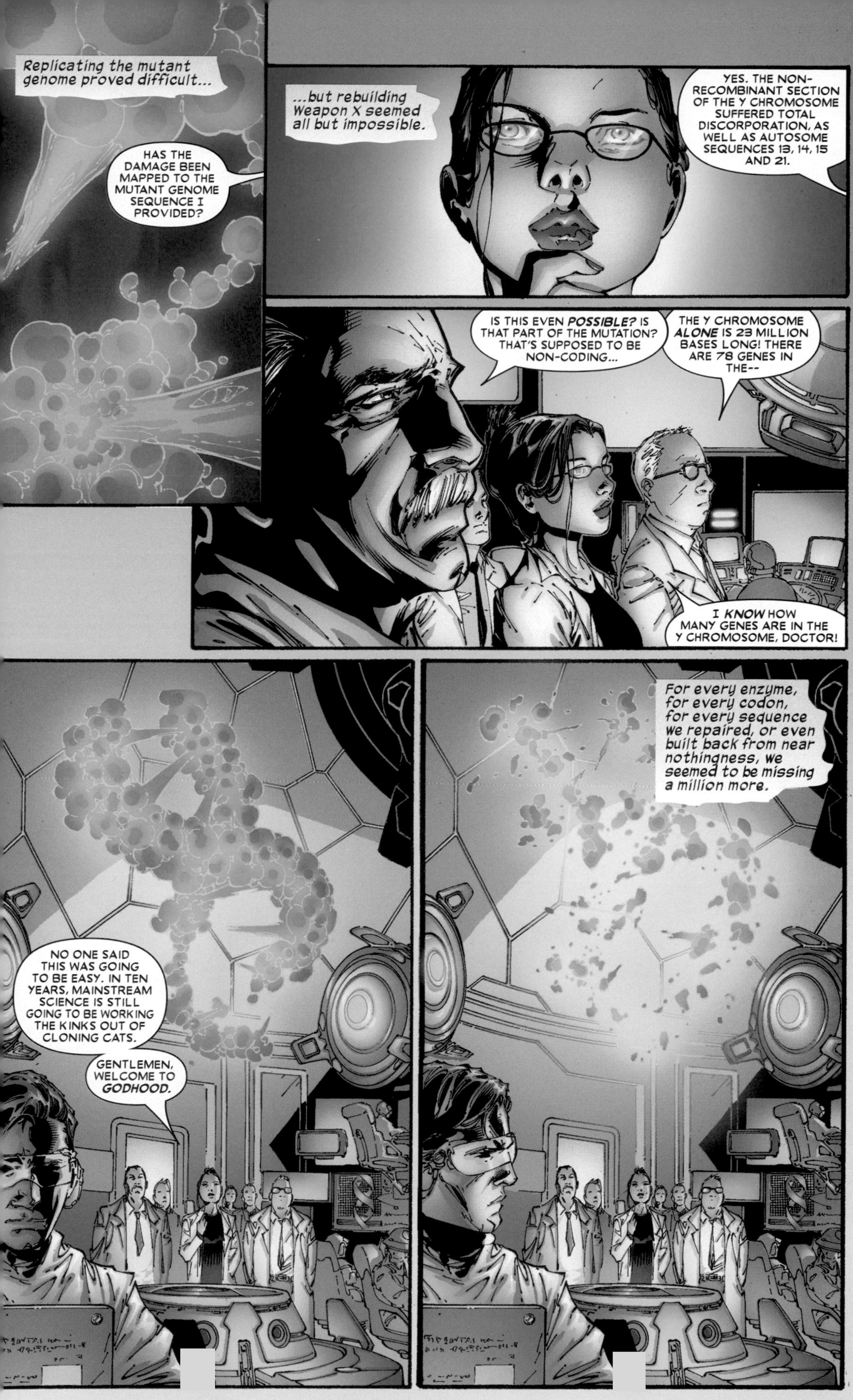

Replicating the mutant genome proved difficult...
HAS THE DAMAGE BEEN MAPPED TO THE MUTANT GENOME SEQUENCE I PROVIDED?
...but rebuilding Weapon X seemed all but impossible.
YES. THE NON-RECOMBINANT SECTION OF THE Y CHROMOSOME SUFFERED TOTAL DISCORPORATION, AS WELL AS AUTOSOME SEQUENCES 13, 14, 15 AND 21.
IS THIS EVEN POSSIBLE? IS THAT PART OF THE MUTATION? THAT'S SUPPOSED TO BE NON-CODING...
THE Y CHROMOSOME ALONE IS 23 MILLION BASES LONG! THERE ARE 78 GENES IN THE--
I KNOW HOW MANY GENES ARE IN THE Y CHROMOSOME, DOCTOR!
NO ONE SAID THIS WAS GOING TO BE EASY. IN TEN YEARS, MAINSTREAM SCIENCE IS STILL GOING TO BE WORKING THE KINKS OUT OF CLONING CATS.
GENTLEMEN, WELCOME TO GODHOOD.
For every enzyme, for every codon, for every sequence we repaired, or even built back from near nothingness, we seemed to be missing a million more.

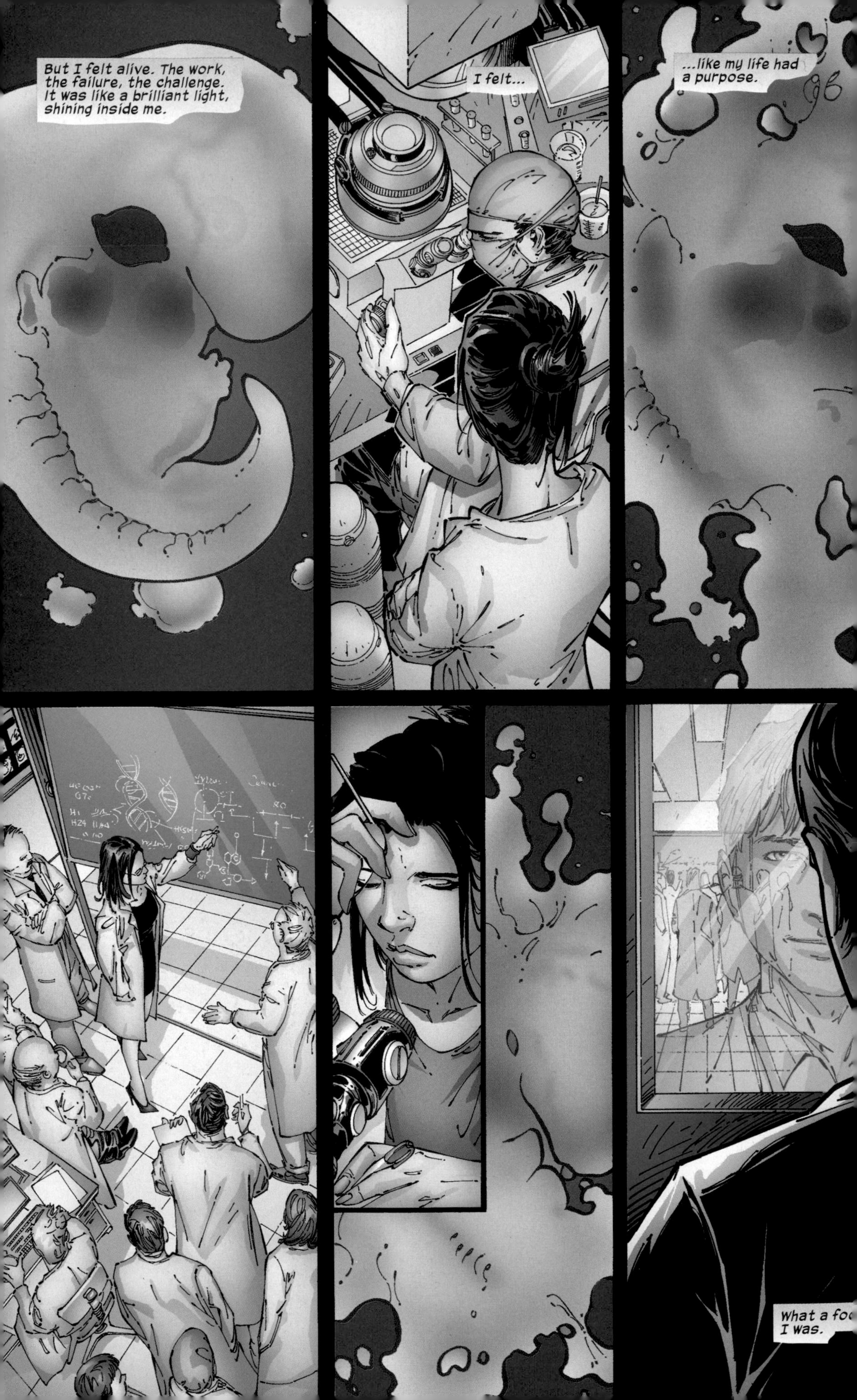

But I felt alive. The work, the failure, the challenge. It was like a brilliant light, shining inside me.
I felt...
...like my life had a purpose.
What a fo
I was.

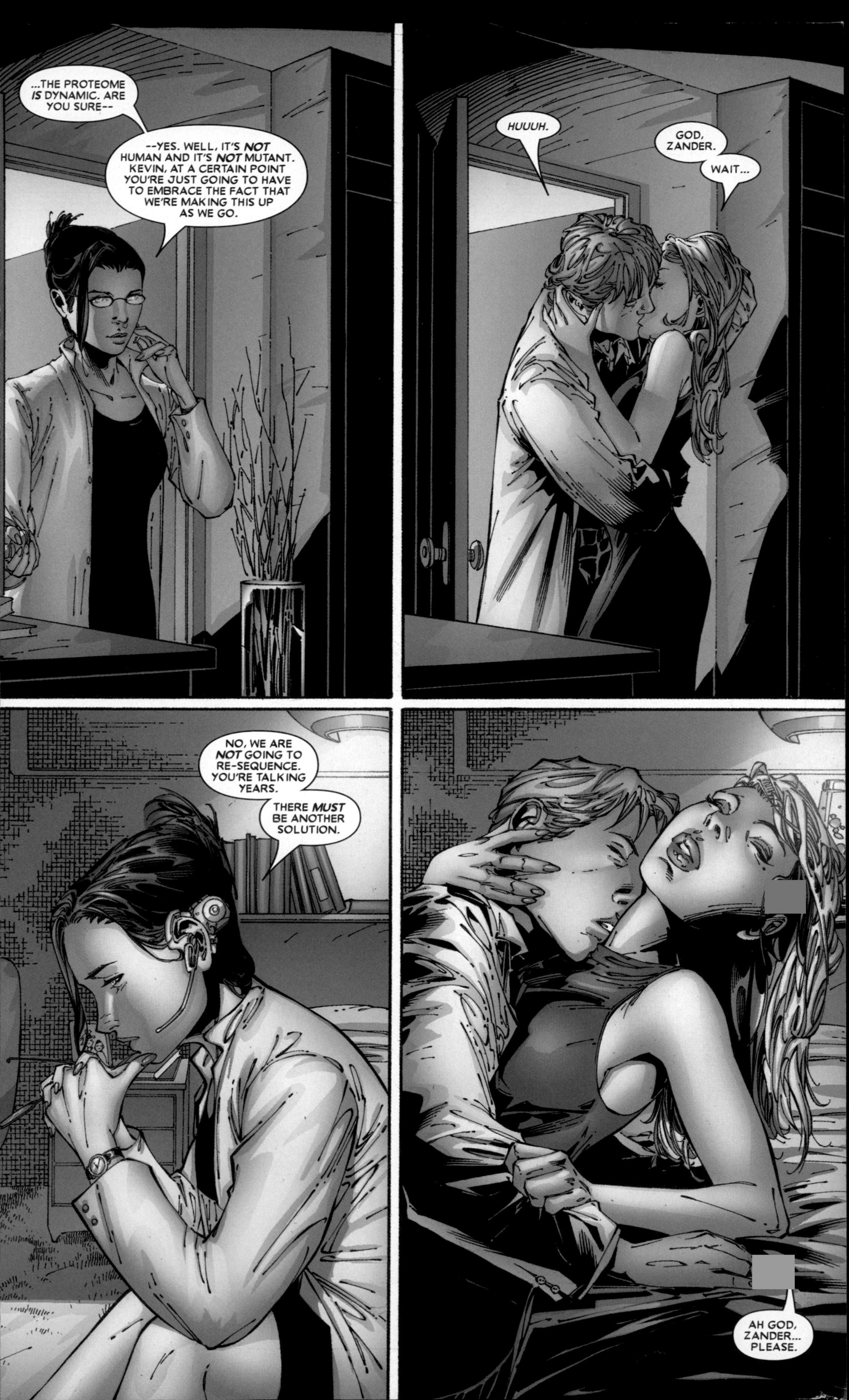
...THE PROTEOME *IS* DYNAMIC. ARE YOU SURE--
--YES. WELL, IT'S *NOT* HUMAN AND IT'S *NOT* MUTANT. KEVIN, AT A CERTAIN POINT YOU'RE JUST GOING TO HAVE TO EMBRACE THE FACT THAT WE'RE MAKING THIS UP AS WE GO.
HUUUH.
GOD, ZANDER.
WAIT...
NO, WE ARE *NOT* GOING TO RE-SEQUENCE. YOU'RE TALKING YEARS.
THERE *MUST* BE ANOTHER SOLUTION.
AH GOD, ZANDER... PLEASE.

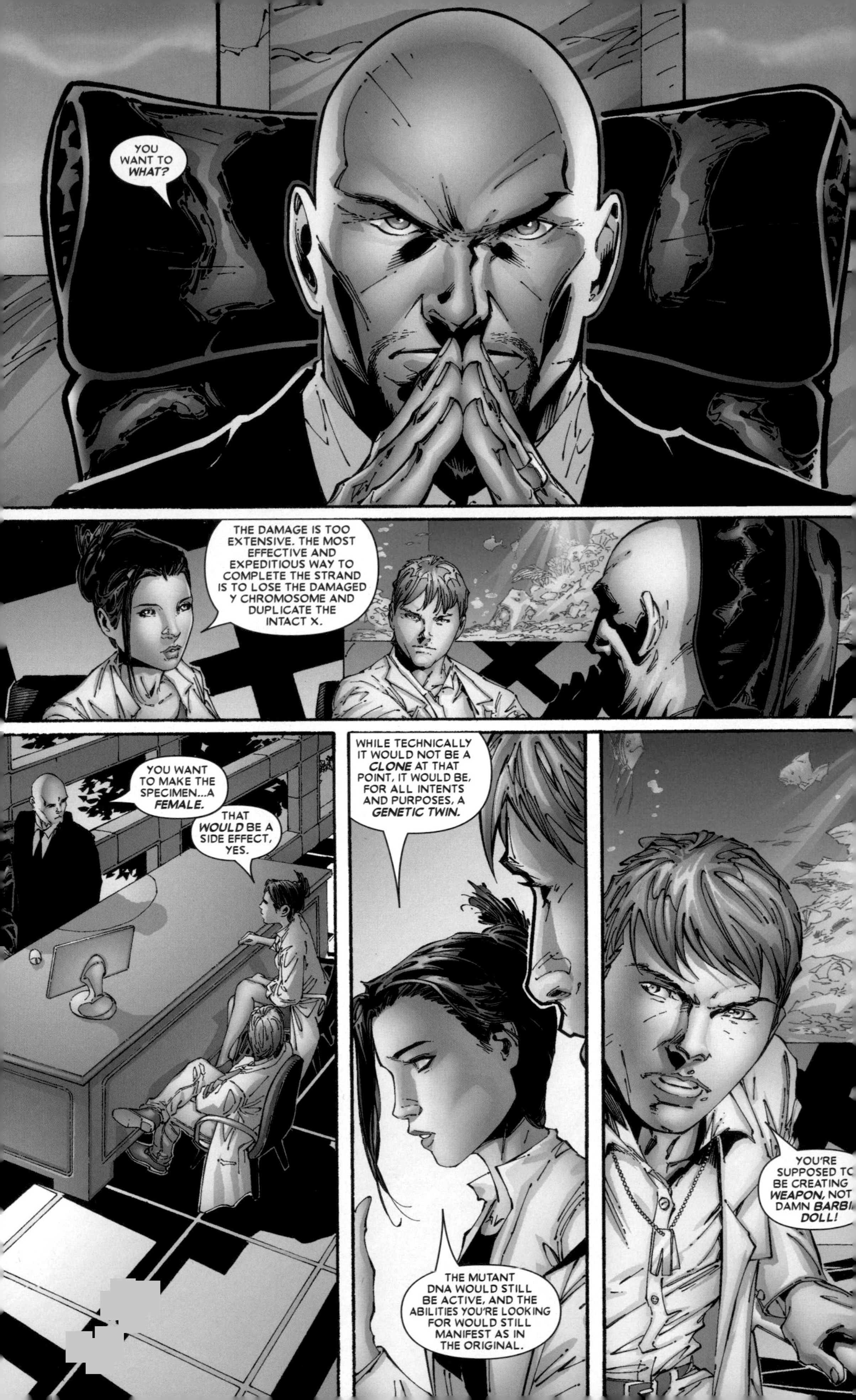

YOU WANT TO WHAT?
THE DAMAGE IS TOO EXTENSIVE. THE MOST EFFECTIVE AND EXPEDITIOUS WAY TO COMPLETE THE STRAND IS TO LOSE THE DAMAGED Y CHROMOSOME AND DUPLICATE THE INTACT X.
YOU WANT TO MAKE THE SPECIMEN...A FEMALE.
THAT WOULD BE A SIDE EFFECT, YES.
WHILE TECHNICALLY IT WOULD NOT BE A CLONE AT THAT POINT, IT WOULD BE, FOR ALL INTENTS AND PURPOSES, A GENETIC TWIN.
THE MUTANT DNA WOULD STILL BE ACTIVE, AND THE ABILITIES YOU'RE LOOKING FOR WOULD STILL MANIFEST AS IN THE ORIGINAL.
YOU'RE SUPPOSED TO BE CREATING WEAPON, NOT DAMN BARBI DOLL!

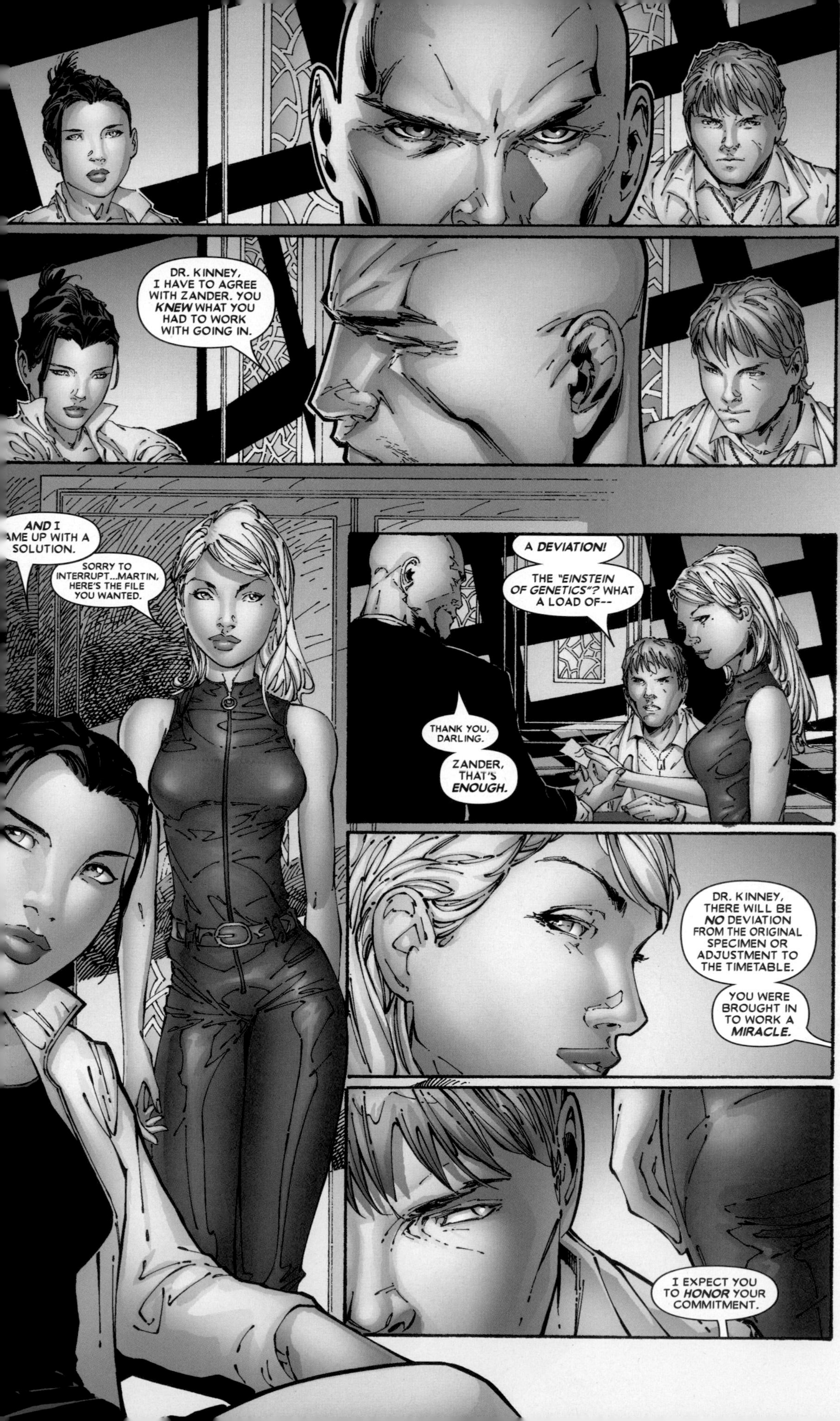
DR. KINNEY, I HAVE TO AGREE WITH ZANDER. YOU *KNEW* WHAT YOU HAD TO WORK WITH GOING IN.
AND I AME UP WITH A SOLUTION.
SORRY TO INTERRUPT...MARTIN, HERE'S THE FILE YOU WANTED.
A *DEVIATION!*
THE *"EINSTEIN OF GENETICS"*? WHAT A LOAD OF--
THANK YOU, DARLING.
ZANDER, THAT'S *ENOUGH.*
DR. KINNEY, THERE WILL BE *NO* DEVIATION FROM THE ORIGINAL SPECIMEN OR ADJUSTMENT TO THE TIMETABLE.
YOU WERE BROUGHT IN TO WORK A *MIRACLE.*
I EXPECT YOU TO *HONOR* YOUR COMMITMENT.

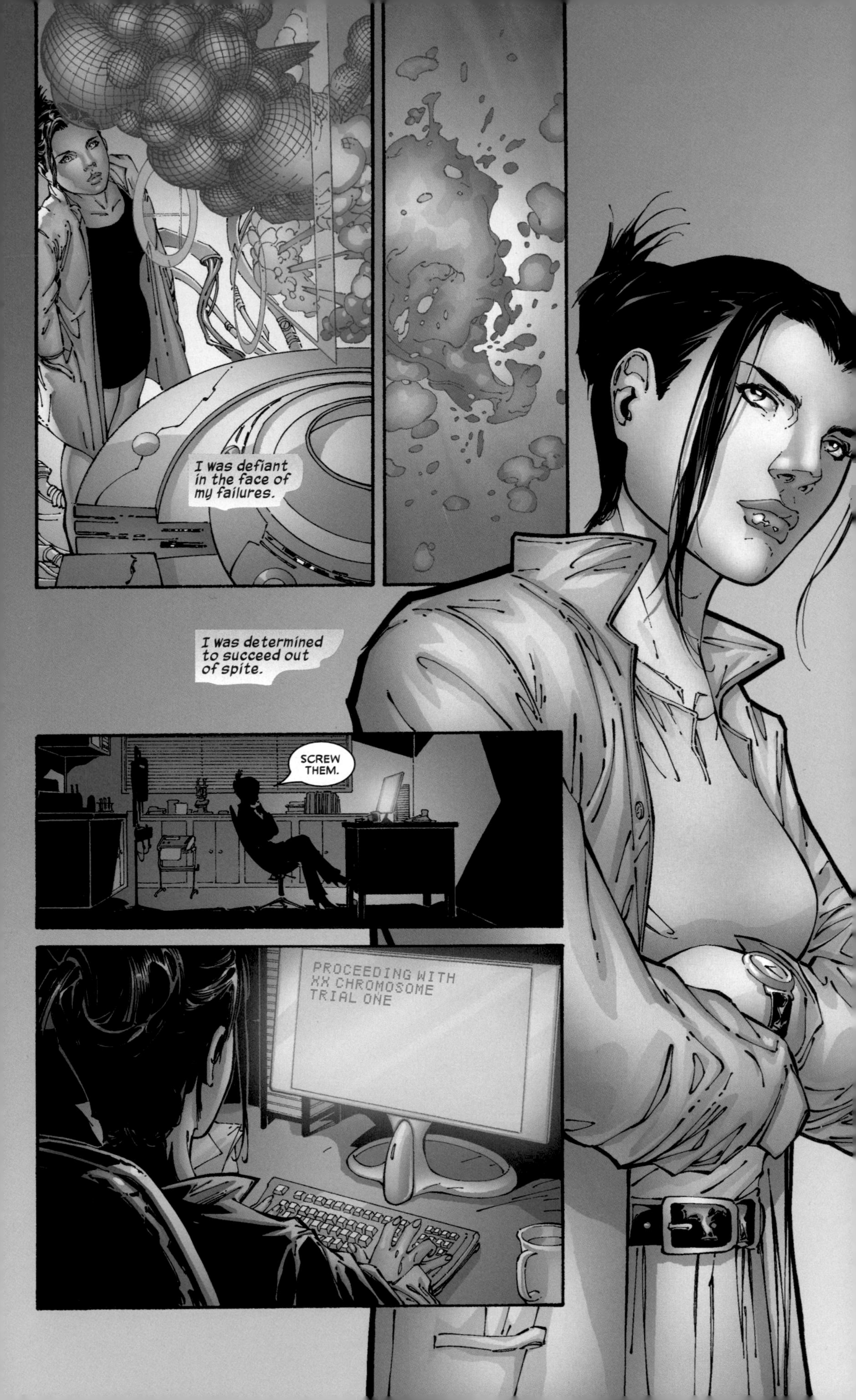
I was defiant in the face of my failures.
I was determined to succeed out of spite.
SCREW THEM.
PROCEEDING WITH XX CHROMOSOME TRIAL ONE

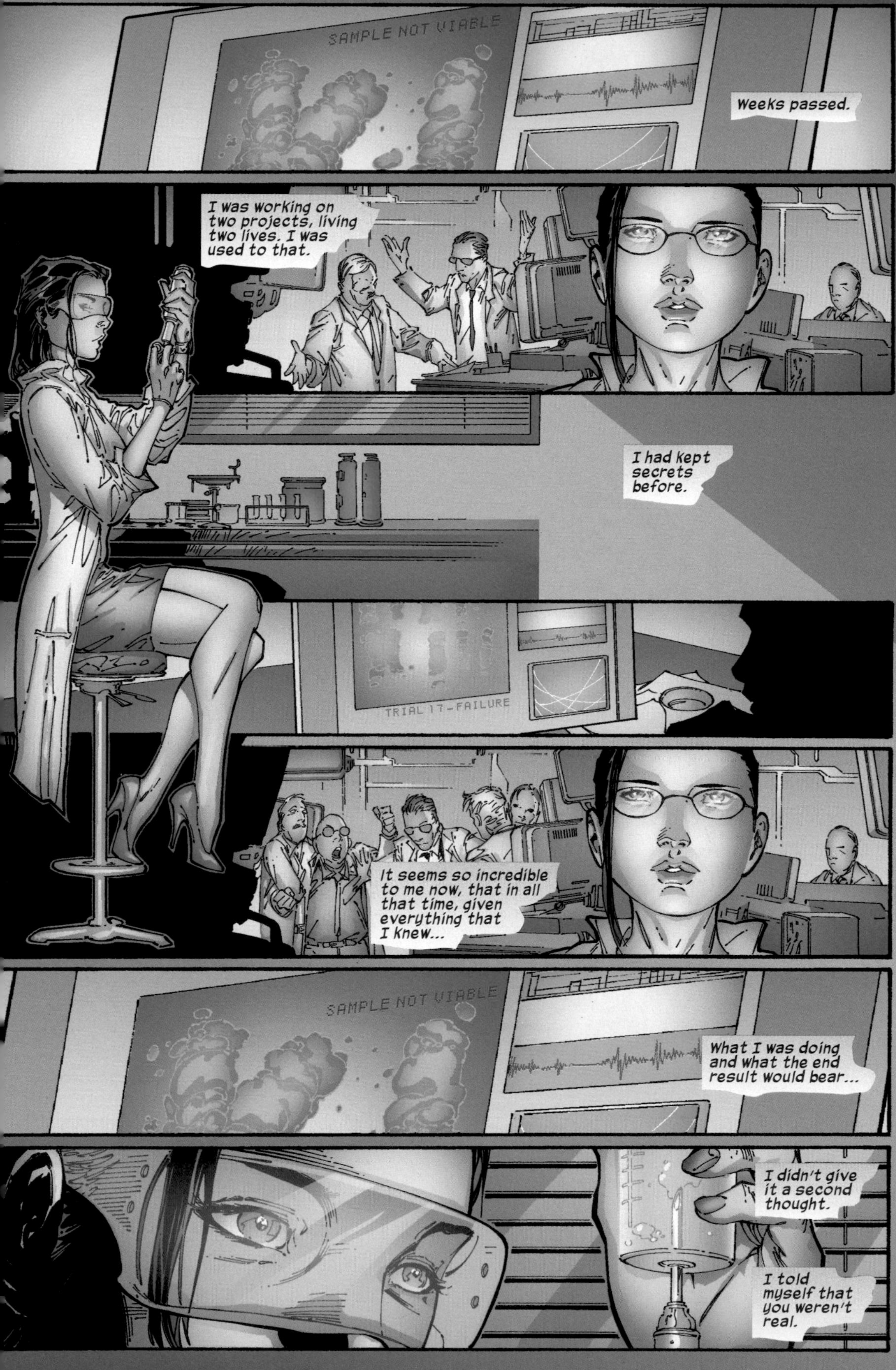
SAMPLE NOT VIABLE
Weeks passed.
I was working on two projects, living two lives. I was used to that.
I had kept secrets before.
TRIAL 17-FAILURE
It seems so incredible to me now, that in all that time, given everything that I knew...
SAMPLE NOT VIABLE
What I was doing and what the end result would bear...
I didn't give it a second thought.
I told myself that you weren't real.

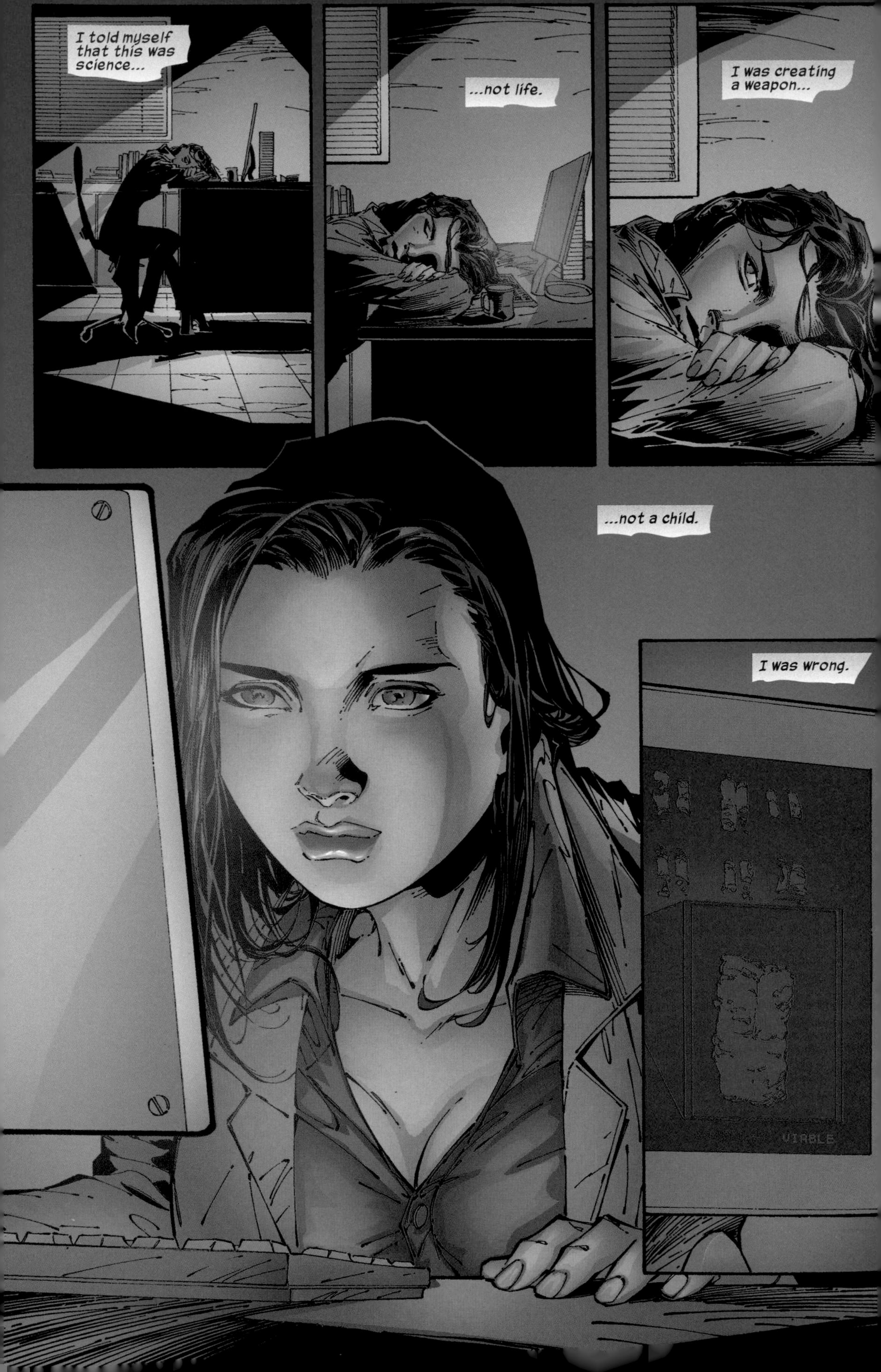

I told myself that this was science...
...not life.
I was creating a weapon...
...not a child.
I was wrong.

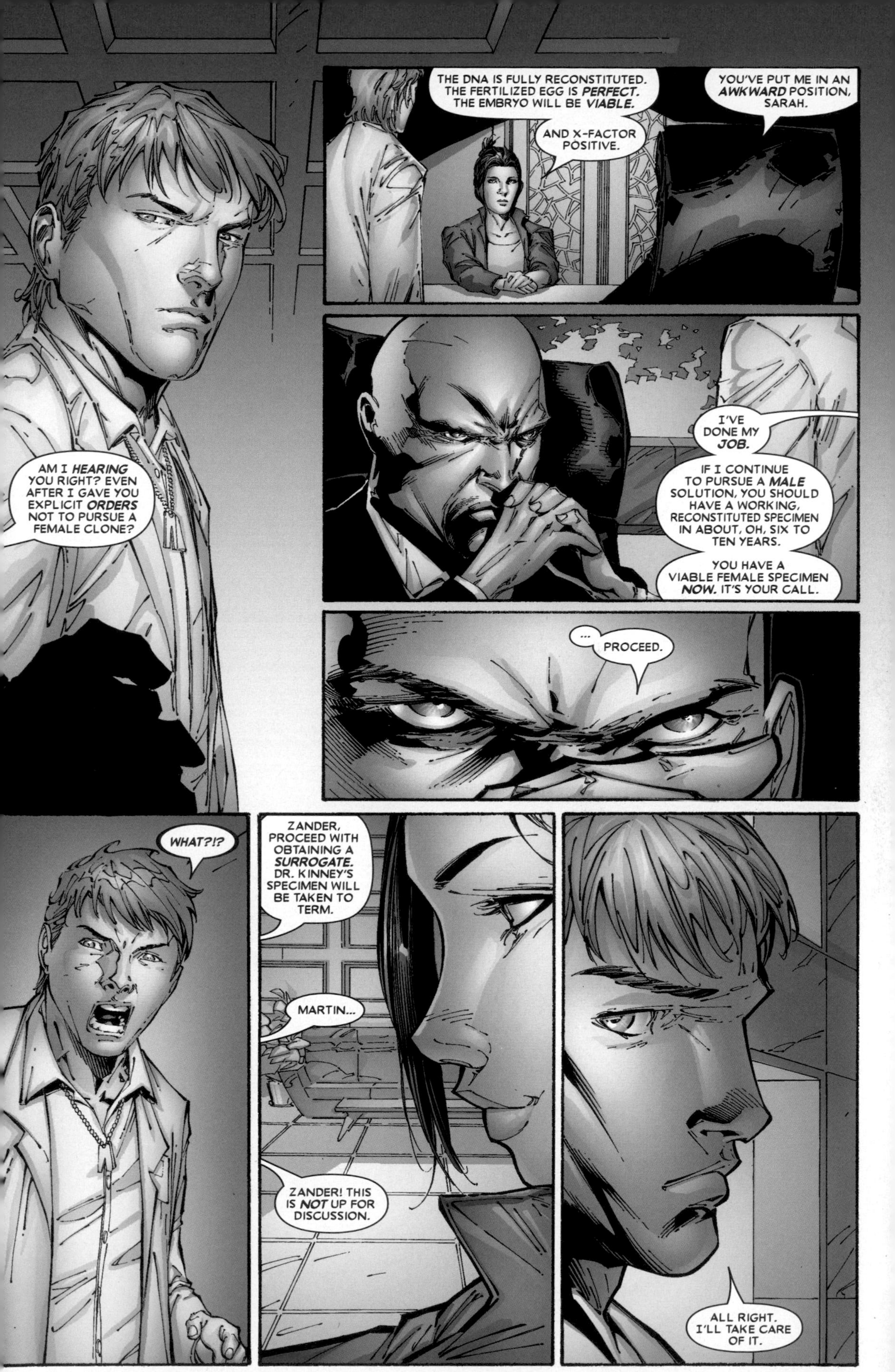
AM I HEARING YOU RIGHT? EVEN AFTER I GAVE YOU EXPLICIT ORDERS NOT TO PURSUE A FEMALE CLONE?
THE DNA IS FULLY RECONSTITUTED. THE FERTILIZED EGG IS PERFECT. THE EMBRYO WILL BE VIABLE.
AND X-FACTOR POSITIVE.
YOU'VE PUT ME IN AN AWKWARD POSITION, SARAH.
I'VE DONE MY JOB.
IF I CONTINUE TO PURSUE A MALE SOLUTION, YOU SHOULD HAVE A WORKING, RECONSTITUTED SPECIMEN IN ABOUT, OH, SIX TO TEN YEARS.
YOU HAVE A VIABLE FEMALE SPECIMEN NOW. IT'S YOUR CALL.
...
PROCEED.
WHAT?!?
ZANDER, PROCEED WITH OBTAINING A SURROGATE. DR. KINNEY'S SPECIMEN WILL BE TAKEN TO TERM.
MARTIN...
ZANDER! THIS IS NOT UP FOR DISCUSSION.
ALL RIGHT. I'LL TAKE CARE OF IT.

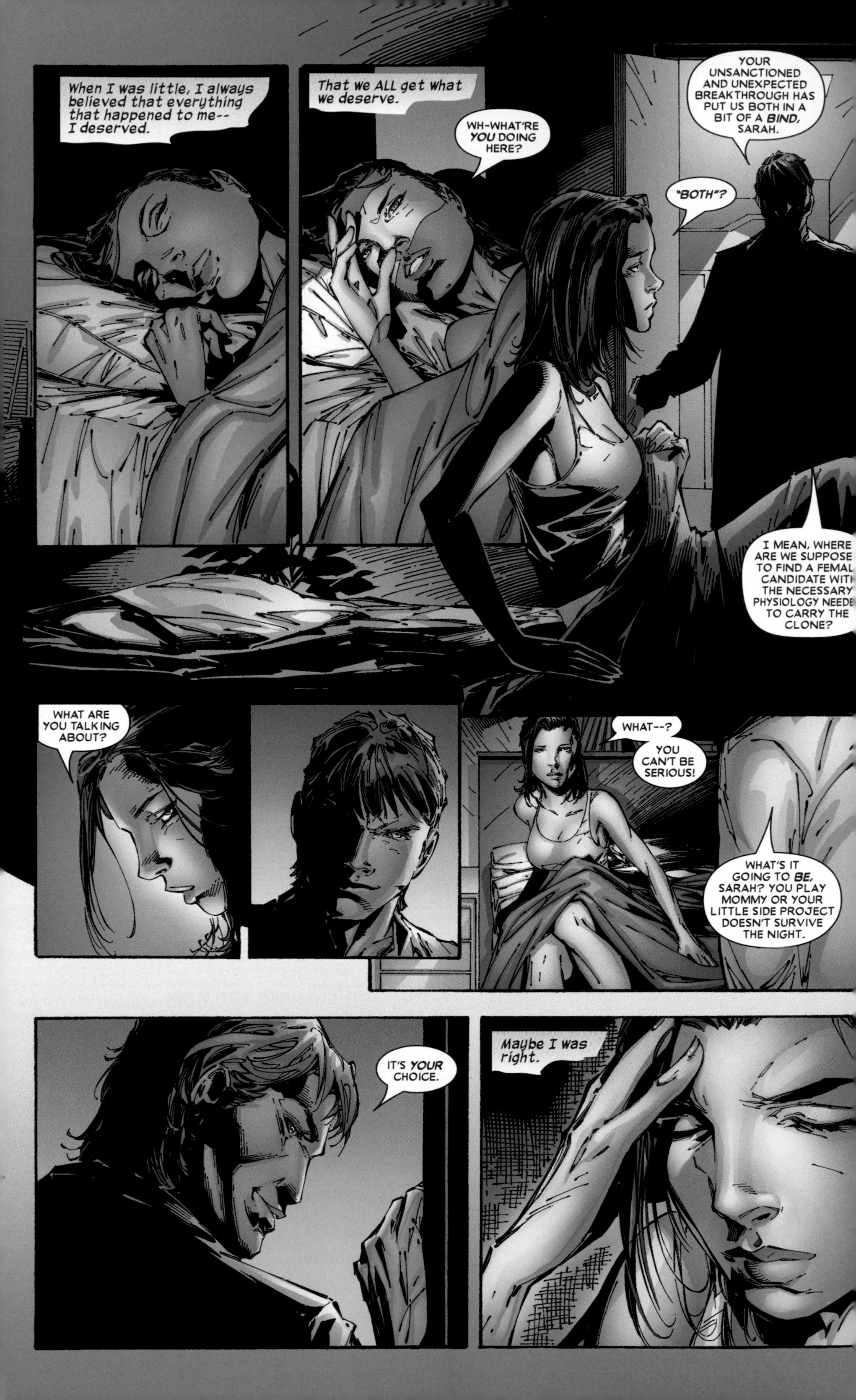
When I was little, I always believed that everything that happened to me-- I deserved.
That we ALL get what we deserve.
WH-WHAT'RE YOU DOING HERE?
YOUR UNSANCTIONED AND UNEXPECTED BREAKTHROUGH HAS PUT US BOTH IN A BIT OF A BIND, SARAH.
"BOTH"?
I MEAN, WHERE ARE WE SUPPOSE TO FIND A FEMAL CANDIDATE WITH THE NECESSARY PHYSIOLOGY NEEDE TO CARRY THE CLONE?
WHAT ARE YOU TALKING ABOUT?
WHAT--?
YOU CAN'T BE SERIOUS!
WHAT'S IT GOING TO BE, SARAH? YOU PLAY MOMMY OR YOUR LITTLE SIDE PROJECT DOESN'T SURVIVE THE NIGHT.
IT'S YOUR CHOICE.
Maybe I was right.

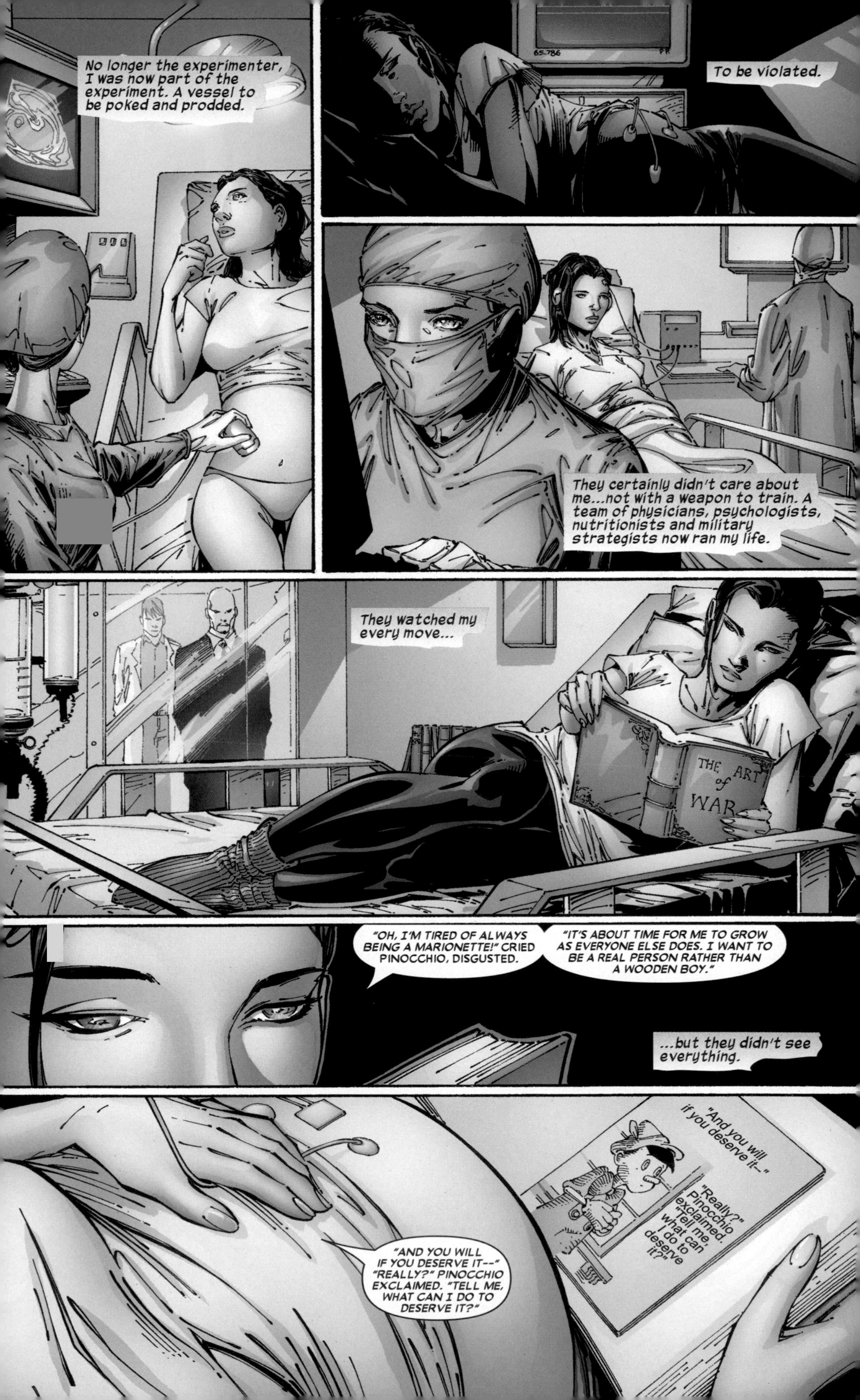
No longer the experimenter, I was now part of the experiment. A vessel to be poked and prodded.
To be violated.
They certainly didn't care about me...not with a weapon to train. A team of physicians, psychologists, nutritionists and military strategists now ran my life.
They watched my every move...
THE ART of WAR
"OH, I'M TIRED OF ALWAYS BEING A MARIONETTE!" CRIED PINOCCHIO, DISGUSTED.
"IT'S ABOUT TIME FOR ME TO GROW AS EVERYONE ELSE DOES. I WANT TO BE A REAL PERSON RATHER THAN A WOODEN BOY."
...but they didn't see everything.
"And you will if you deserve it–"
"Really?" Pinocchio exclaimed. "Tell me, what can I do to deserve it?"
"AND YOU WILL IF YOU DESERVE IT--" "REALLY?" PINOCCHIO EXCLAIMED. "TELL ME, WHAT CAN I DO TO DESERVE IT?"

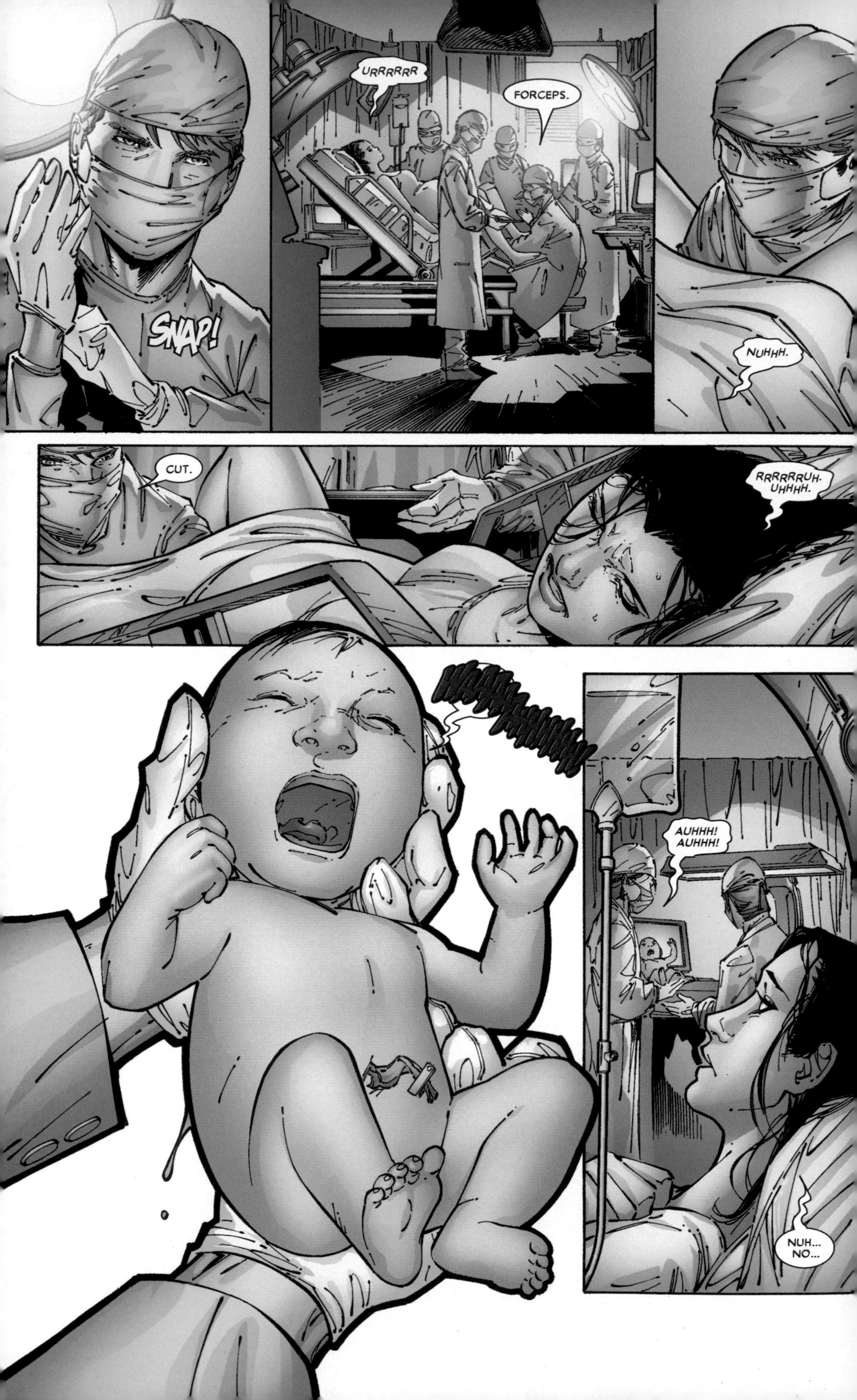
SNAP!
URRRRRR
FORCEPS.
NUHHH.
CUT.
RRRRRRUH-UHHHH.
AUHHH! AUHHH!
NUH... NO...

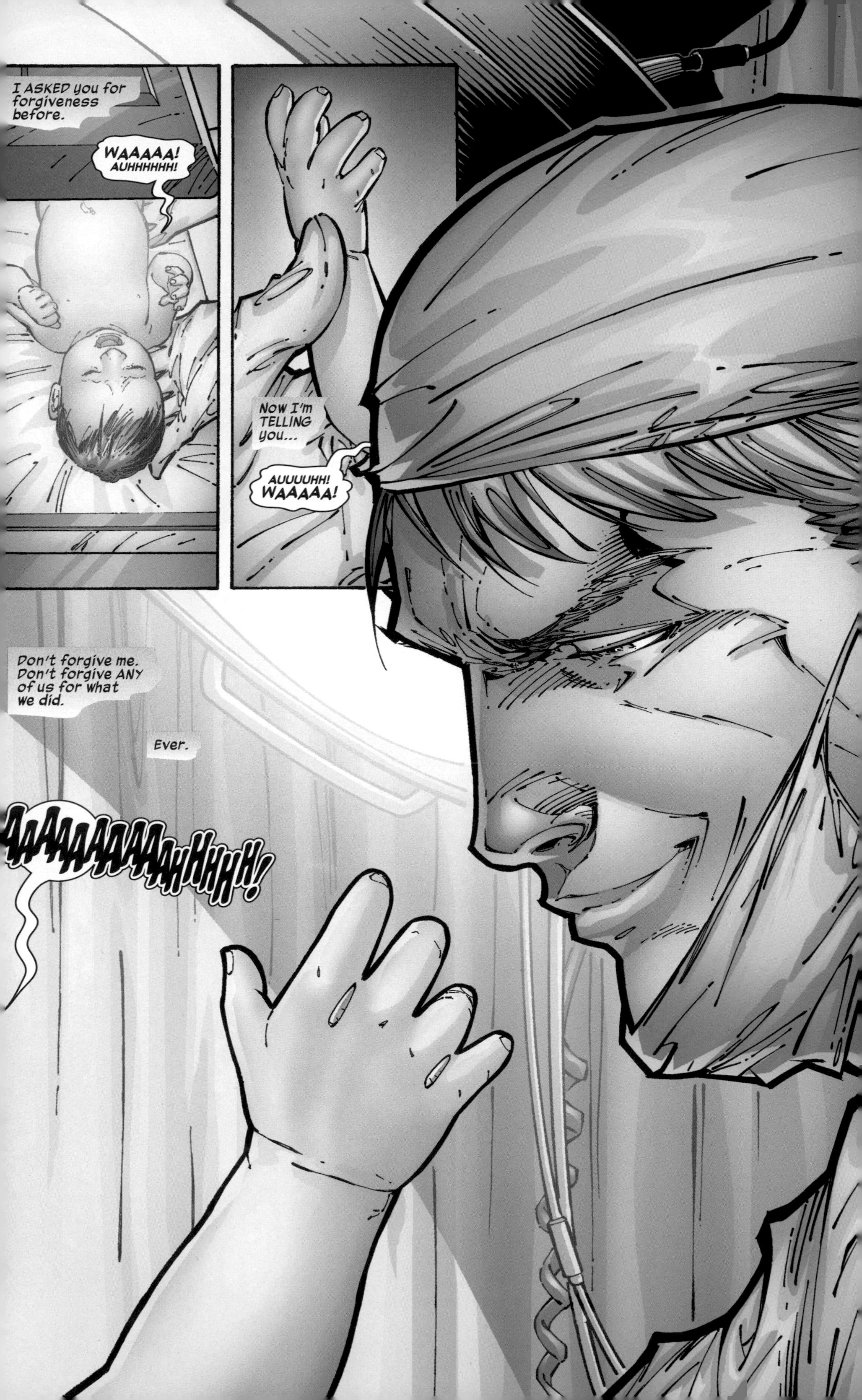

I ASKED you for forgiveness before.
WAAAAA! AUHHHHHH!
Now I'm TELLING you...
AUUUUHH! WAAAAA!
Don't forgive me. Don't forgive ANY of us for what we did.
Ever.
AAAAAAAAAAAAHHHHH!

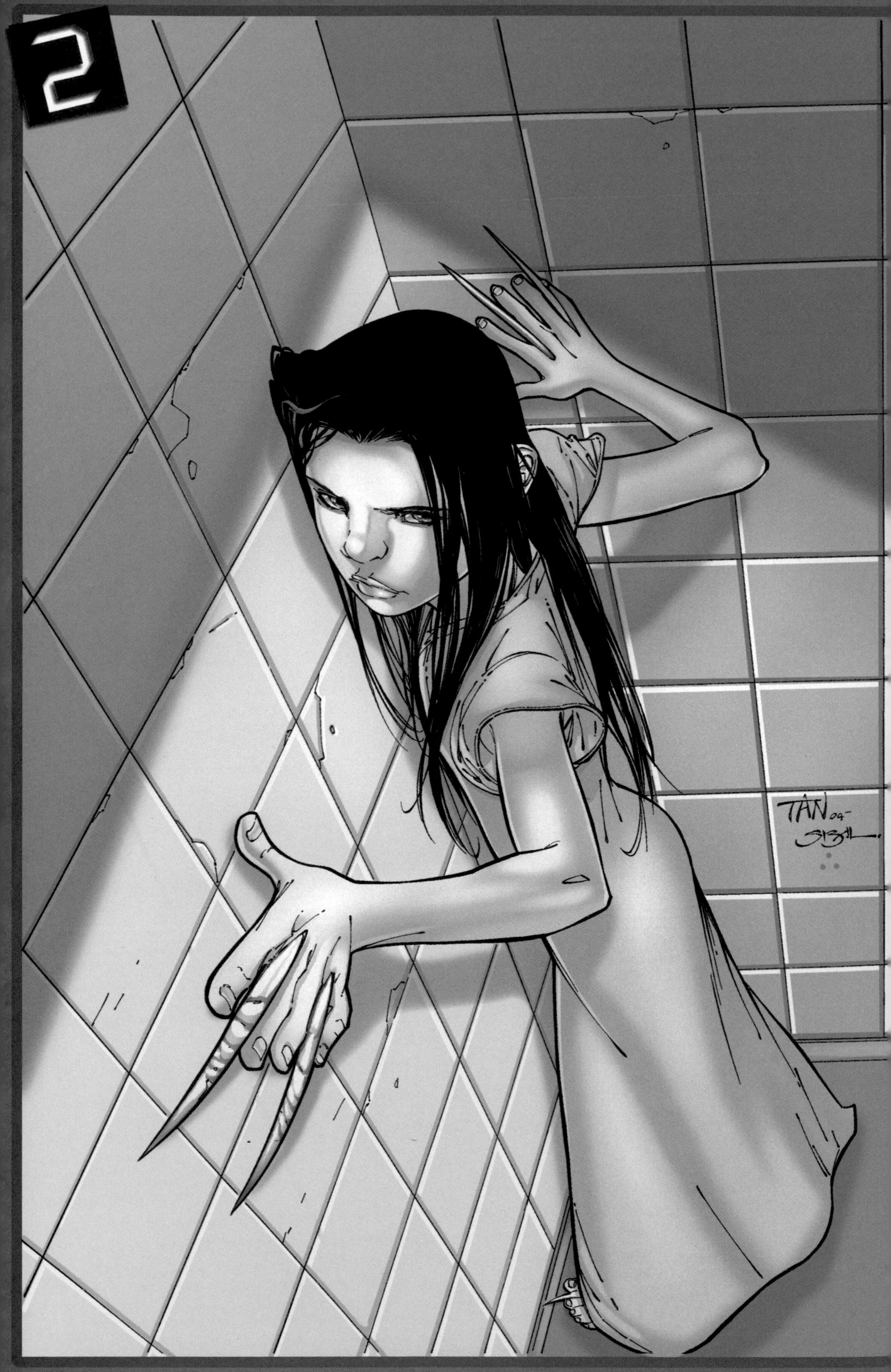
2
TAN 04

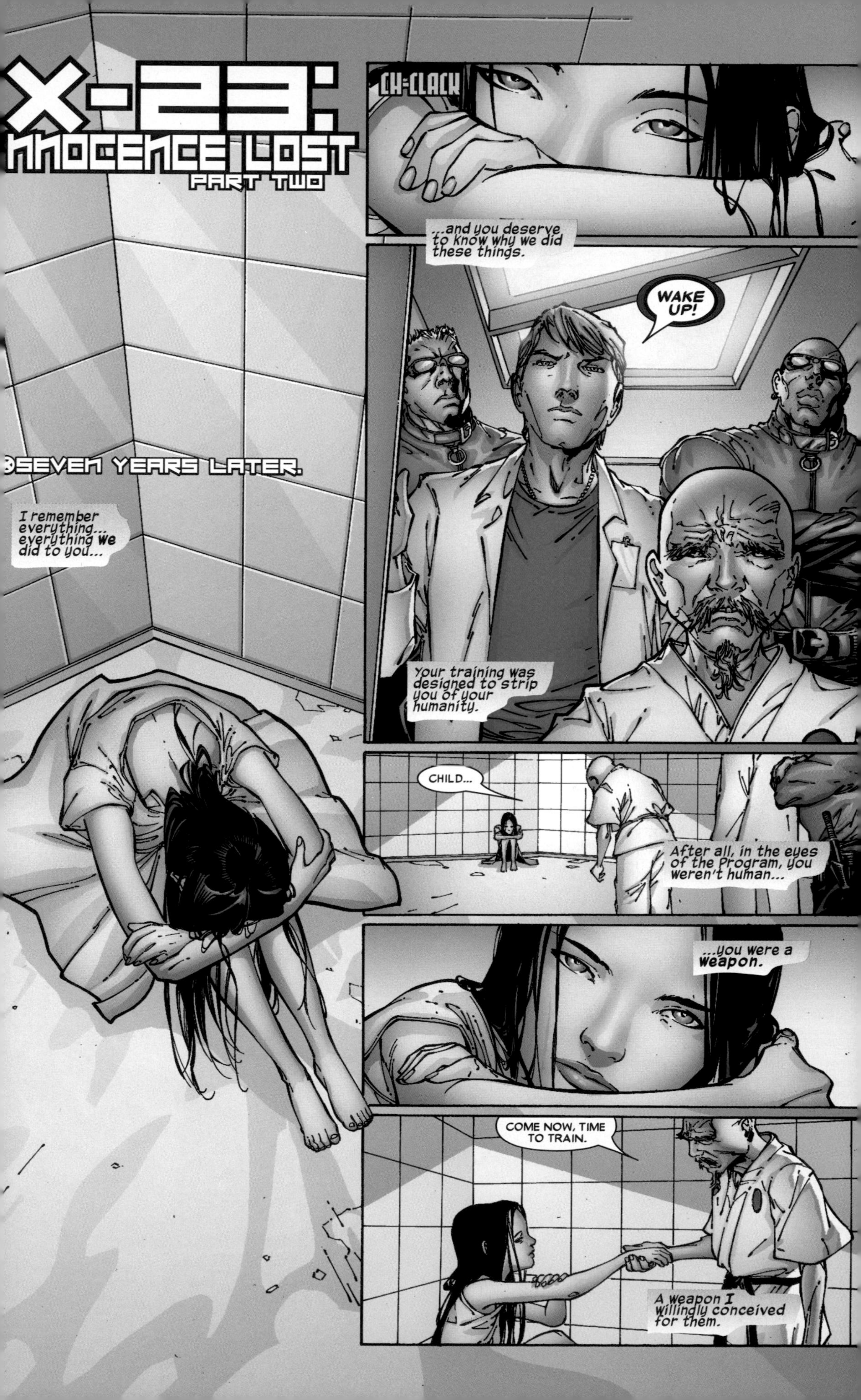

X-23:
INNOCENCE LOST
PART TWO
SEVEN YEARS LATER.
I remember everything... everything we did to you...
CH-CLACK
...and you deserve to know why we did these things.
WAKE UP!
Your training was designed to strip you of your humanity.
CHILD...
After all, in the eyes of the Program, you weren't human...
...you were a weapon.
COME NOW, TIME TO TRAIN.
A weapon I willingly conceived for them.

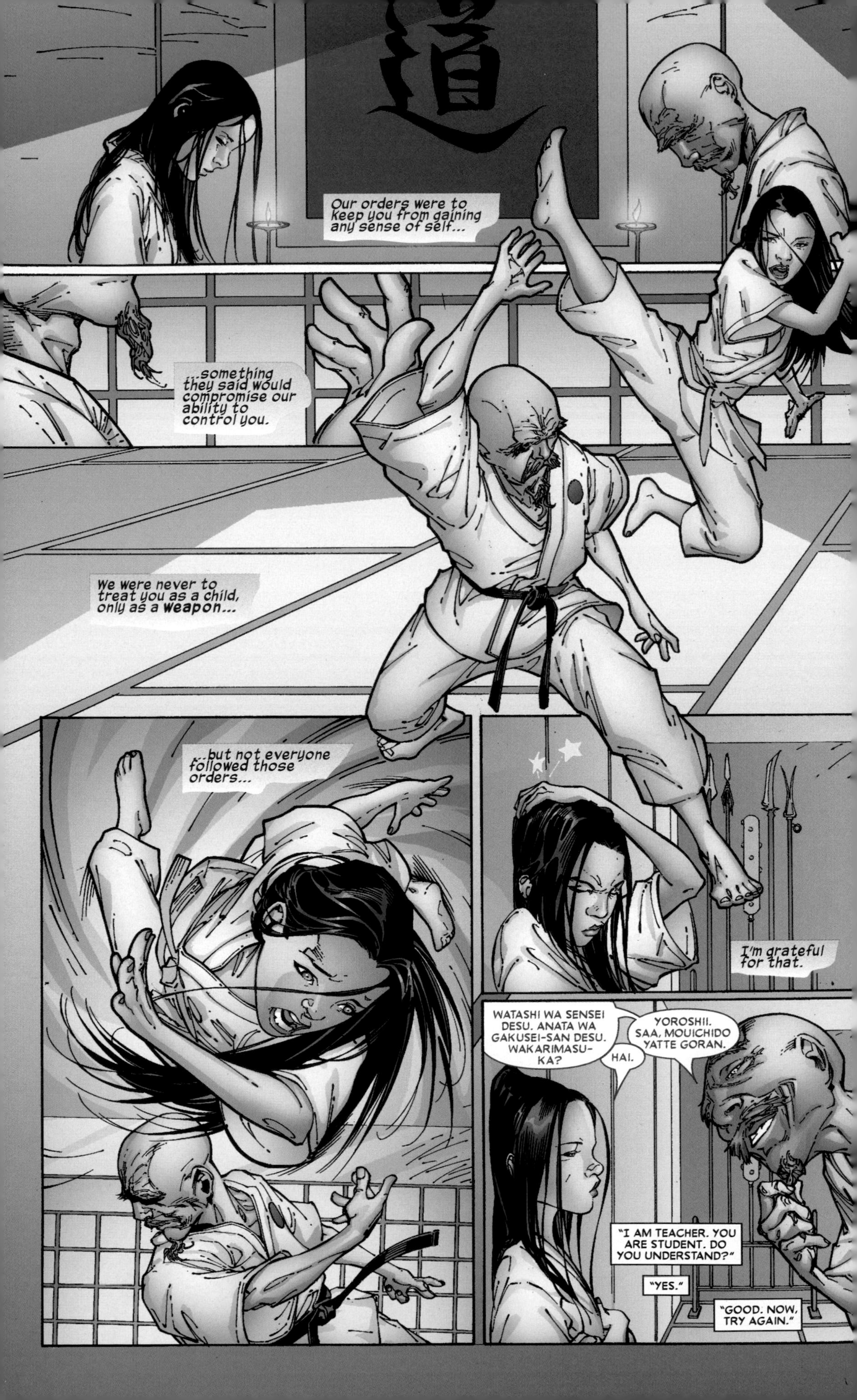

Our orders were to keep you from gaining any sense of self...
...something they said would compromise our ability to control you.
We were never to treat you as a child, only as a weapon...
...but not everyone followed those orders...
I'm grateful for that.
WATASHI WA SENSEI DESU. ANATA WA GAKUSEI-SAN DESU. WAKARIMASU-KA?
HAI.
YOROSHII. SAA, MOUICHIDO YATTE GORAN.
"I AM TEACHER. YOU ARE STUDENT. DO YOU UNDERSTAND?"
"YES."
"GOOD. NOW, TRY AGAIN."

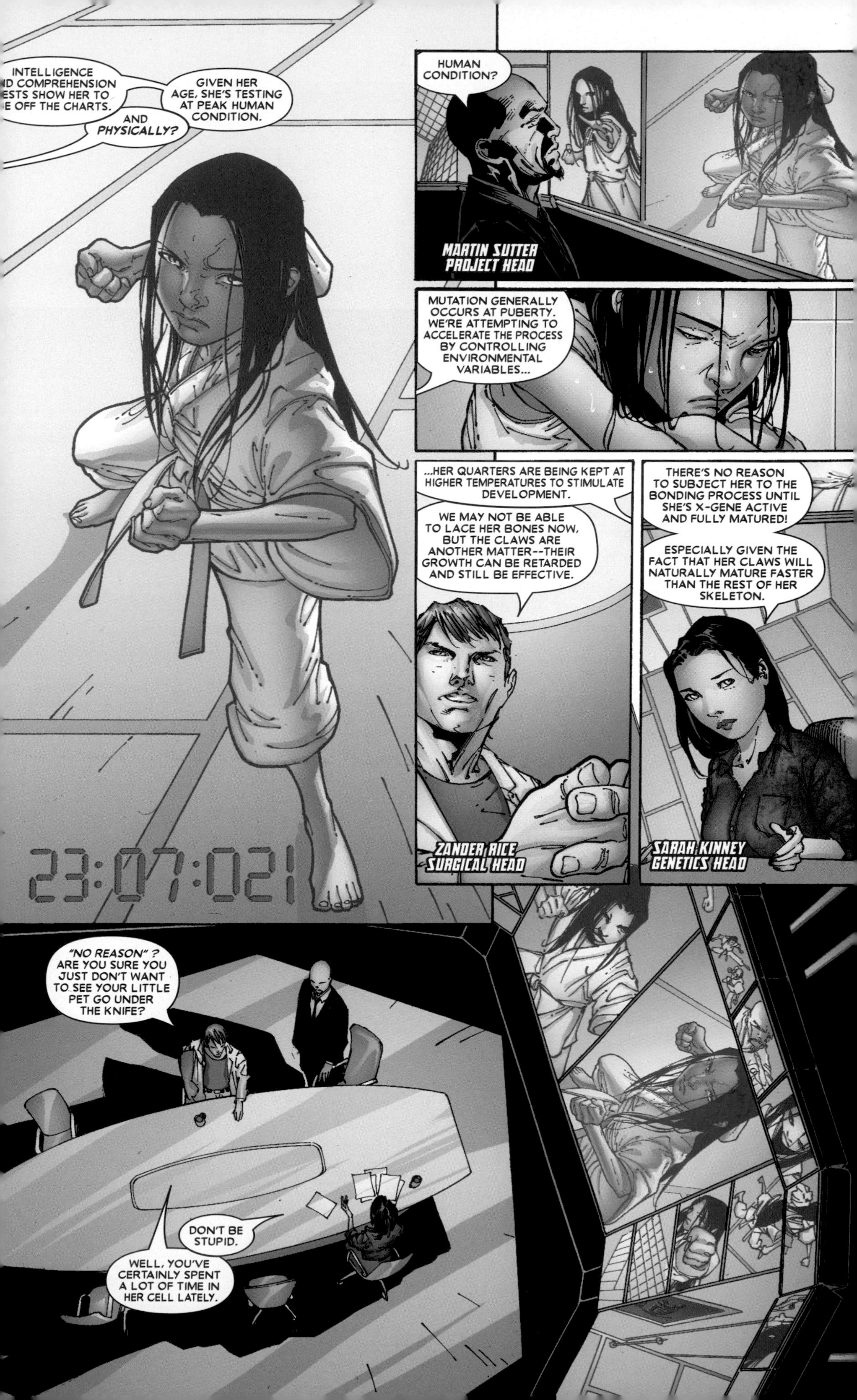

INTELLIGENCE
ND COMPREHENSION
ESTS SHOW HER TO
E OFF THE CHARTS.
AND PHYSICALLY?
GIVEN HER AGE, SHE'S TESTING AT PEAK HUMAN CONDITION.
HUMAN CONDITION?
MARTIN SUTTER PROJECT HEAD
MUTATION GENERALLY OCCURS AT PUBERTY. WE'RE ATTEMPTING TO ACCELERATE THE PROCESS BY CONTROLLING ENVIRONMENTAL VARIABLES...
...HER QUARTERS ARE BEING KEPT AT HIGHER TEMPERATURES TO STIMULATE DEVELOPMENT.
WE MAY NOT BE ABLE TO LACE HER BONES NOW, BUT THE CLAWS ARE ANOTHER MATTER--THEIR GROWTH CAN BE RETARDED AND STILL BE EFFECTIVE.
ZANDER RICE SURGICAL HEAD
THERE'S NO REASON TO SUBJECT HER TO THE BONDING PROCESS UNTIL SHE'S X-GENE ACTIVE AND FULLY MATURED!
ESPECIALLY GIVEN THE FACT THAT HER CLAWS WILL NATURALLY MATURE FASTER THAN THE REST OF HER SKELETON.
SARAH KINNEY GENETICS HEAD
23:07:021
"NO REASON"? ARE YOU SURE YOU JUST DON'T WANT TO SEE YOUR LITTLE PET GO UNDER THE KNIFE?
DON'T BE STUPID.
WELL, YOU'VE CERTAINLY SPENT A LOT OF TIME IN HER CELL LATELY.

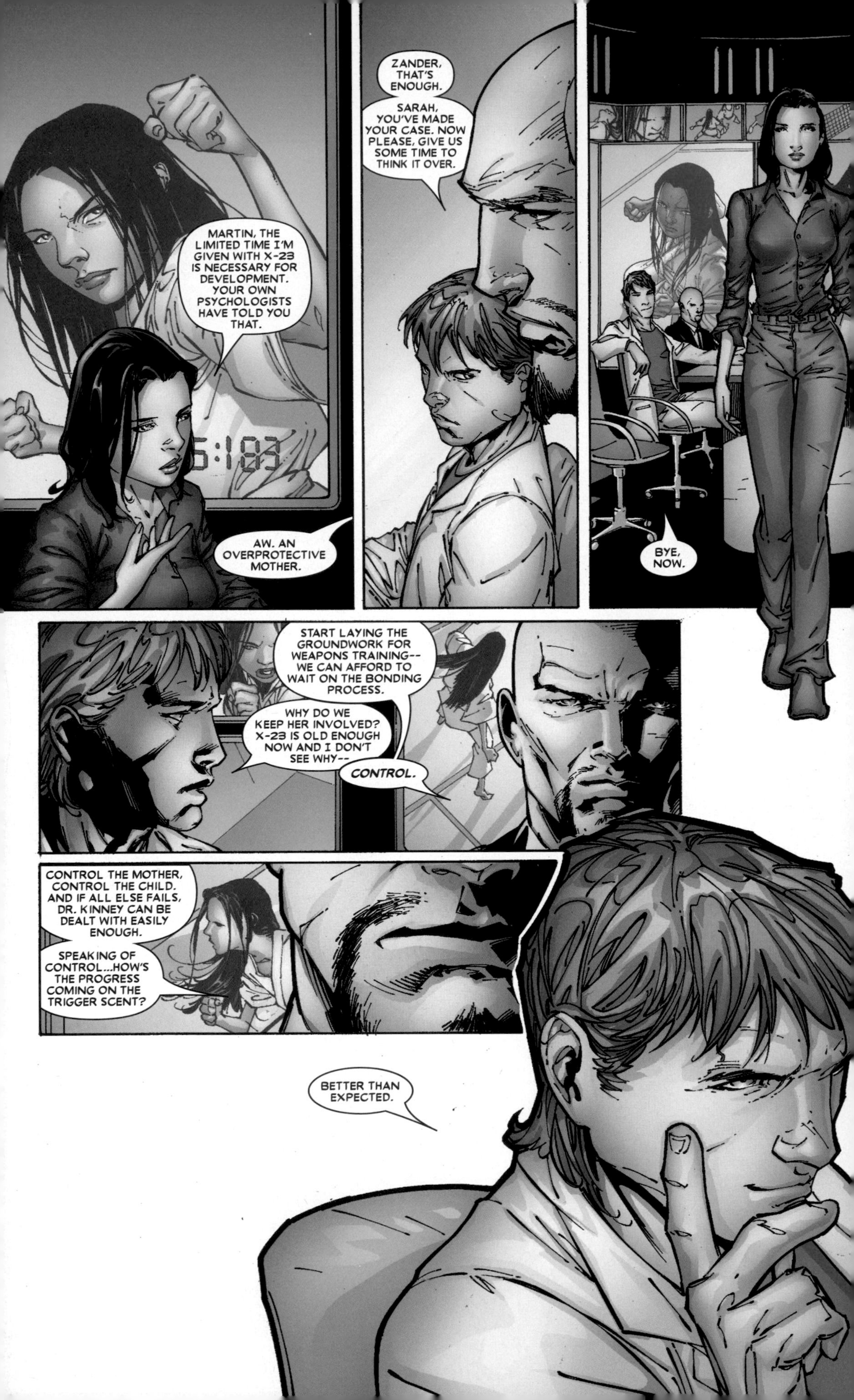
MARTIN, THE LIMITED TIME I'M GIVEN WITH X-23 IS NECESSARY FOR DEVELOPMENT. YOUR OWN PSYCHOLOGISTS HAVE TOLD YOU THAT.
AW. AN OVERPROTECTIVE MOTHER.
ZANDER, THAT'S ENOUGH.
SARAH, YOU'VE MADE YOUR CASE. NOW PLEASE, GIVE US SOME TIME TO THINK IT OVER.
BYE, NOW.
START LAYING THE GROUNDWORK FOR WEAPONS TRAINING-- WE CAN AFFORD TO WAIT ON THE BONDING PROCESS.
WHY DO WE KEEP HER INVOLVED? X-23 IS OLD ENOUGH NOW AND I DON'T SEE WHY--
CONTROL.
CONTROL THE MOTHER, CONTROL THE CHILD. AND IF ALL ELSE FAILS, DR. KINNEY CAN BE DEALT WITH EASILY ENOUGH.
SPEAKING OF CONTROL...HOW'S THE PROGRESS COMING ON THE TRIGGER SCENT?
BETTER THAN EXPECTED.

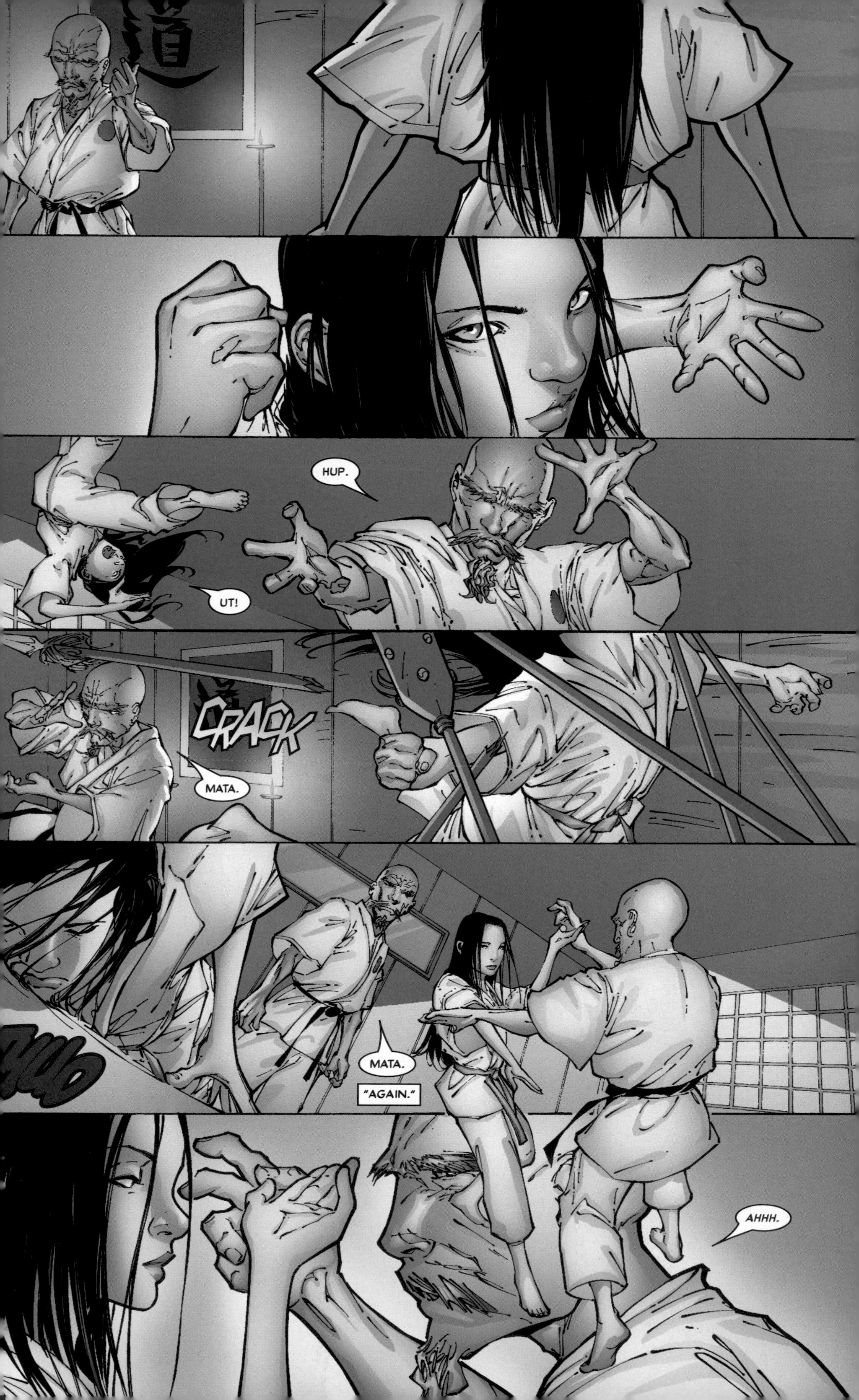
HUP.
UT!
CRACK
MATA.
MATA.
"AGAIN."
AHHH.

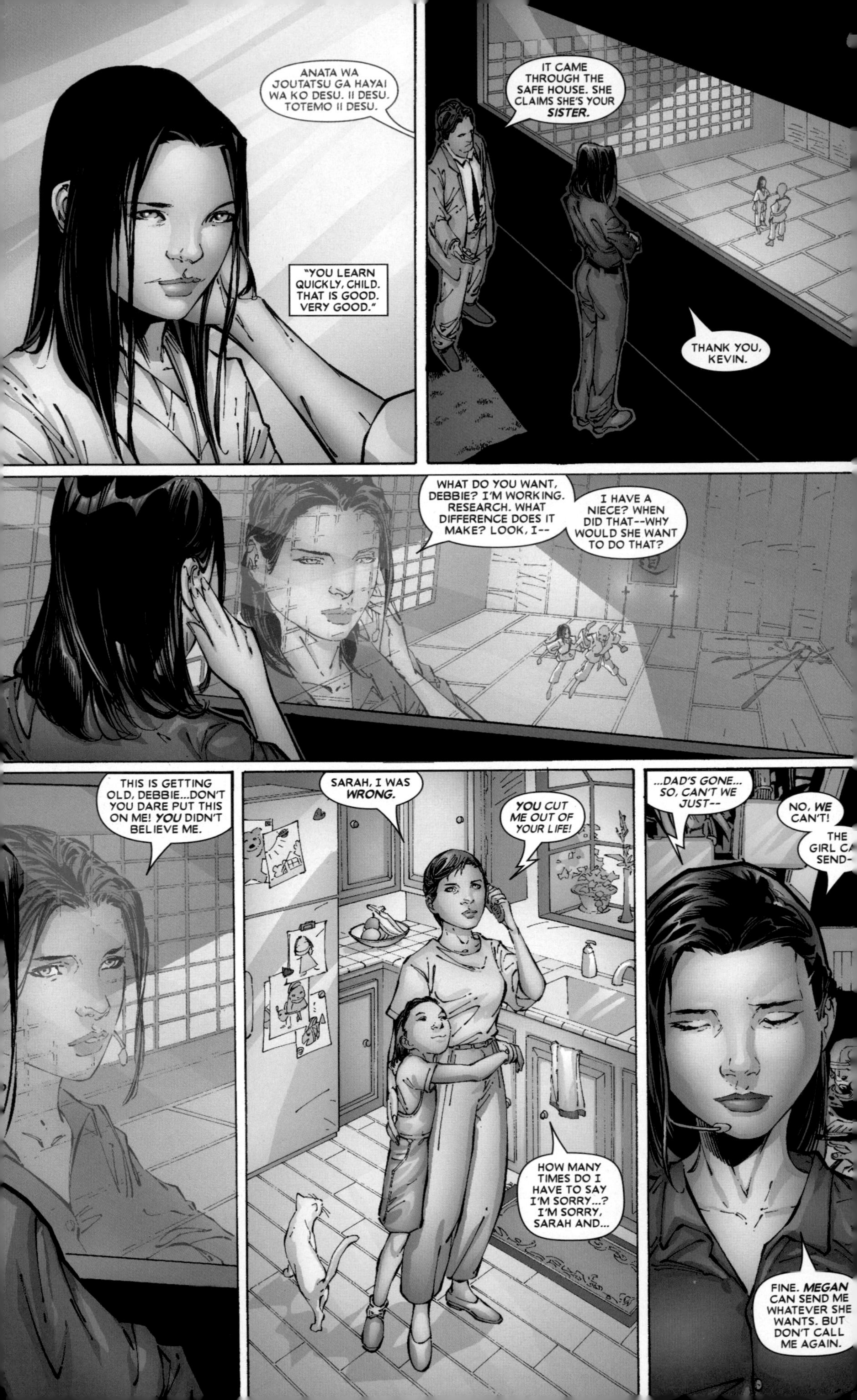
ANATA WA JOUTATSU GA HAYAI WA KO DESU. II DESU. TOTEMO II DESU.
"YOU LEARN QUICKLY, CHILD. THAT IS GOOD. VERY GOOD."
IT CAME THROUGH THE SAFE HOUSE. SHE CLAIMS SHE'S YOUR *SISTER.*
THANK YOU, KEVIN.
WHAT DO YOU WANT, DEBBIE? I'M WORKING. RESEARCH. WHAT DIFFERENCE DOES IT MAKE? LOOK, I--
I HAVE A NIECE? WHEN DID THAT--WHY WOULD SHE WANT TO DO THAT?
THIS IS GETTING OLD, DEBBIE...DON'T YOU DARE PUT THIS ON ME! *YOU* DIDN'T BELIEVE ME.
SARAH, I WAS *WRONG.*
YOU CUT ME OUT OF YOUR LIFE!
HOW MANY TIMES DO I HAVE TO SAY I'M SORRY...? I'M SORRY, SARAH AND...
...DAD'S GONE... SO, CAN'T WE JUST--
NO, *WE* CAN'T!
FINE. *MEGAN* CAN SEND ME WHATEVER SHE WANTS. BUT DON'T CALL ME AGAIN.

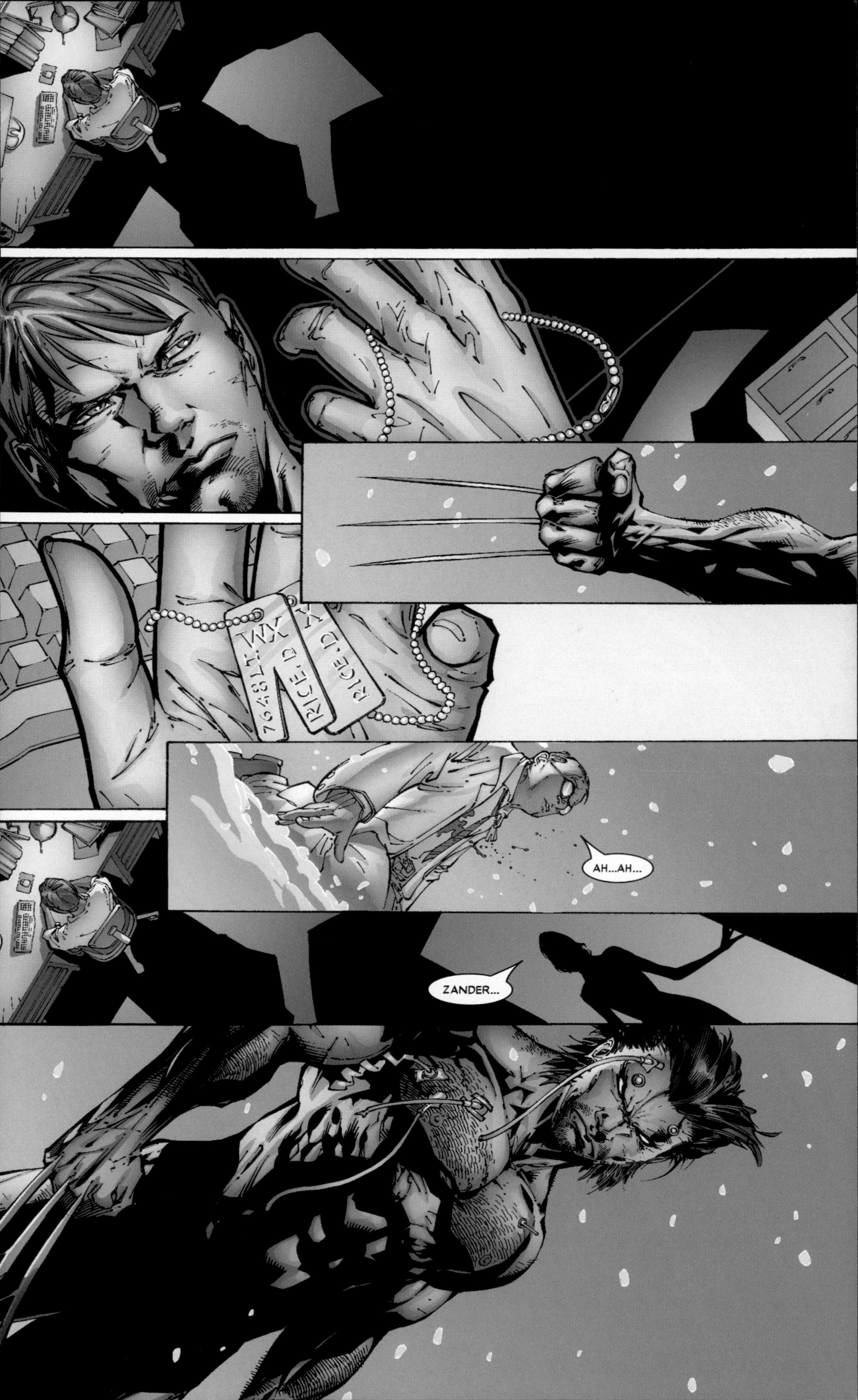
AH...AH...
ZANDER...

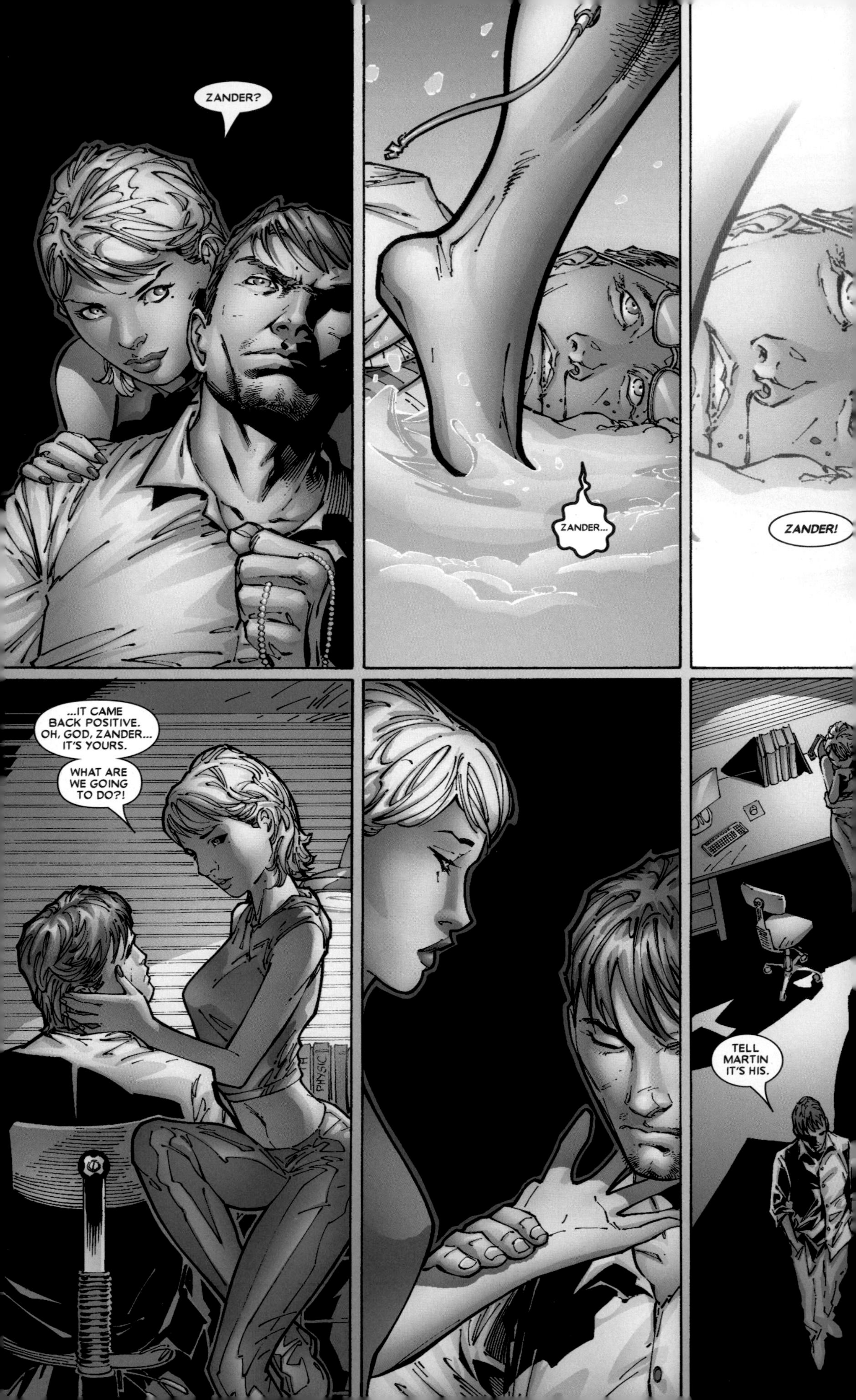
ZANDER?
ZANDER...
ZANDER!
...IT CAME BACK POSITIVE. OH, GOD, ZANDER... IT'S YOURS.
WHAT ARE WE GOING TO DO?!
TELL MARTIN IT'S HIS.

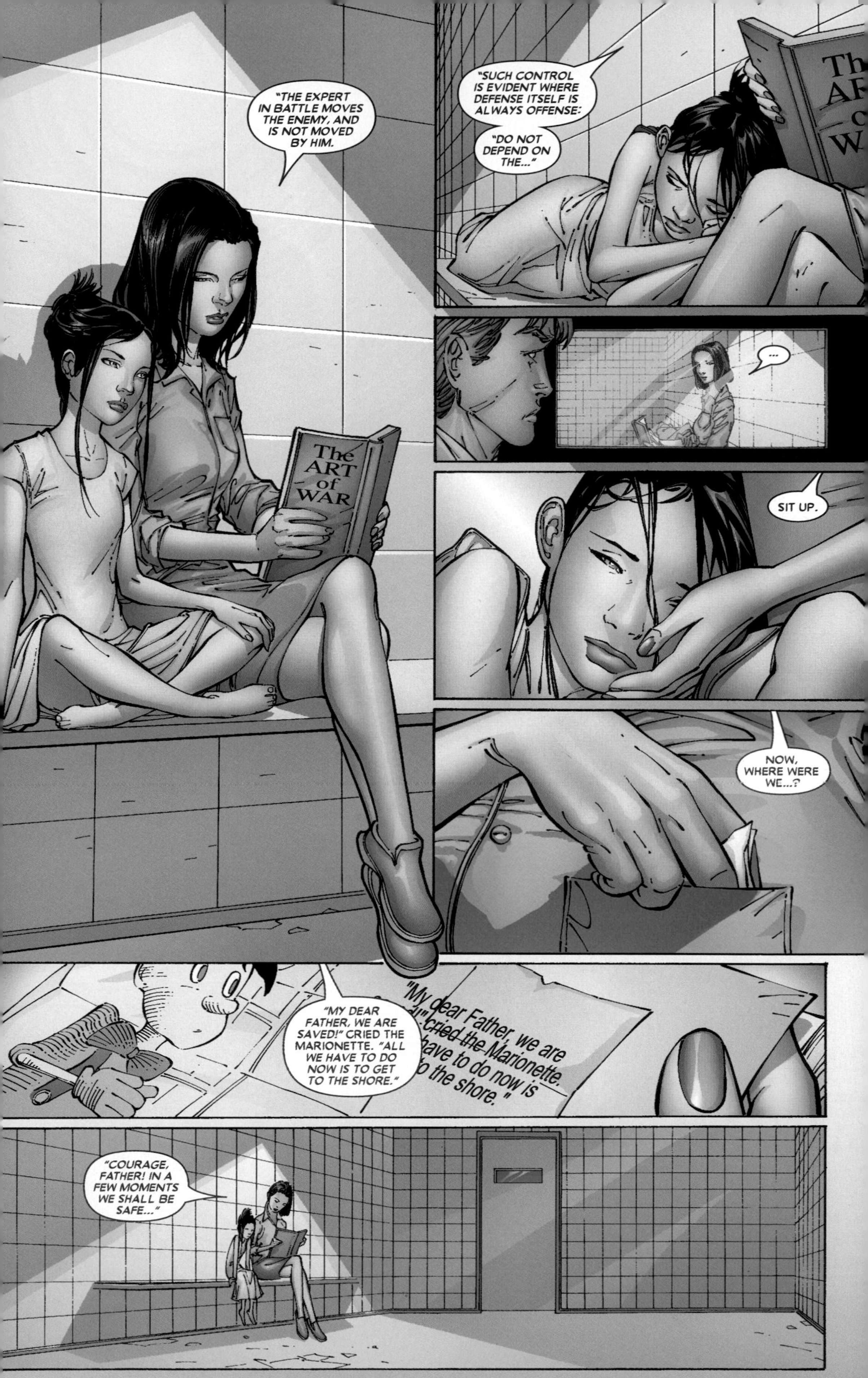
"THE EXPERT IN BATTLE MOVES THE ENEMY, AND IS NOT MOVED BY HIM.
The ART of WAR
"SUCH CONTROL IS EVIDENT WHERE DEFENSE ITSELF IS ALWAYS OFFENSE:
"DO NOT DEPEND ON THE..."
...
SIT UP.
NOW, WHERE WERE WE...?
"MY DEAR FATHER, WE ARE SAVED!" CRIED THE MARIONETTE. "ALL WE HAVE TO DO NOW IS TO GET TO THE SHORE."
"COURAGE, FATHER! IN A FEW MOMENTS WE SHALL BE SAFE..."

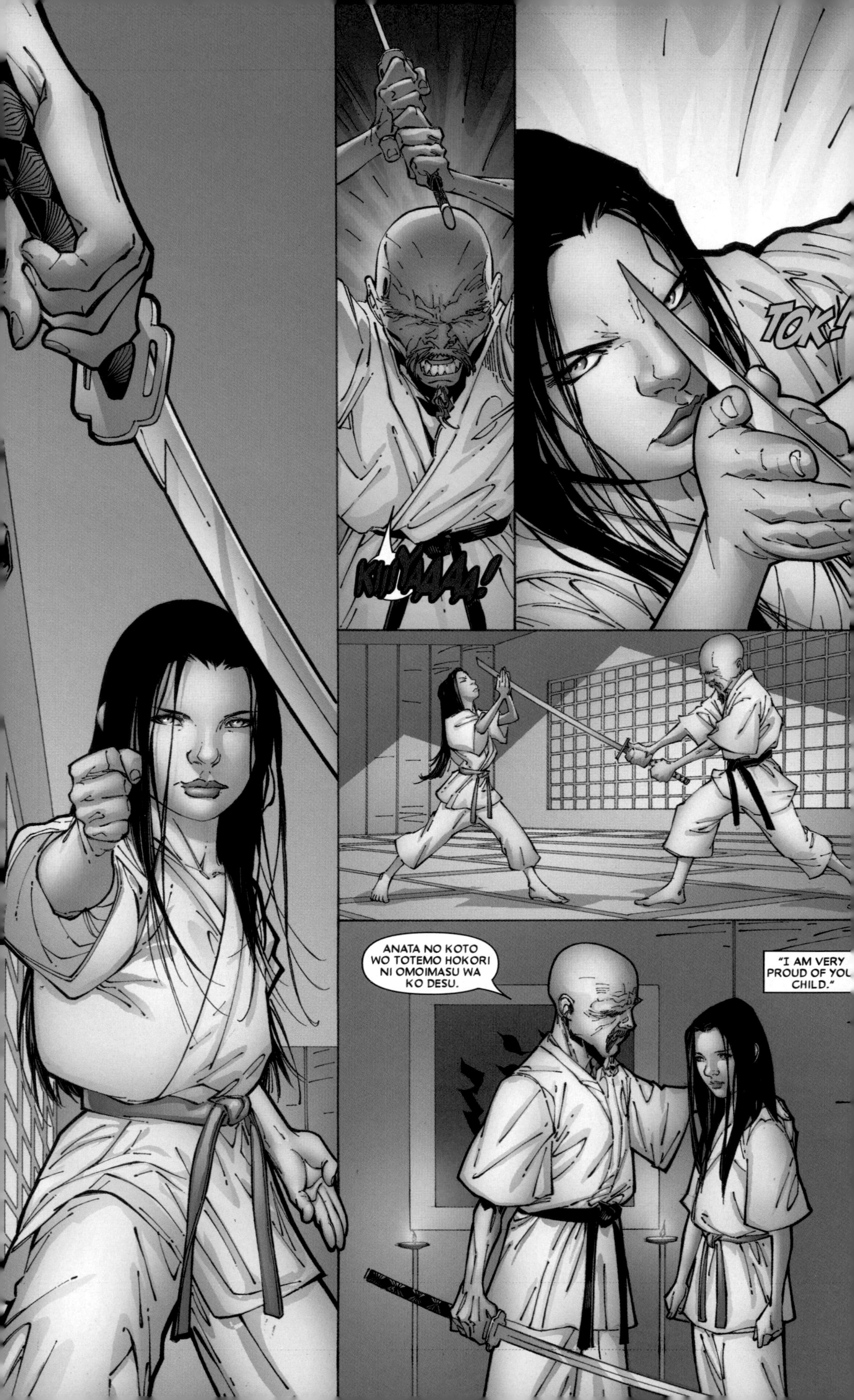

KIIYAAAA!
TOK!
ANATA NO KOTO WO TOTEMO HOKORI NI OMOIMASU WA KO DESU.
"I AM VERY PROUD OF YOU CHILD."

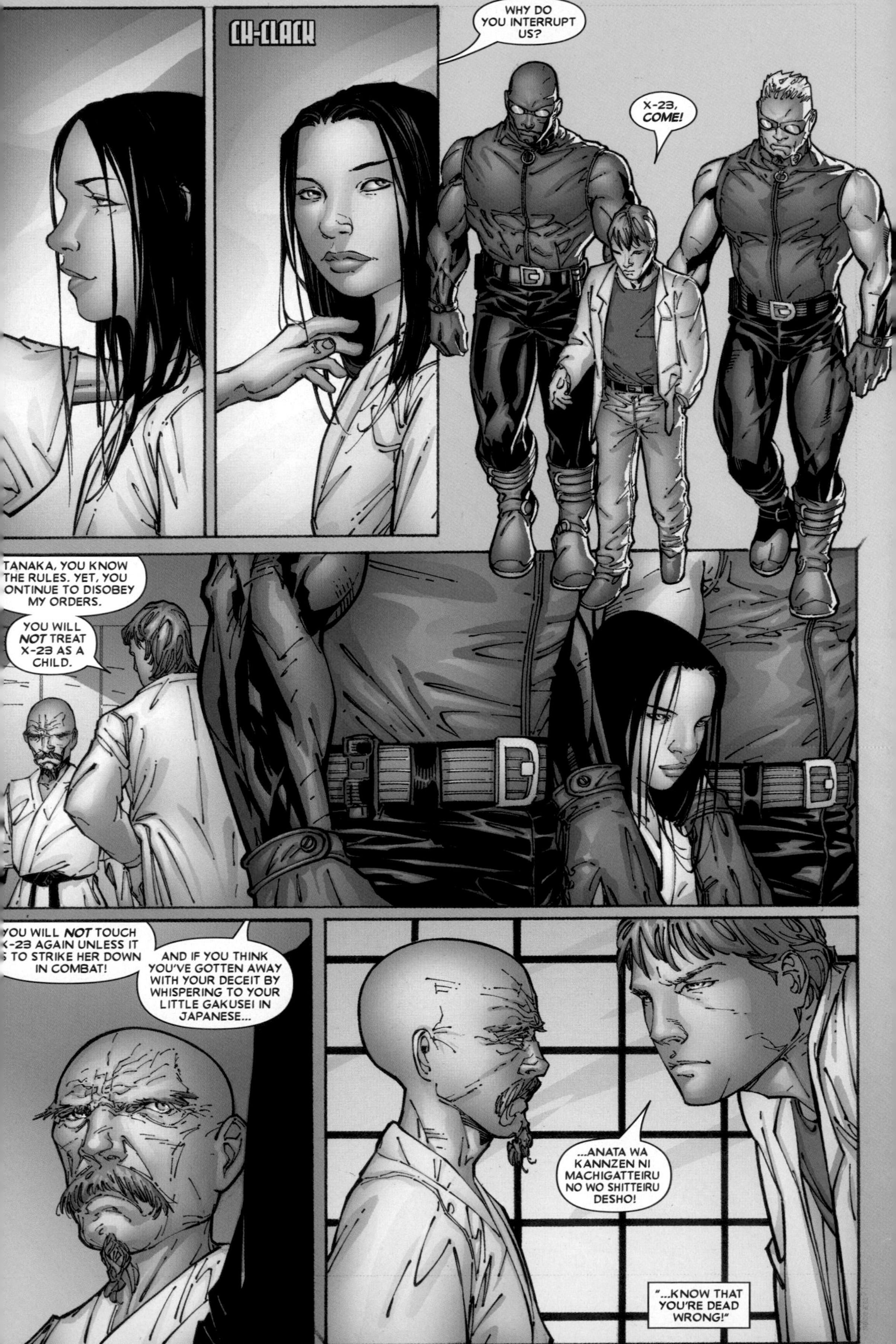
CH-CLACK
WHY DO YOU INTERRUPT US?
X-23, COME!
TANAKA, YOU KNOW THE RULES. YET, YOU ONTINUE TO DISOBEY MY ORDERS.
YOU WILL NOT TREAT X-23 AS A CHILD.
YOU WILL NOT TOUCH X-23 AGAIN UNLESS IT S TO STRIKE HER DOWN IN COMBAT!
AND IF YOU THINK YOU'VE GOTTEN AWAY WITH YOUR DECEIT BY WHISPERING TO YOUR LITTLE GAKUSEI IN JAPANESE...
...ANATA WA KANNZEN NI MACHIGATTEIRU NO WO SHITTEIRU DESHO!
"...KNOW THAT YOU'RE DEAD WRONG!"

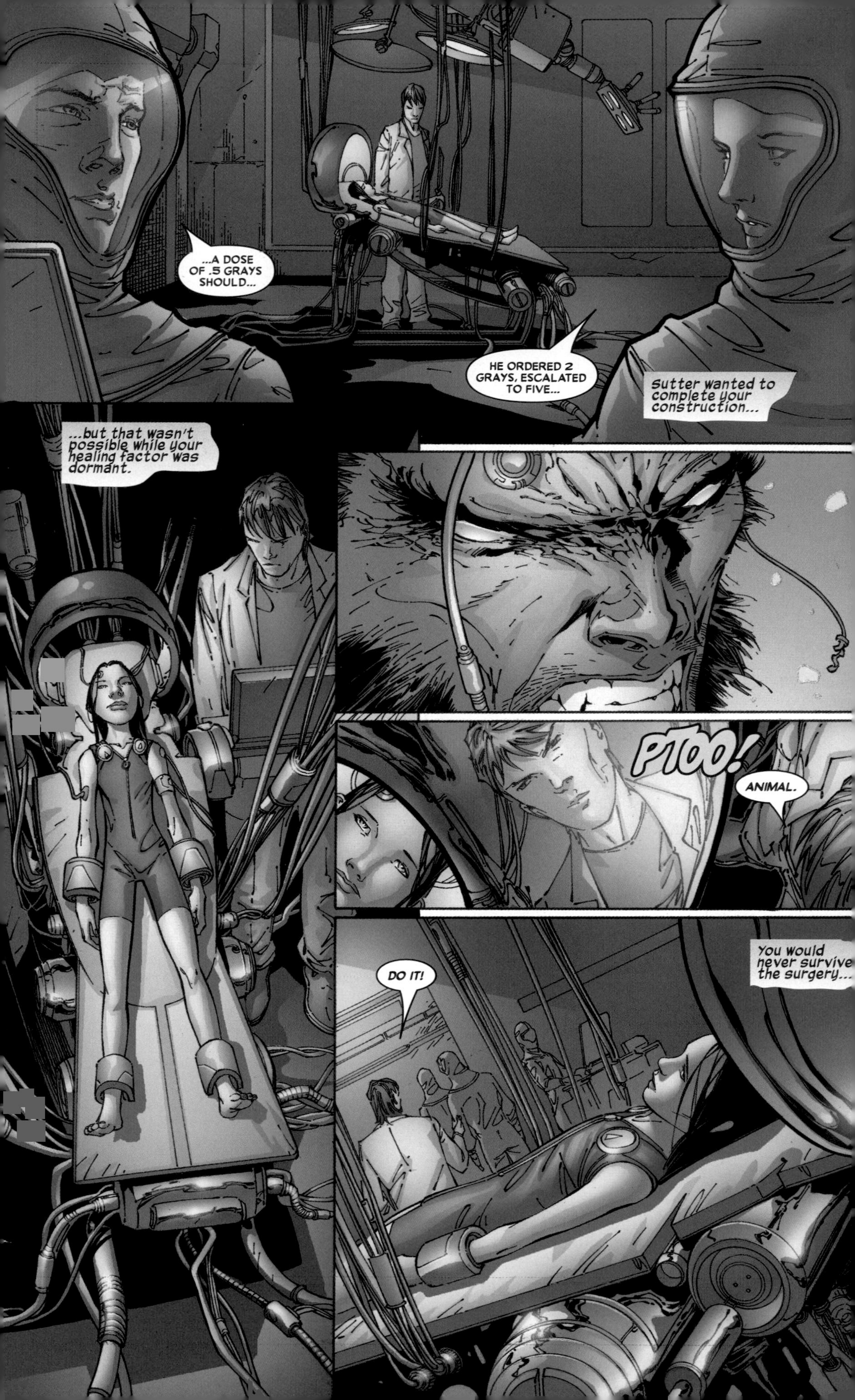
...A DOSE OF .5 GRAYS SHOULD...
HE ORDERED 2 GRAYS, ESCALATED TO FIVE...
Sutter wanted to complete your construction...
...but that wasn't possible while your healing factor was dormant.
PTOO!
ANIMAL.
DO IT!
You would never survive the surgery...

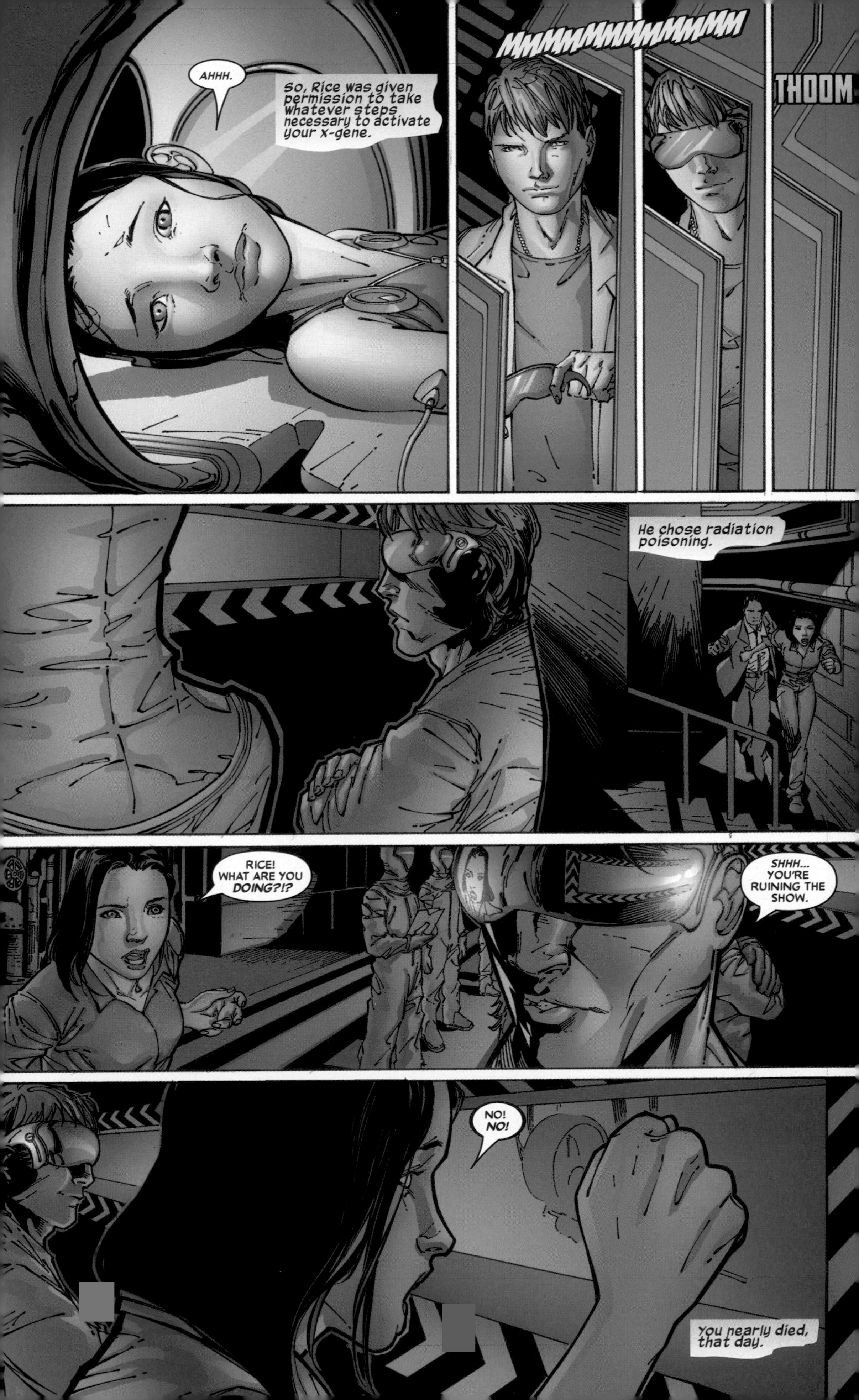
AHHH.
So, Rice was given permission to take whatever steps necessary to activate your x-gene.
MMMMMMMMMMMMMM
THOOM
He chose radiation poisoning.
RICE! WHAT ARE YOU DOING?!?
SHHH... YOU'RE RUINING THE SHOW.
NO! NO!
You nearly died, that day.

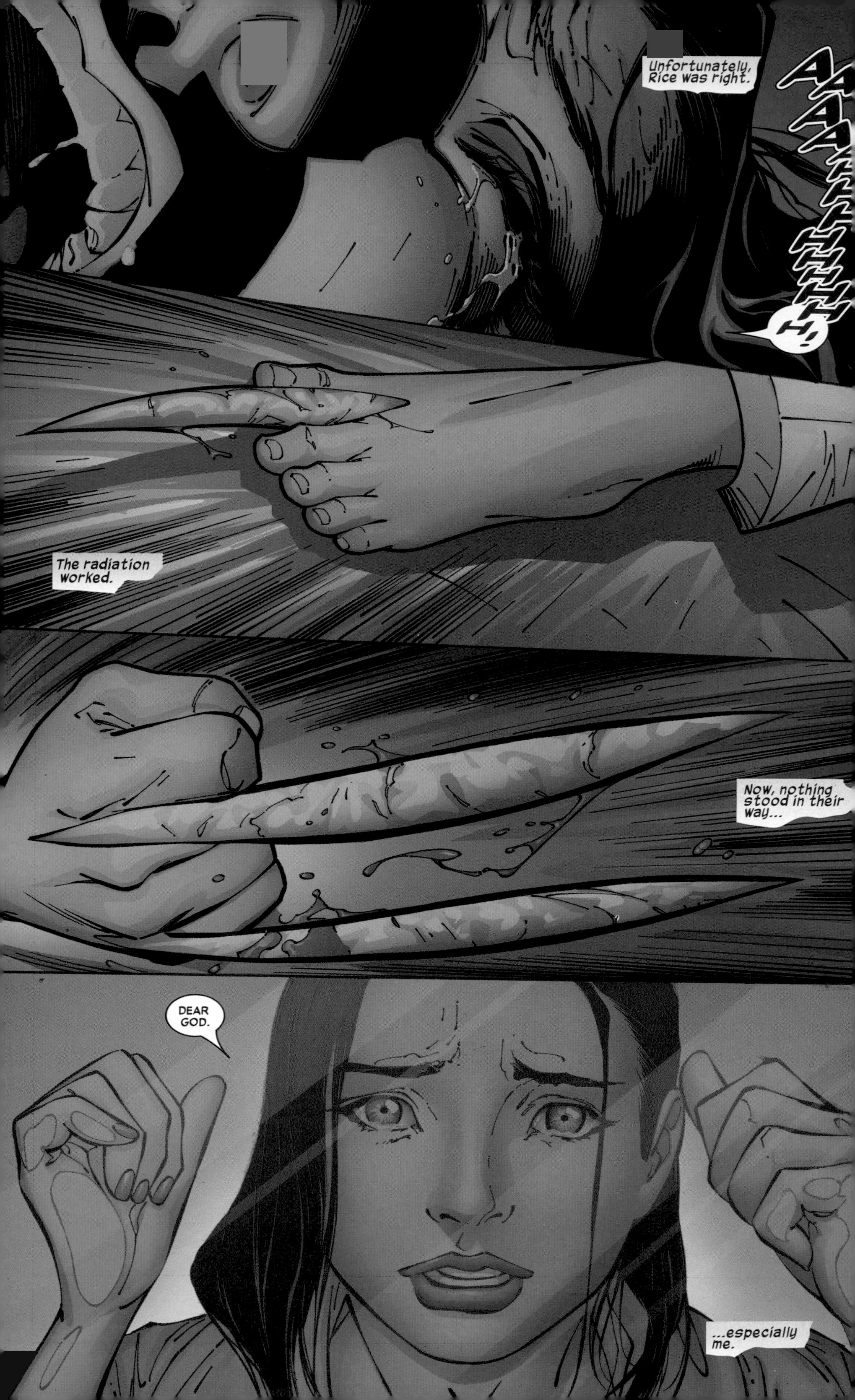

Unfortunately, Rice was right.
AAAAHHHHHHH!
The radiation worked.
Now, nothing stood in their way...
DEAR GOD.
...especially me.

ABSOLUTELY NOT! ZANDER HAS PREPARED FOR THIS HIS WHOLE LIFE. THERE'S NO REASON TO TAKE HIM OFF THE SURGERY.

MARTIN, YOU DON'T UNDERSTAND. HE'S BECOME TOO EMOTIONALLY MOTIVATED. HE'S LOST IT!

SARAH--

PLEASE...LET SOMEONE ELSE... LET ME HANDLE THE SURGERY! RICE CAN OVERSEE THE BONDING, BUT PLEASE...

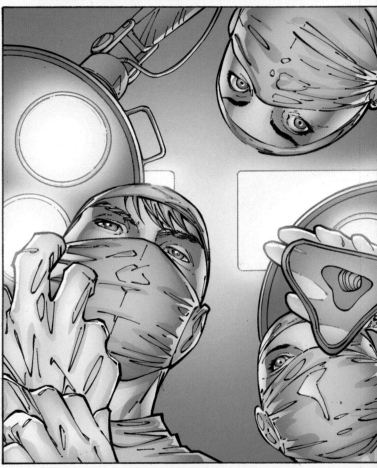

OUT OF THE QUESTION. NO ONE KNOWS ZANDER BETTER THAN ME. AND IF ANYONE HAS BECOME EMOTIONALLY INVESTED, SARAH...

...IT'S YOU.

STOP.

NO ANESTHESIA.

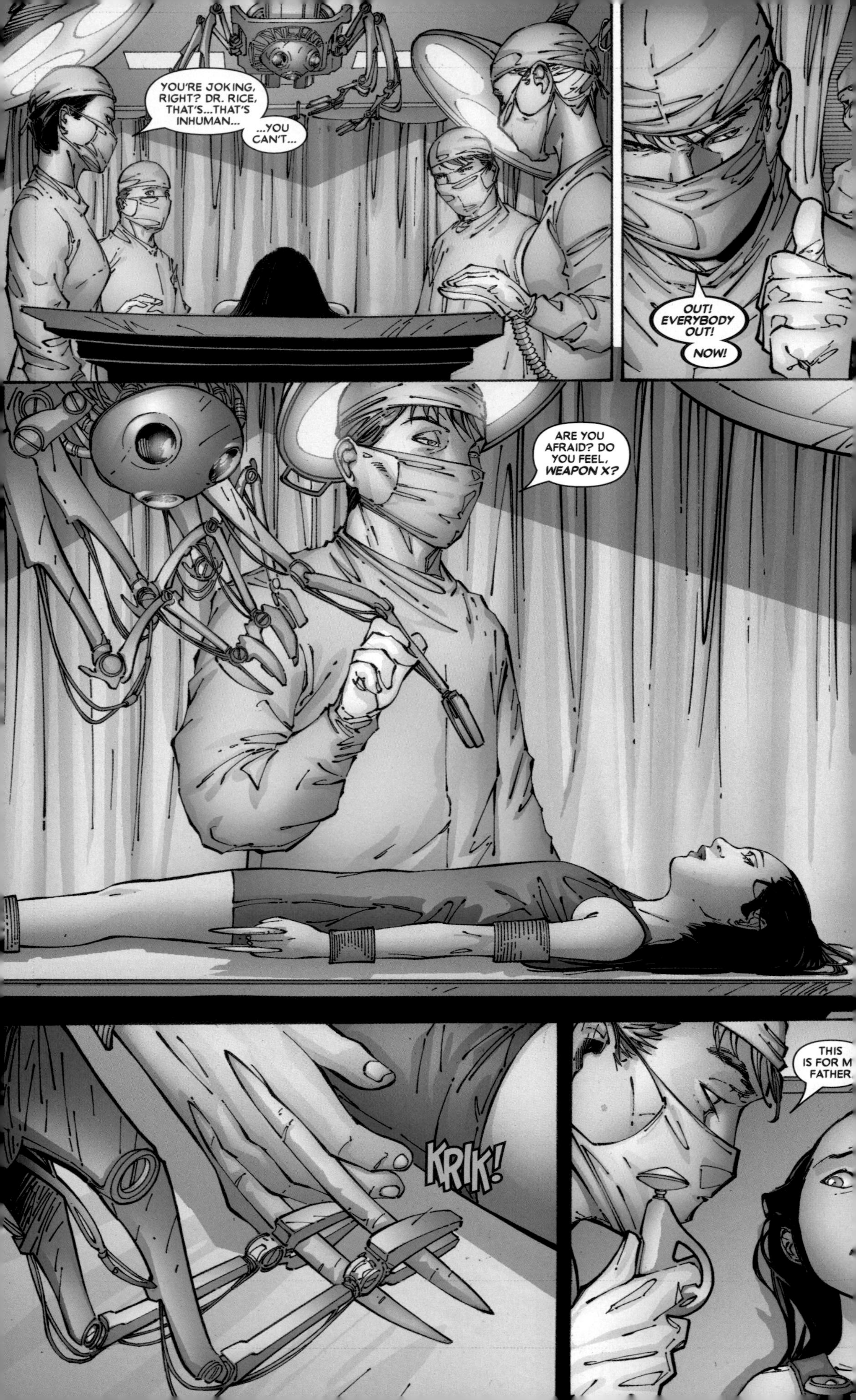
YOU'RE JOKING, RIGHT? DR. RICE, THAT'S...THAT'S INHUMAN...
...YOU CAN'T...
OUT! EVERYBODY OUT!
NOW!
ARE YOU AFRAID? DO YOU FEEL, WEAPON X?
KRIK!
THIS IS FOR M FATHER.

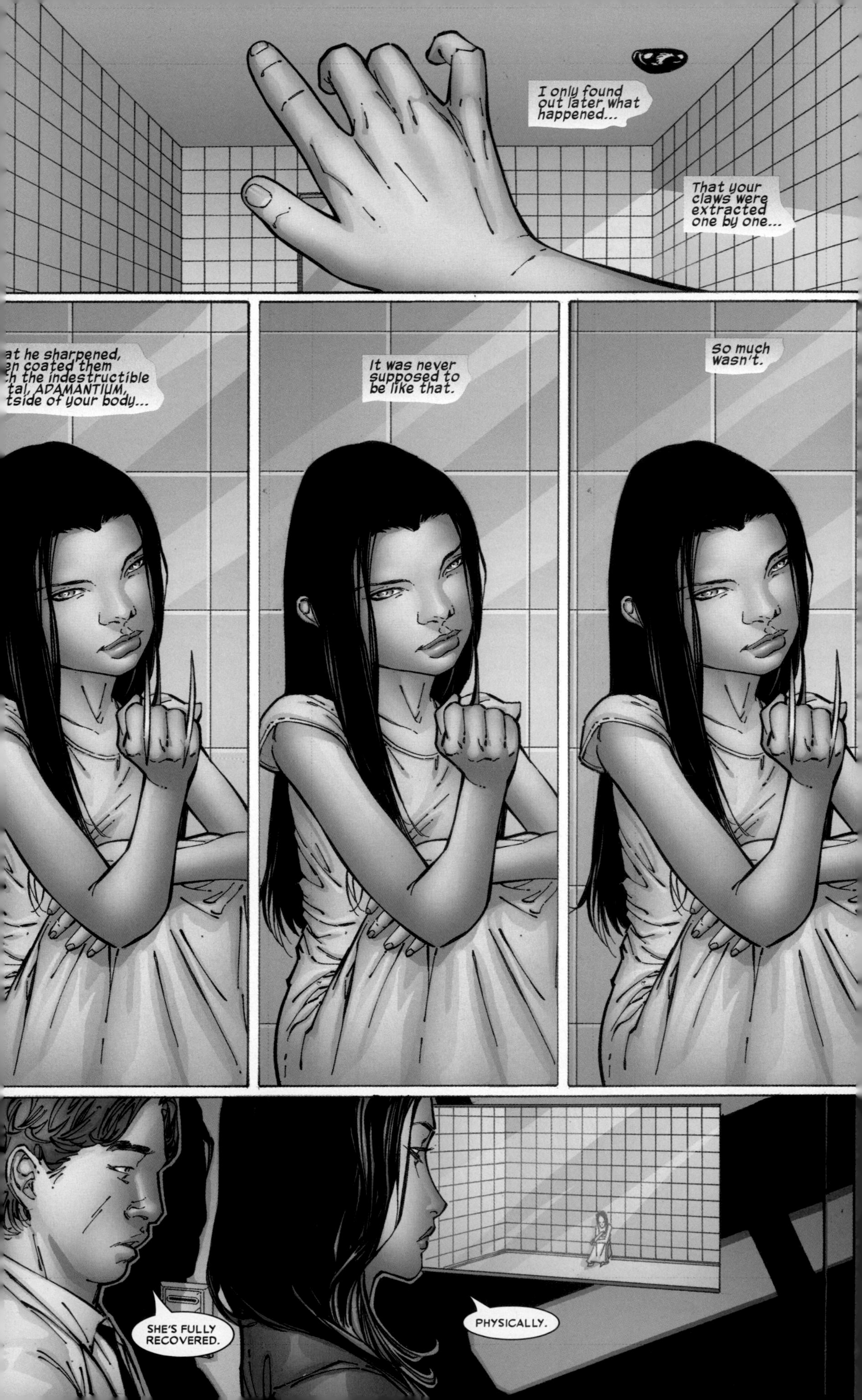

I only found out later what happened...
That your claws were extracted one by one...
at he sharpened, en coated them h the indestructible tal, ADAMANTIUM, tside of your body...
It was never supposed to be like that.
So much wasn't.
SHE'S FULLY RECOVERED.
PHYSICALLY.

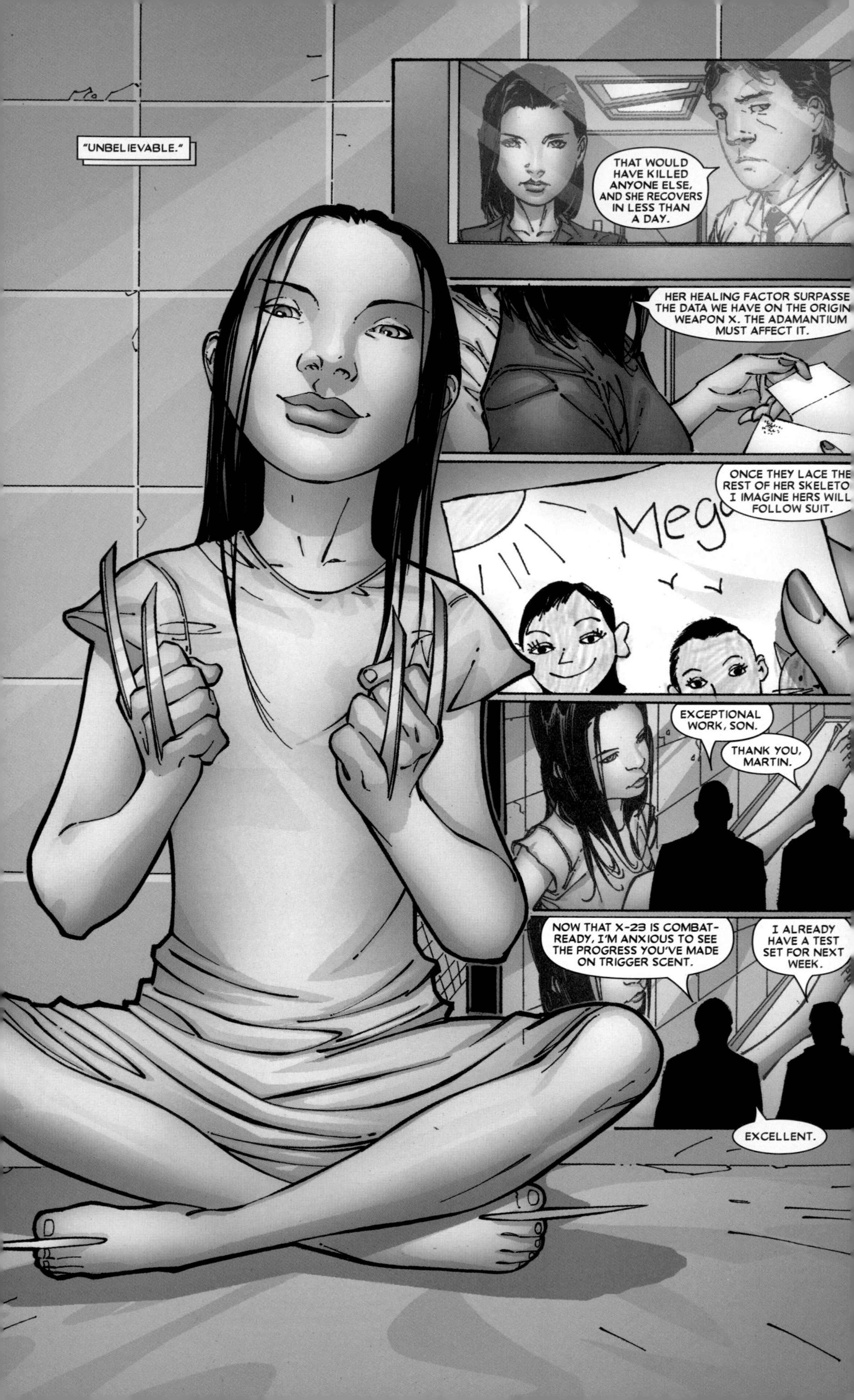
"UNBELIEVABLE."
THAT WOULD HAVE KILLED ANYONE ELSE, AND SHE RECOVERS IN LESS THAN A DAY.
HER HEALING FACTOR SURPASSE THE DATA WE HAVE ON THE ORIGIN WEAPON X. THE ADAMANTIUM MUST AFFECT IT.
ONCE THEY LACE THE REST OF HER SKELETO I IMAGINE HERS WILL FOLLOW SUIT.
Meg
EXCEPTIONAL WORK, SON.
THANK YOU, MARTIN.
NOW THAT X-23 IS COMBAT-READY, I'M ANXIOUS TO SEE THE PROGRESS YOU'VE MADE ON TRIGGER SCENT.
I ALREADY HAVE A TEST SET FOR NEXT WEEK.
EXCELLENT.

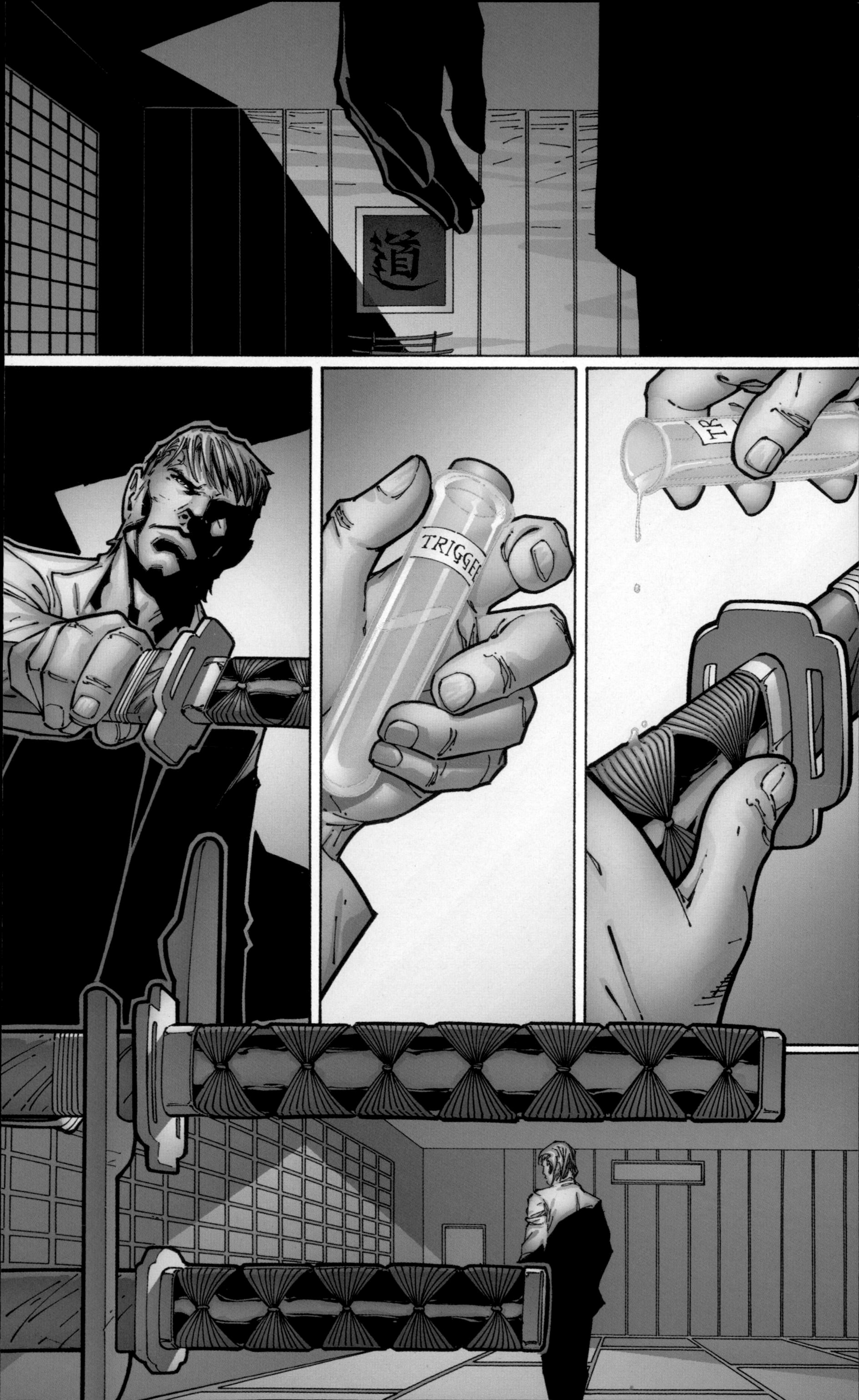

道
TRIGGE
TR

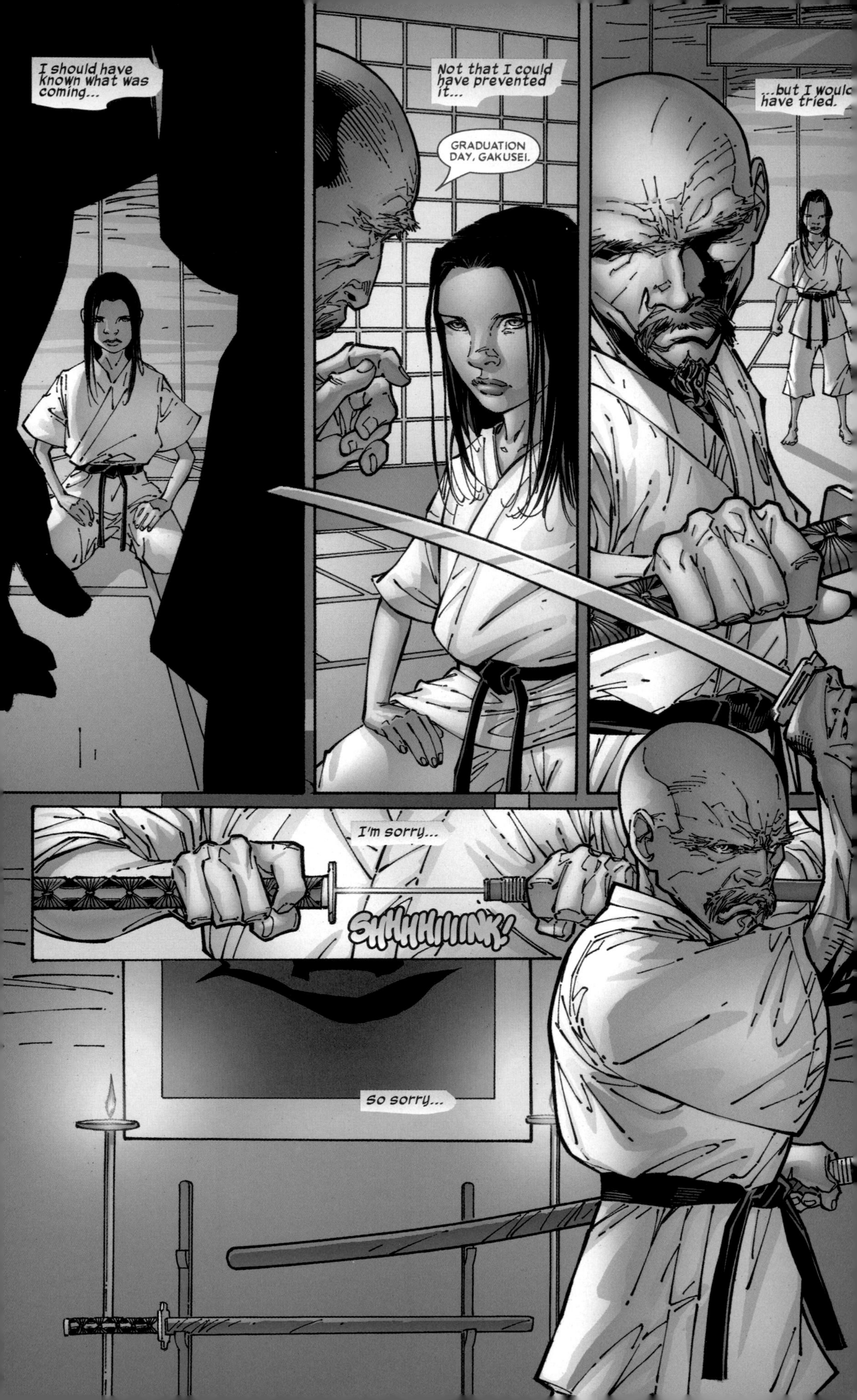
I should have known what was coming...
Not that I could have prevented it...
GRADUATION DAY, GAKUSEI.
...but I would have tried.
I'm sorry...
SHHHHIIIINK!
So sorry...

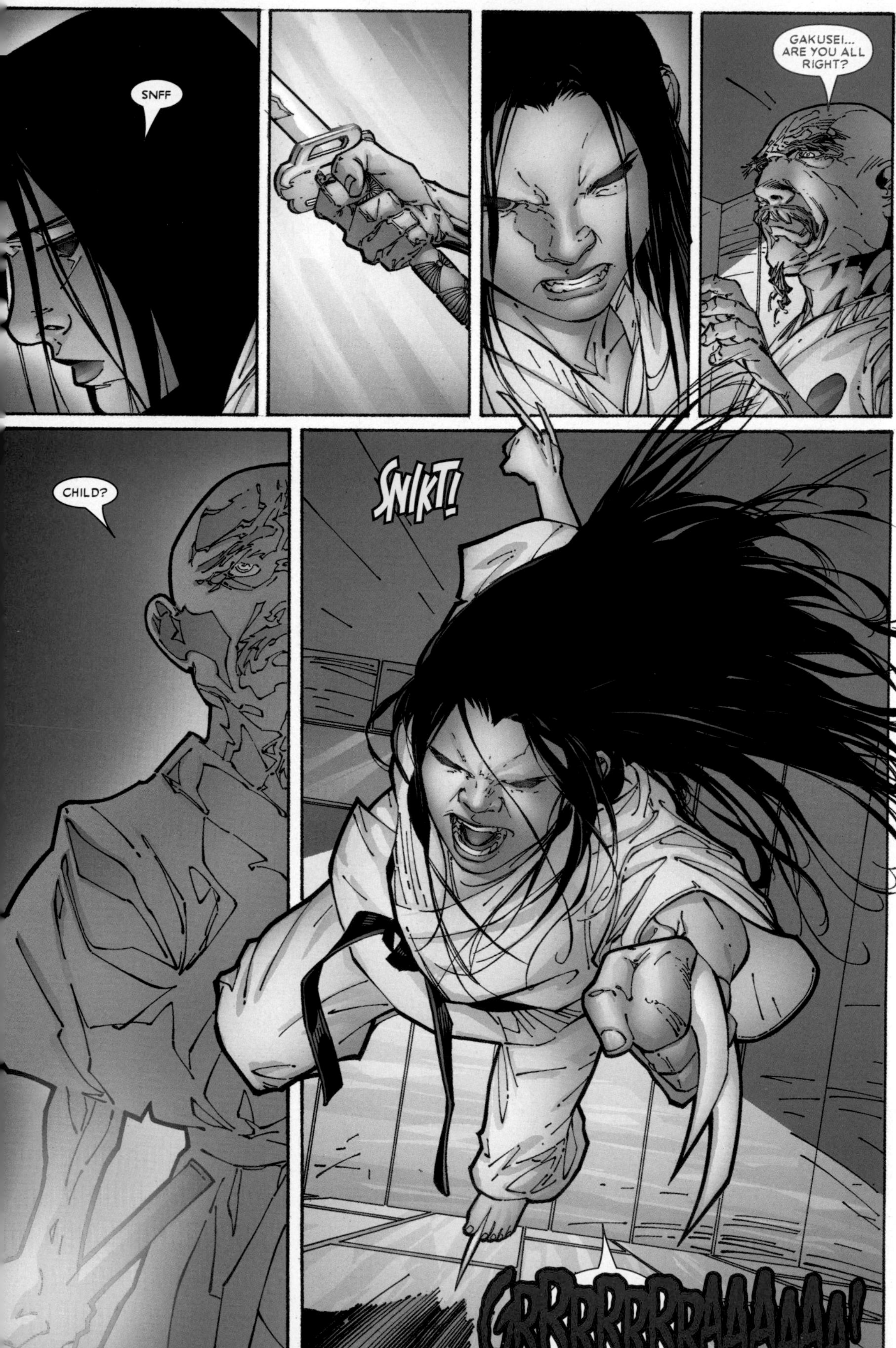
SNFF
GAKUSEI... ARE YOU ALL RIGHT?
CHILD?
SNIKT!
GRRRRRRRAAAAAA!

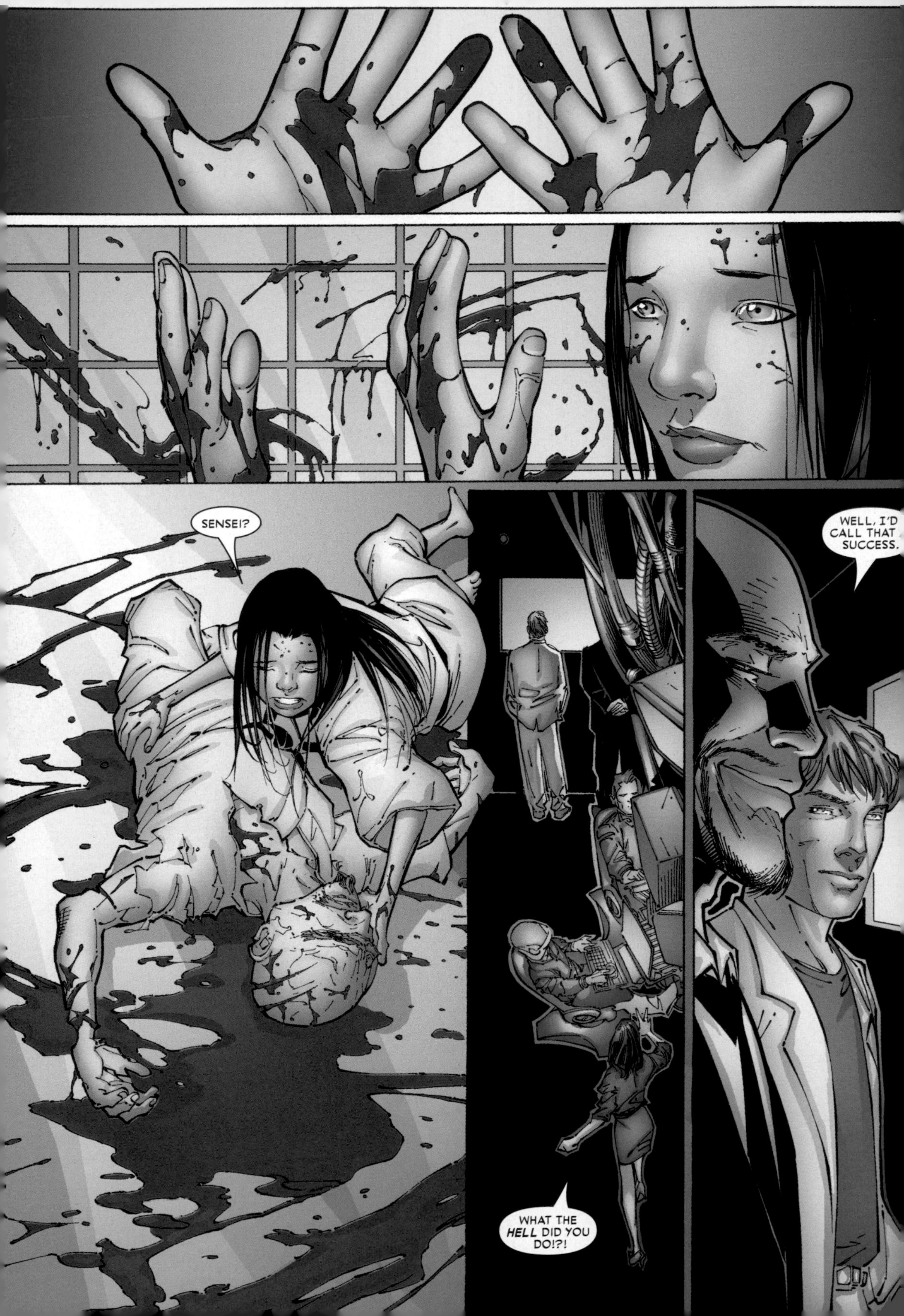
SENSEI!?
WHAT THE *HELL* DID YOU DO!?!
WELL, I'D CALL THAT SUCCESS.

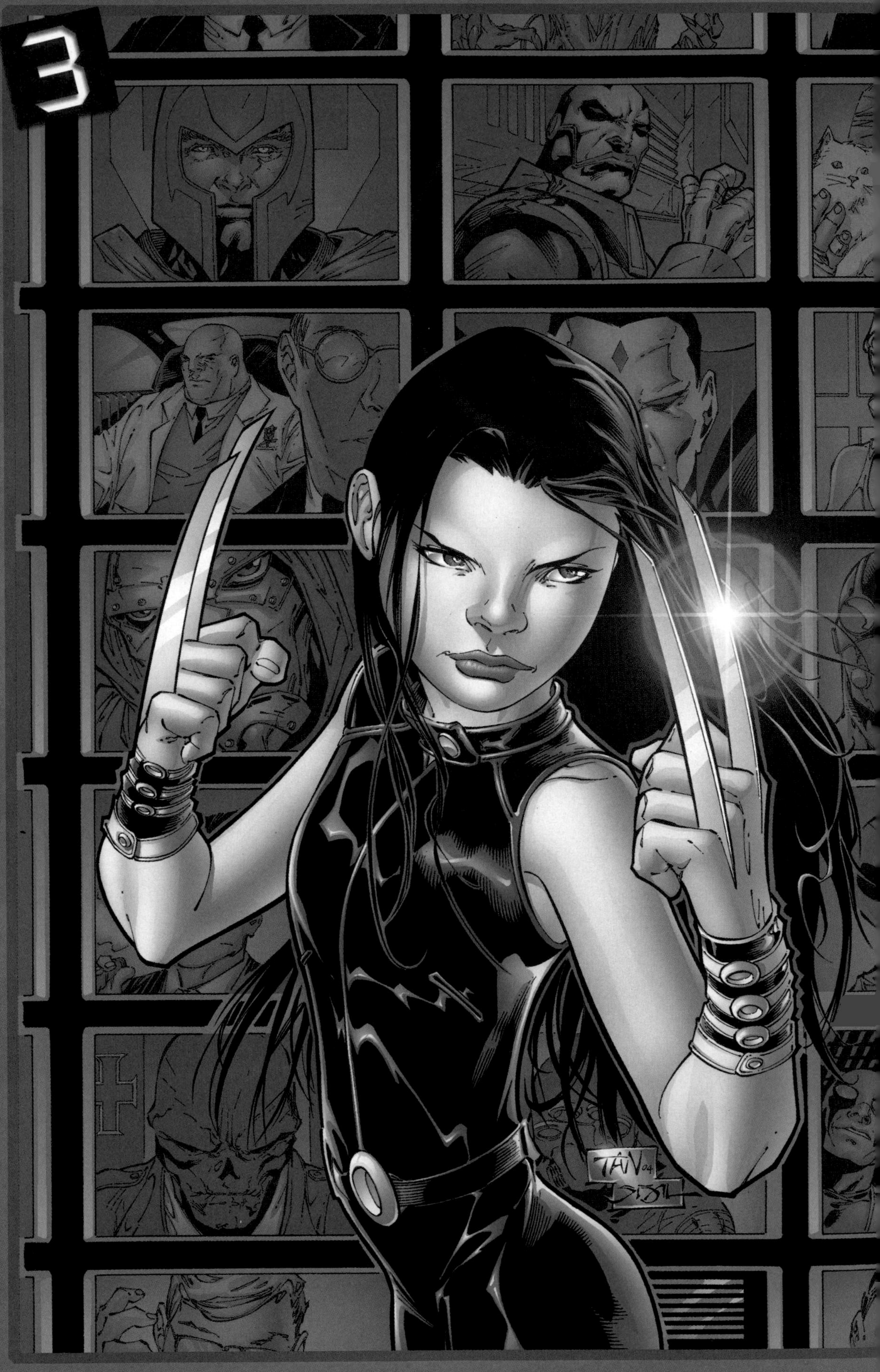
3

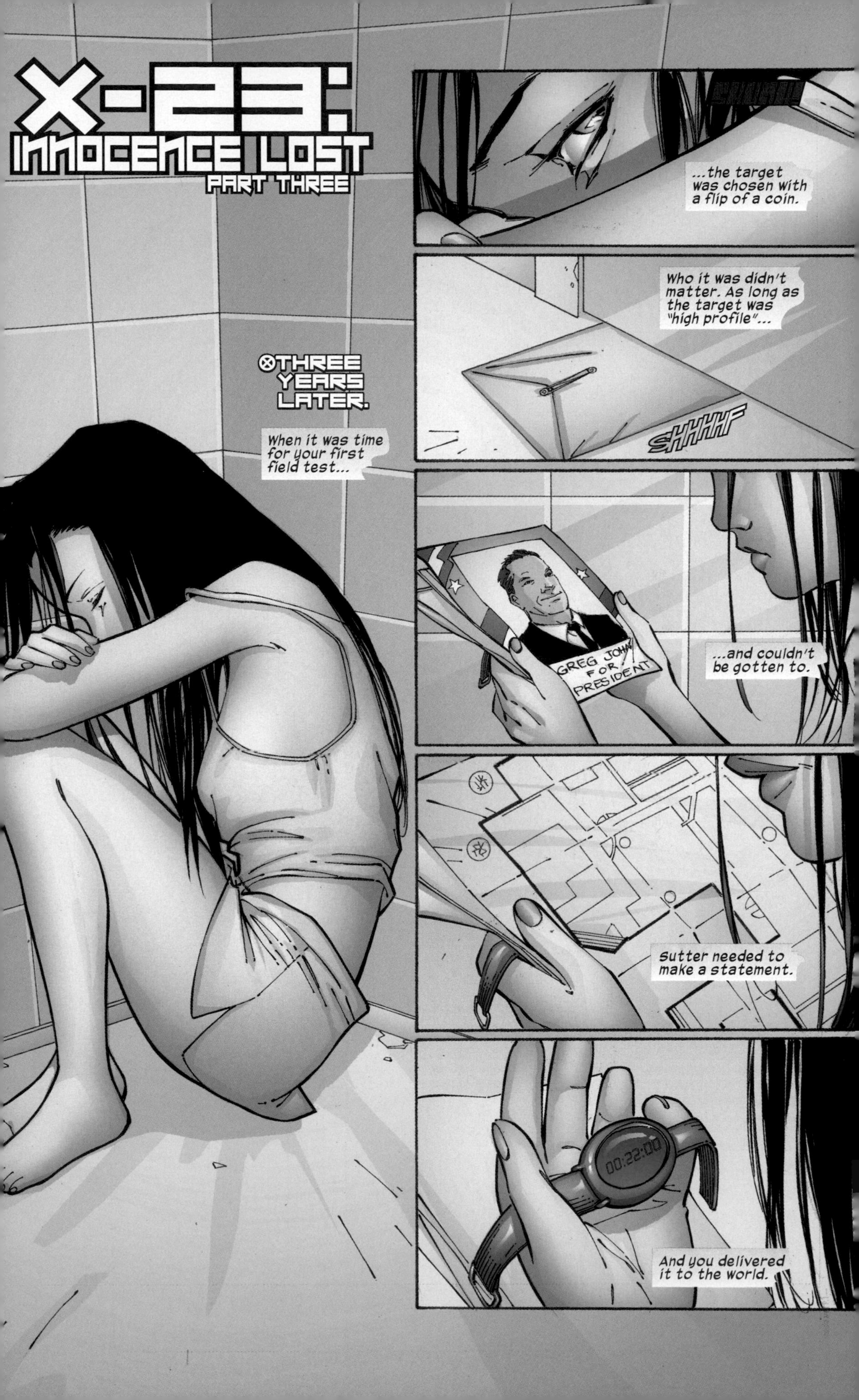

X-23:
INNOCENCE LOST
PART THREE
THREE YEARS LATER.
When it was time for your first field test...
...the target was chosen with a flip of a coin.
Who it was didn't matter. As long as the target was "high profile"...
SHHHHF
...and couldn't be gotten to.
GREG JOHN FOR PRESIDENT
Sutter needed to make a statement.
00:22:00
And you delivered it to the world.

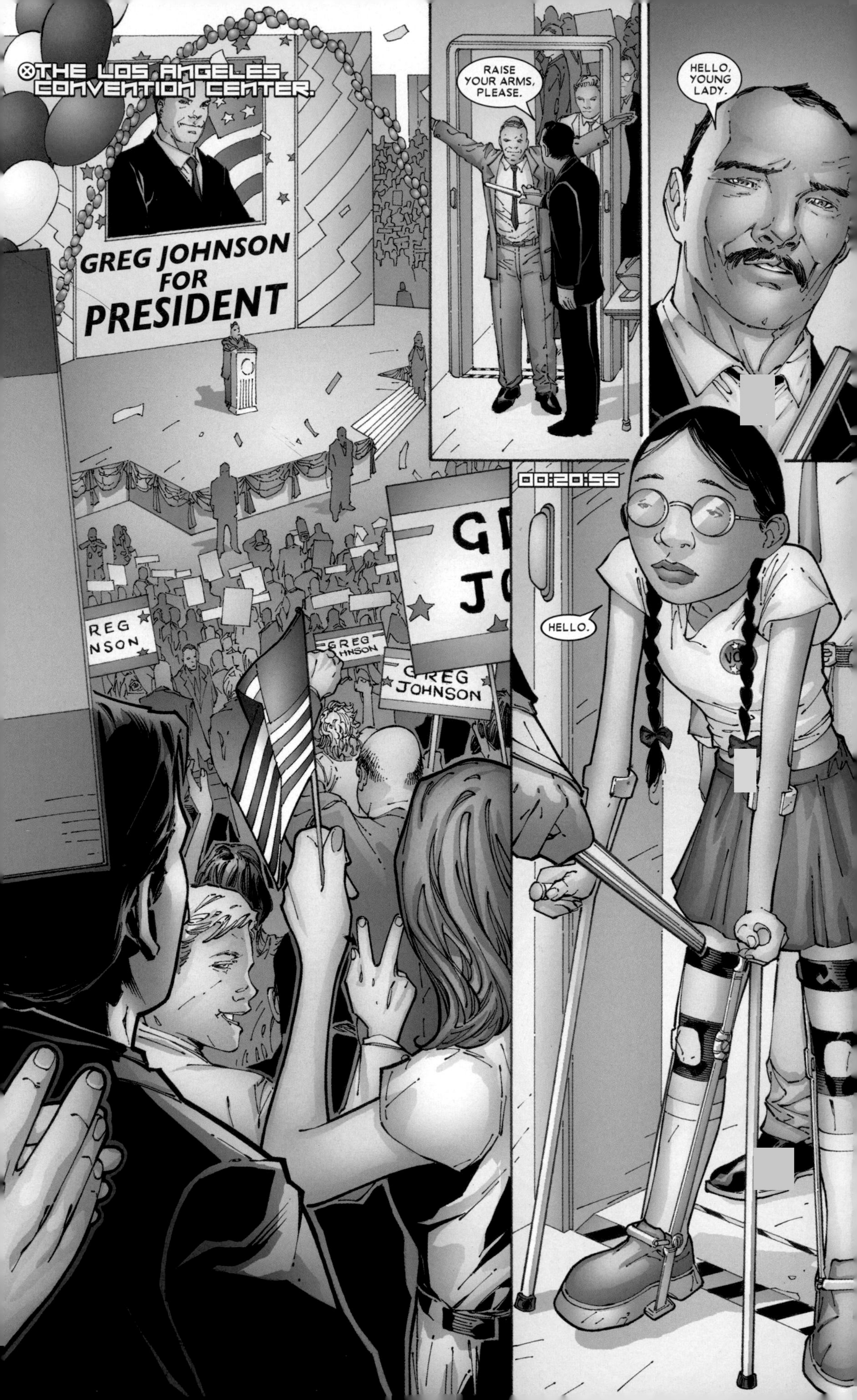
THE LOS ANGELES CONVENTION CENTER.
GREG JOHNSON FOR PRESIDENT
REG NSON
GREG JOHNSON
GREG JOHNSON
RAISE YOUR ARMS, PLEASE.
HELLO, YOUNG LADY.
00:20:55
HELLO.

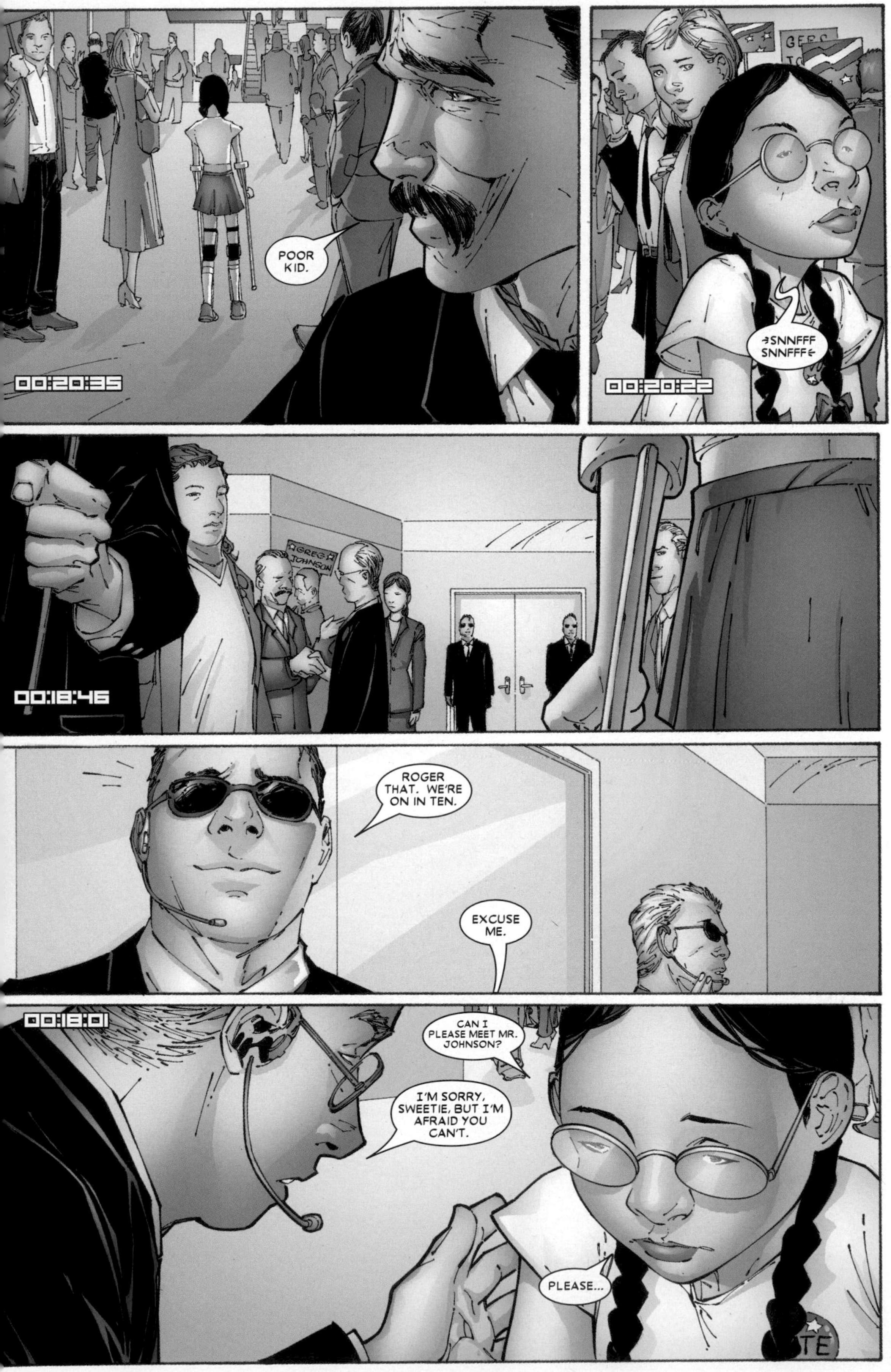
00:20:35
POOR KID.
00:20:22
SNNFFF SNNFFF
GREG JOHNSON
00:18:46
ROGER THAT. WE'RE ON IN TEN.
EXCUSE ME.
00:18:01
CAN I PLEASE MEET MR. JOHNSON?
I'M SORRY, SWEETIE, BUT I'M AFRAID YOU CAN'T.
PLEASE...

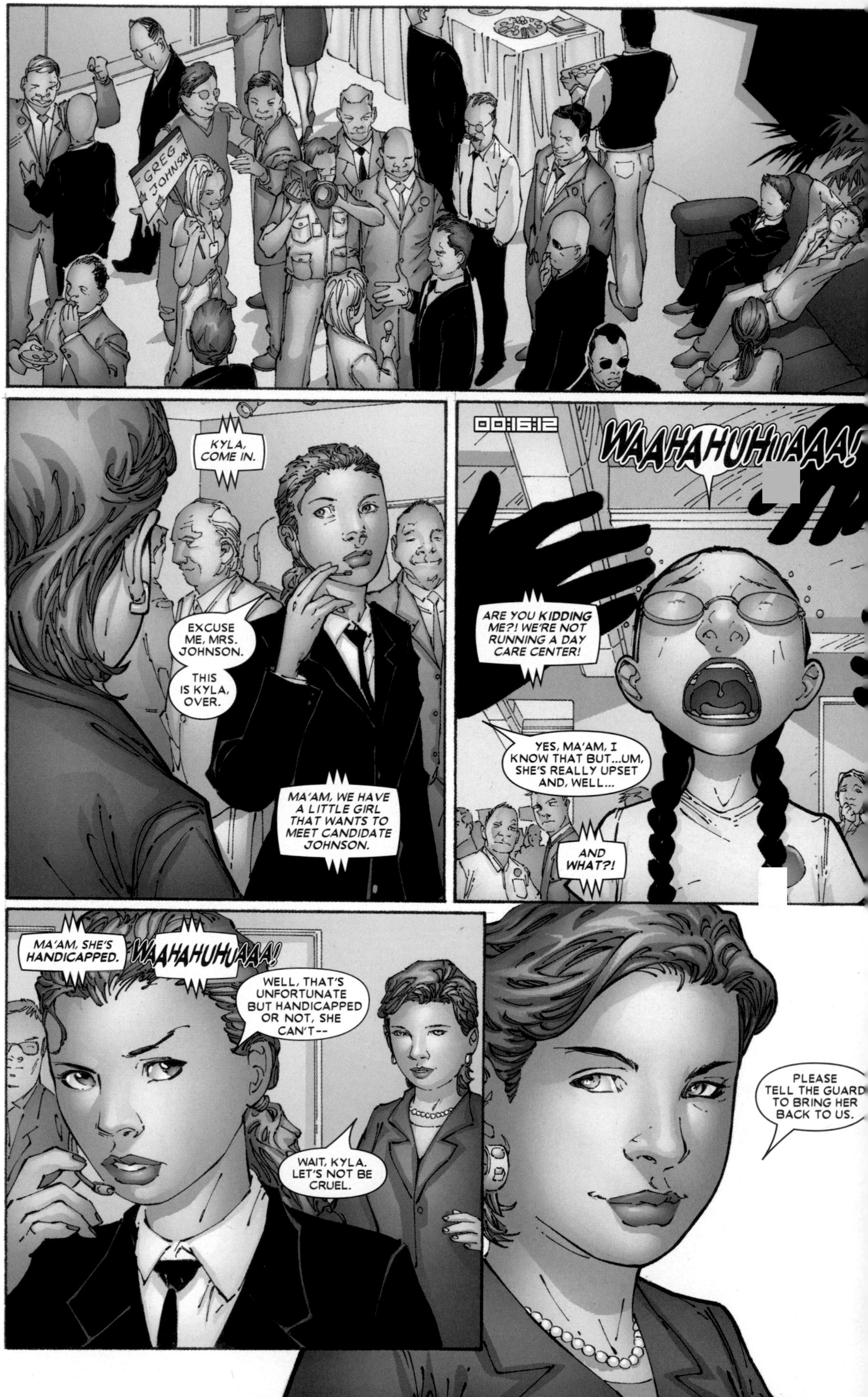
GREG JOHNSON
KYLA, COME IN.
EXCUSE ME, MRS. JOHNSON.
THIS IS KYLA, OVER.
MA'AM, WE HAVE A LITTLE GIRL THAT WANTS TO MEET CANDIDATE JOHNSON.
00:16:12
WAAHAHUHUAAA!
ARE YOU KIDDING ME?! WE'RE NOT RUNNING A DAY CARE CENTER!
YES, MA'AM, I KNOW THAT BUT...UM, SHE'S REALLY UPSET AND, WELL...
AND WHAT?!
MA'AM, SHE'S HANDICAPPED.
WAAHAHUHUAAA!
WELL, THAT'S UNFORTUNATE BUT HANDICAPPED OR NOT, SHE CAN'T--
WAIT, KYLA. LET'S NOT BE CRUEL.
PLEASE TELL THE GUARD TO BRING HER BACK TO US.

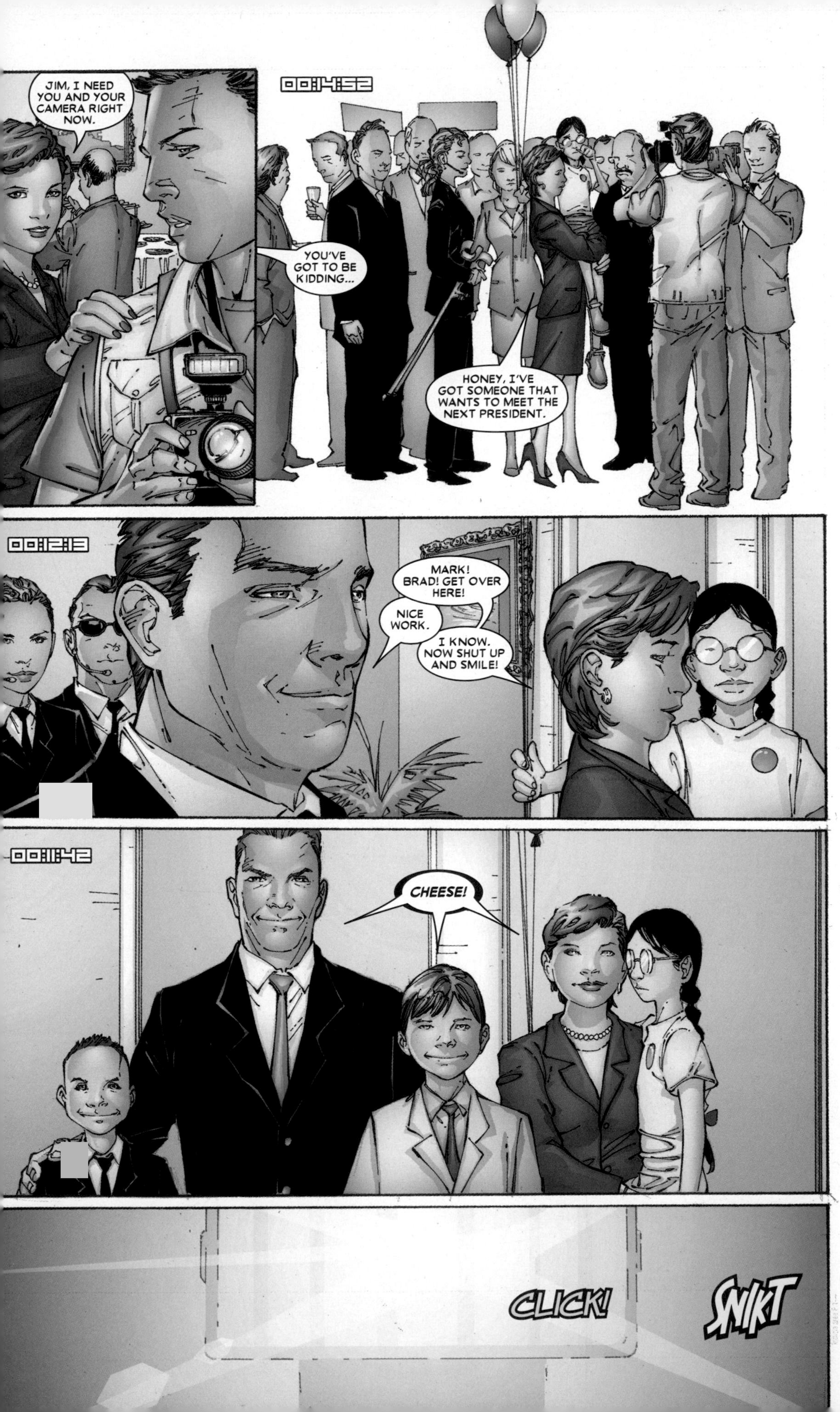
JIM, I NEED YOU AND YOUR CAMERA RIGHT NOW.
00:14:52
YOU'VE GOT TO BE KIDDING...
HONEY, I'VE GOT SOMEONE THAT WANTS TO MEET THE NEXT PRESIDENT.
00:12:13
MARK! BRAD! GET OVER HERE!
NICE WORK.
I KNOW. NOW SHUT UP AND SMILE!
00:11:42
CHEESE!
CLICK!
SNIKT

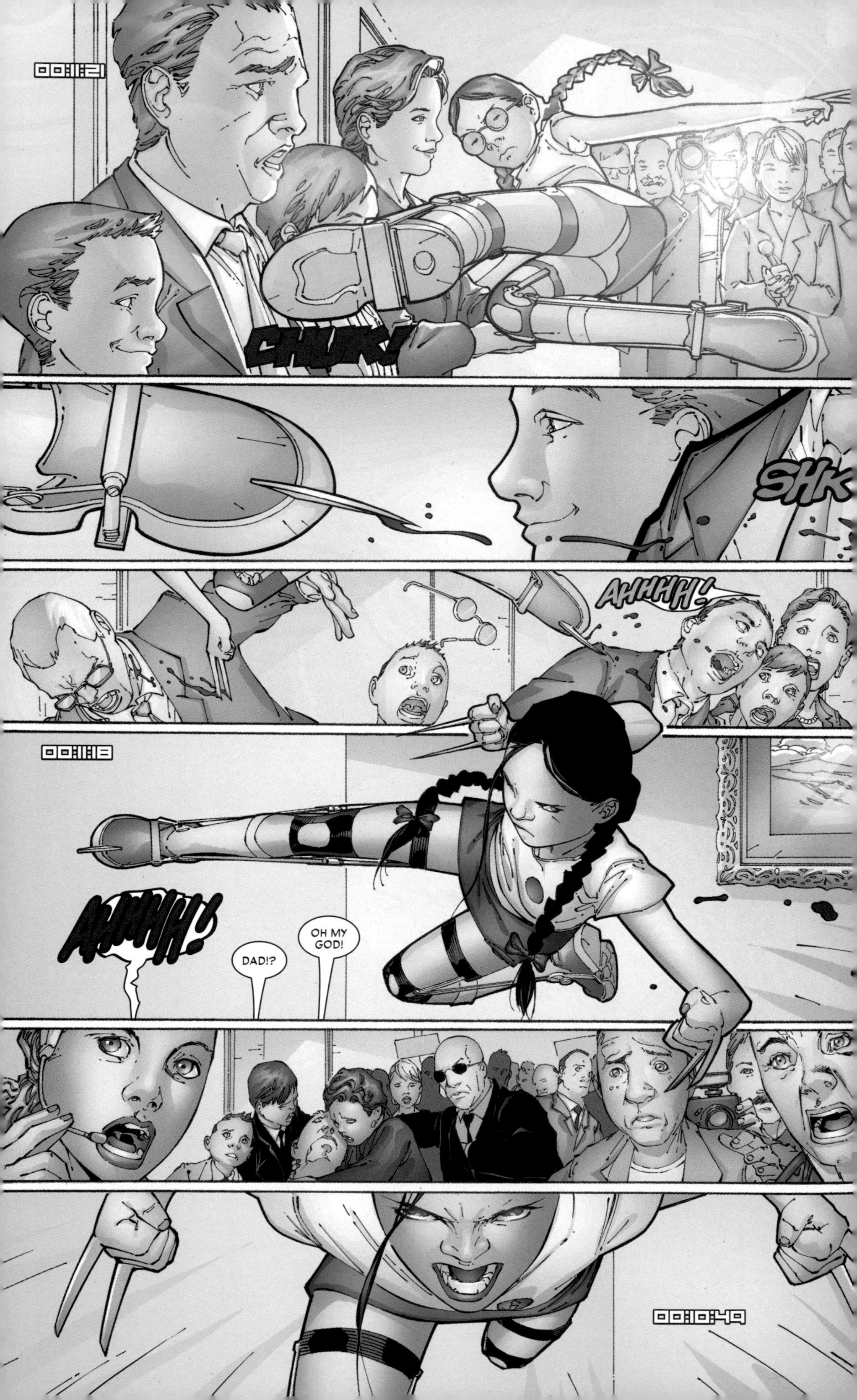

00:11:21
CHUK!
SHK
AHHHH!
00:11:18
AHHHH!
DAD!?
OH MY GOD!
00:10:49

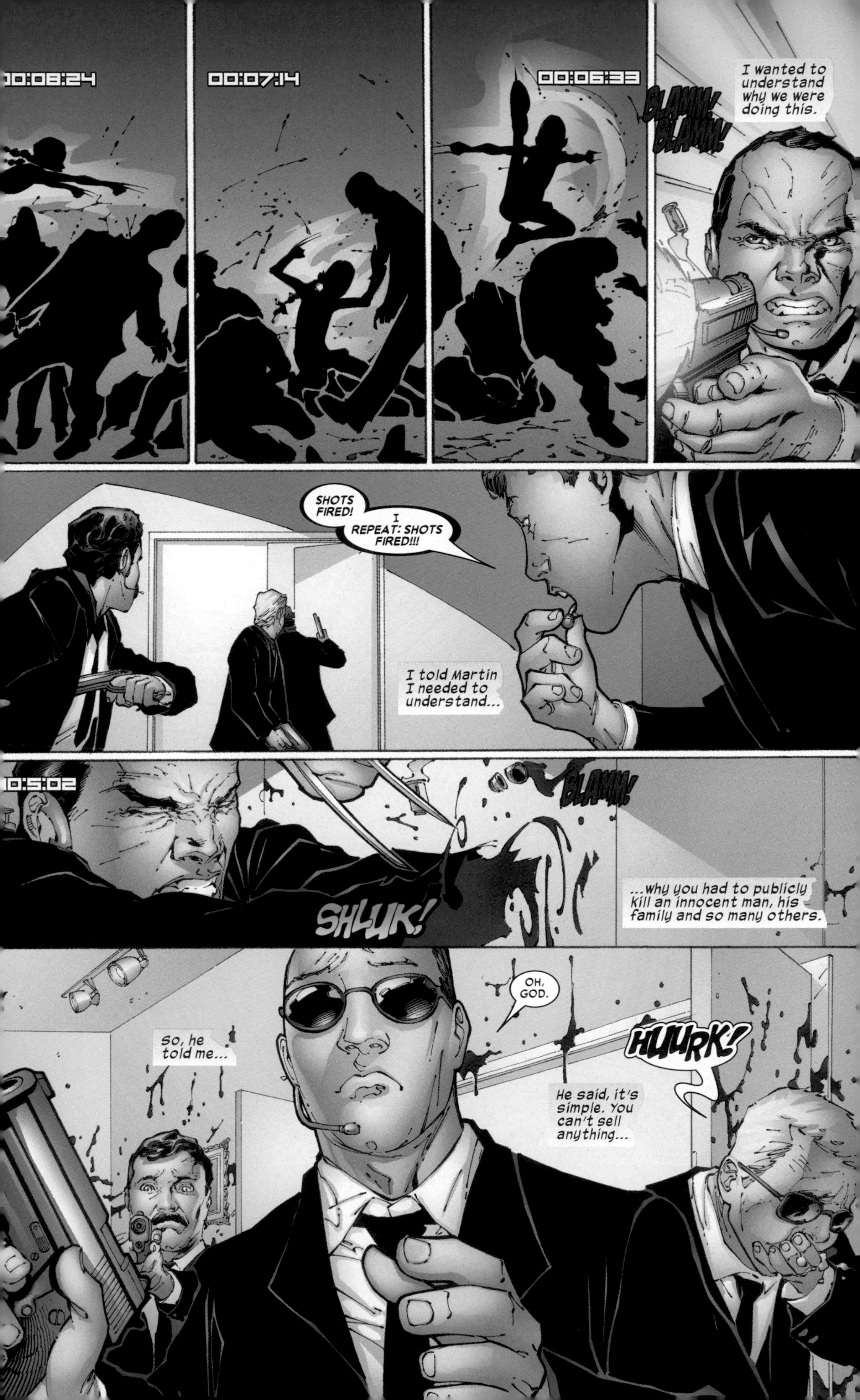
00:08:24
00:07:14
00:06:33
BLAMM! BLAMM!
I wanted to understand why we were doing this.
SHOTS FIRED!
I REPEAT: SHOTS FIRED!!!
I told Martin I needed to understand...
0:5:02
BLAMM!
SHLUK!
...why you had to publicly kill an innocent man, his family and so many others.
So, he told me...
OH, GOD.
HUURK!
He said, it's simple. You can't sell anything...

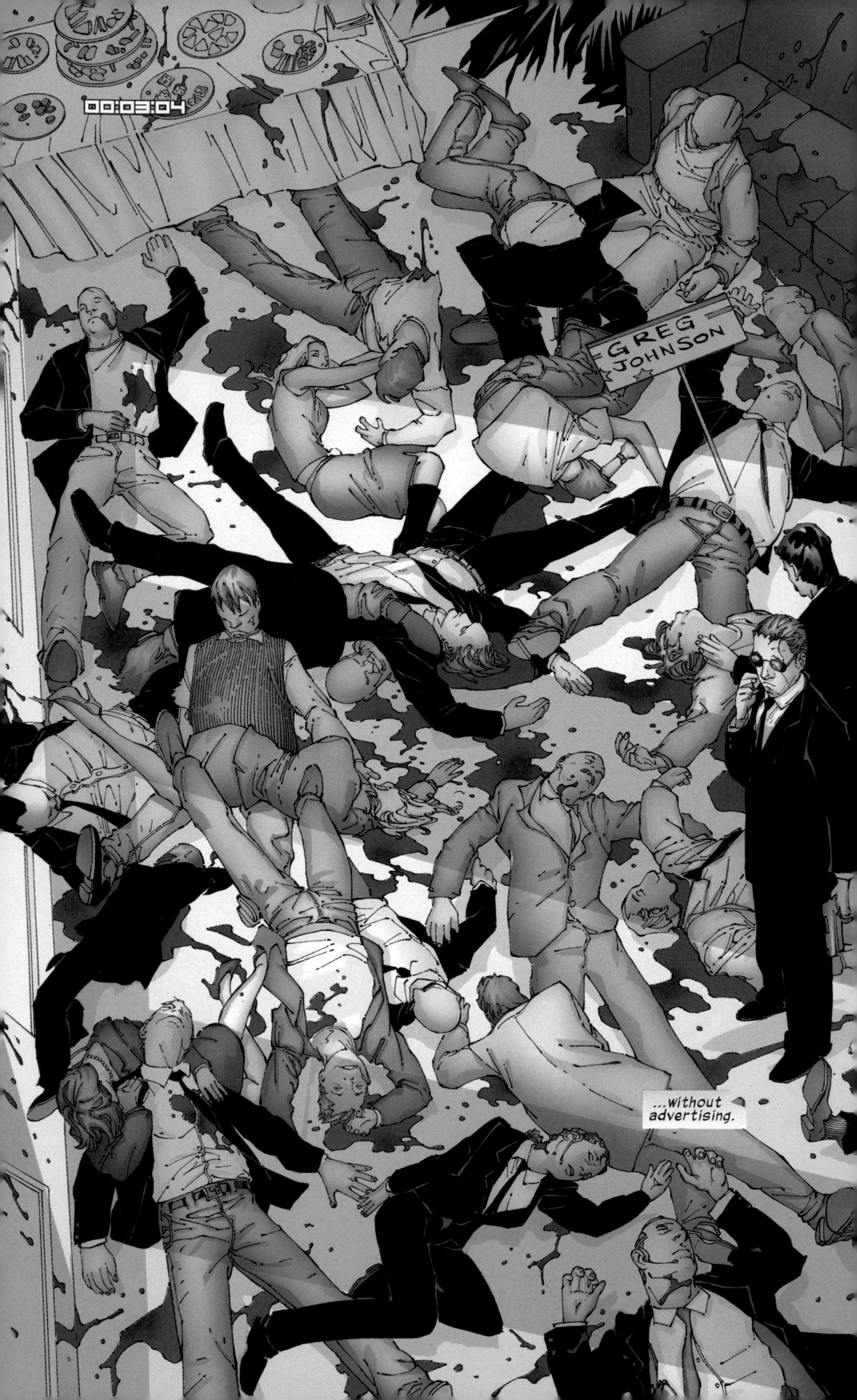
00:03:04
GREG JOHNSON
...without advertising.

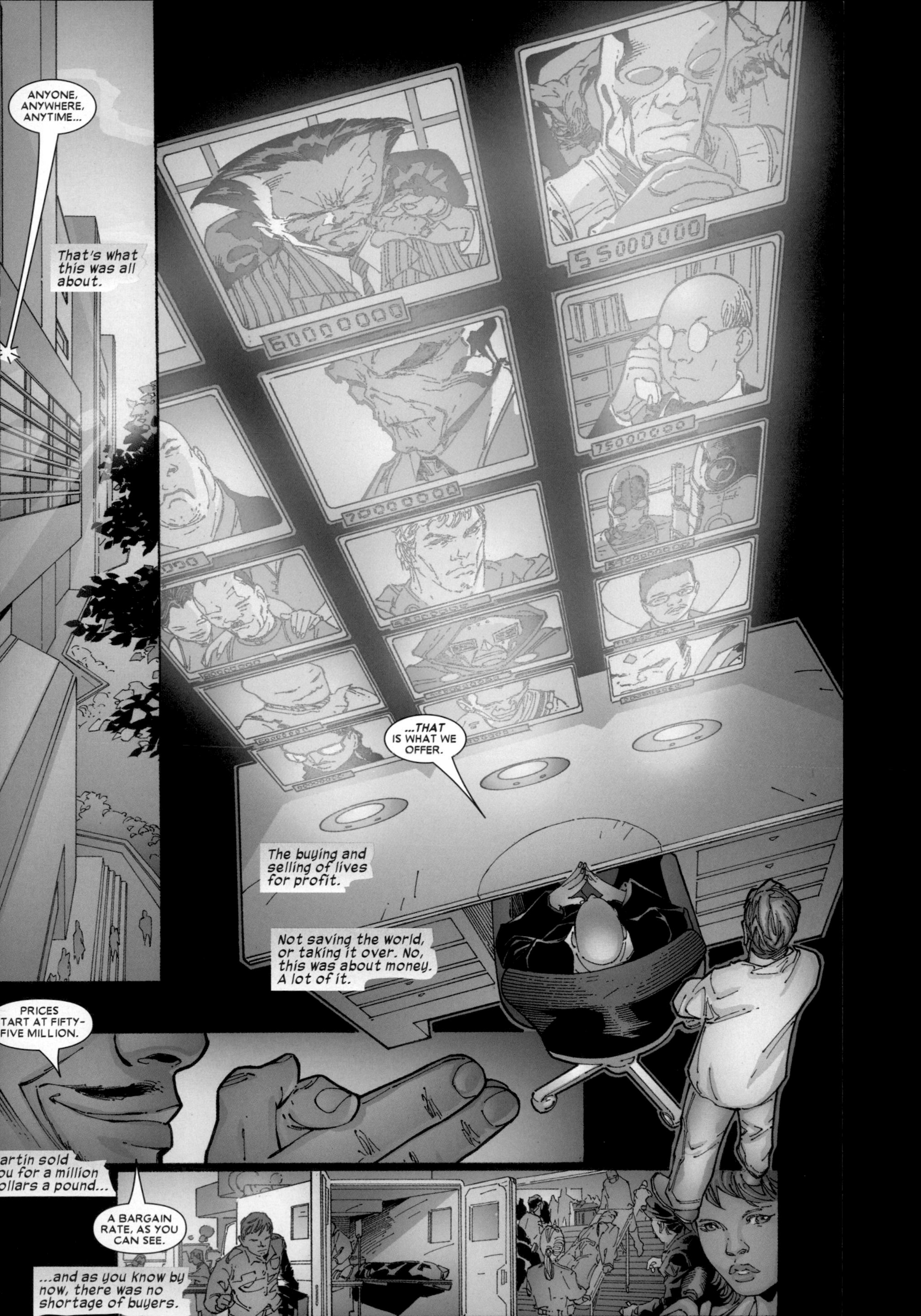
ANYONE, ANYWHERE, ANYTIME...
That's what this was all about.
55000000
60000000
75000000
70000000
...THAT IS WHAT WE OFFER.
The buying and selling of lives for profit.
Not saving the world, or taking it over. No, this was about money. A lot of it.
PRICES TART AT FIFTY-FIVE MILLION.
artin sold ou for a million ollars a pound...
A BARGAIN RATE, AS YOU CAN SEE.
...and as you know by now, there was no shortage of buyers.

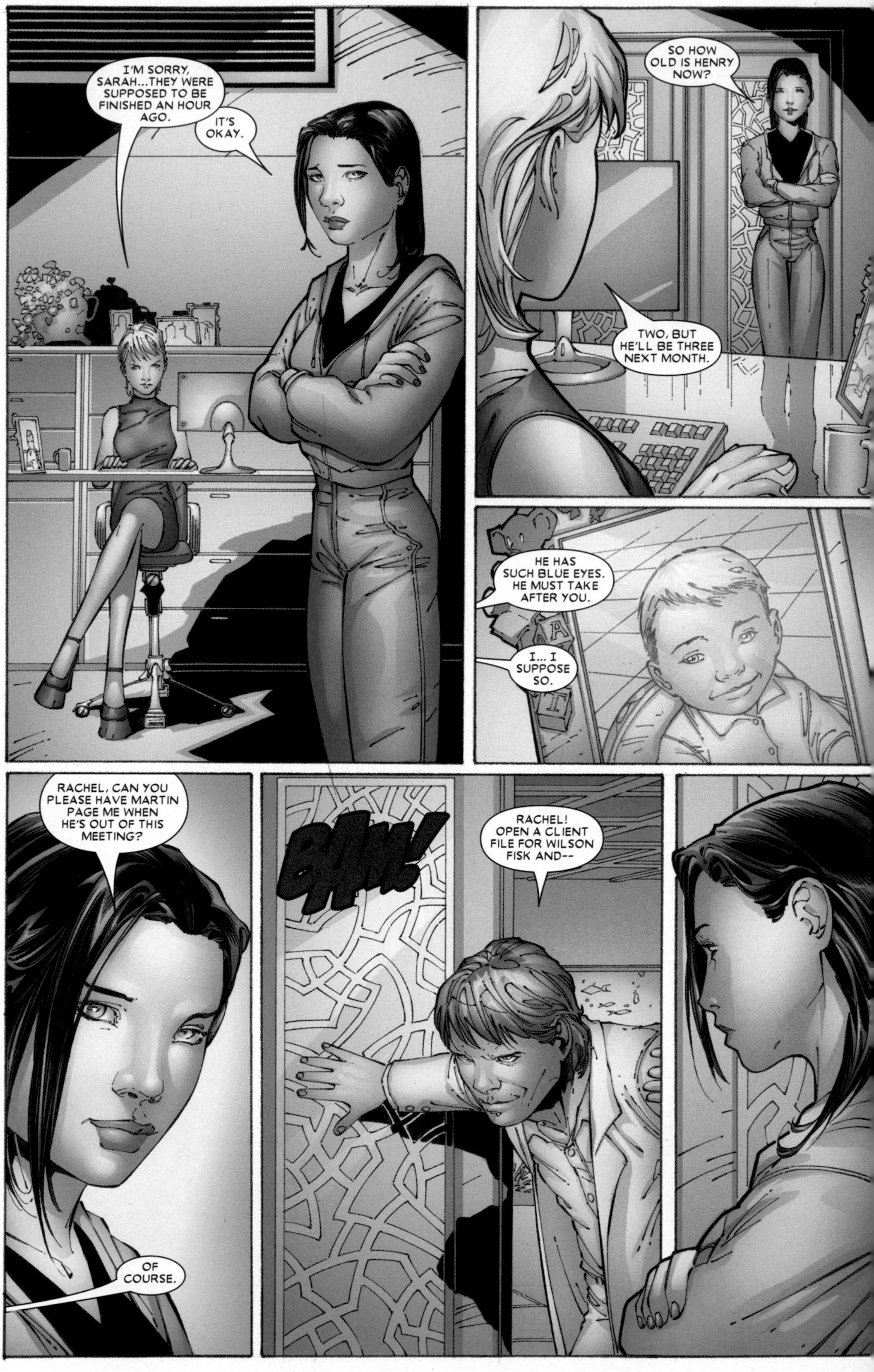
I'M SORRY, SARAH...THEY WERE SUPPOSED TO BE FINISHED AN HOUR AGO.
IT'S OKAY.
SO HOW OLD IS HENRY NOW?
TWO, BUT HE'LL BE THREE NEXT MONTH.
HE HAS SUCH BLUE EYES. HE MUST TAKE AFTER YOU.
I... I SUPPOSE SO.
RACHEL, CAN YOU PLEASE HAVE MARTIN PAGE ME WHEN HE'S OUT OF THIS MEETING?
OF COURSE.
BAM!
RACHEL! OPEN A CLIENT FILE FOR WILSON FISK AND--

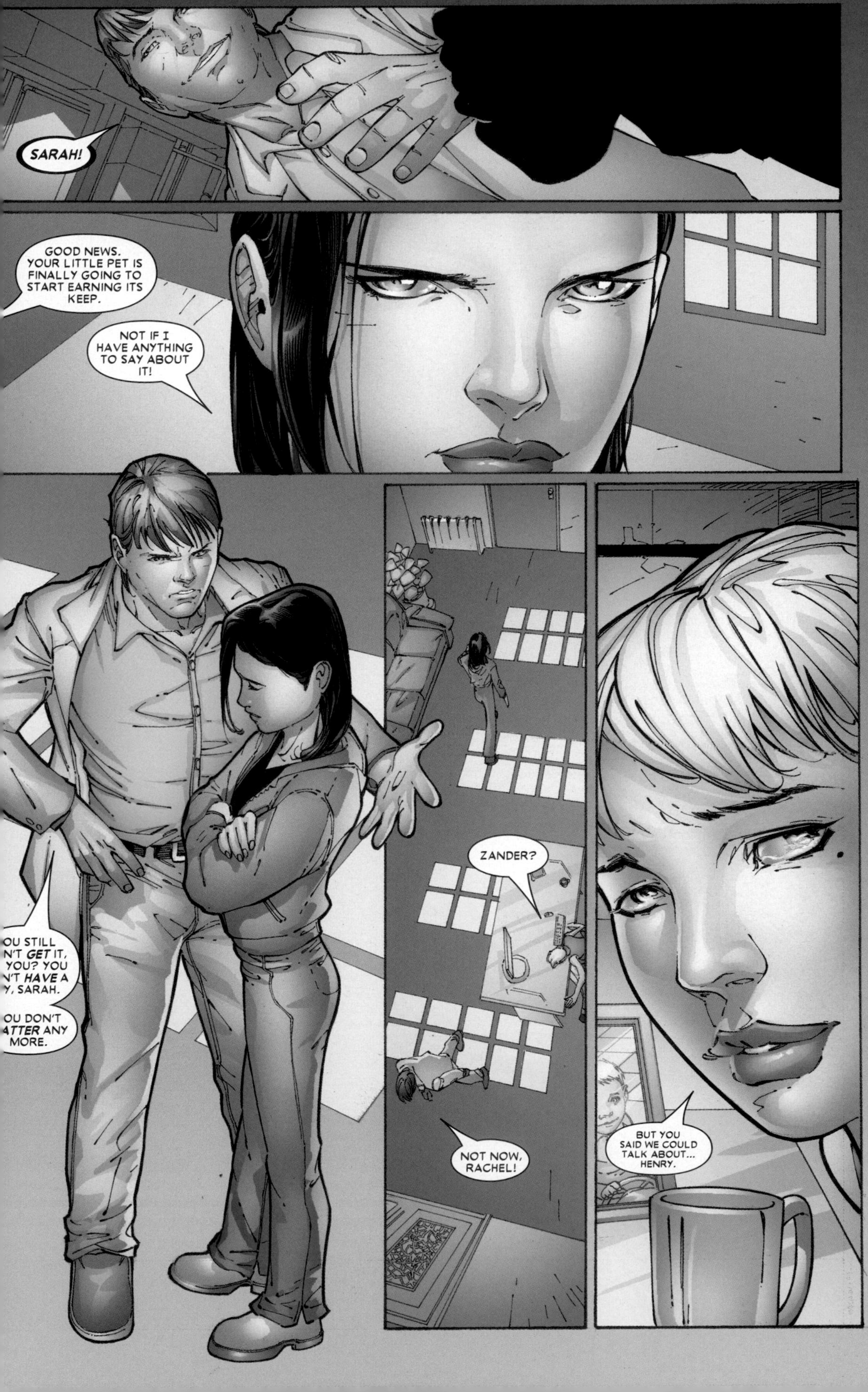
SARAH!
GOOD NEWS. YOUR LITTLE PET IS FINALLY GOING TO START EARNING ITS KEEP.
NOT IF I HAVE ANYTHING TO SAY ABOUT IT!
OU STILL N'T GET IT, YOU? YOU N'T HAVE A Y, SARAH.
OU DON'T ATTER ANY MORE.
ZANDER?
NOT NOW, RACHEL!
BUT YOU SAID WE COULD TALK ABOUT... HENRY.

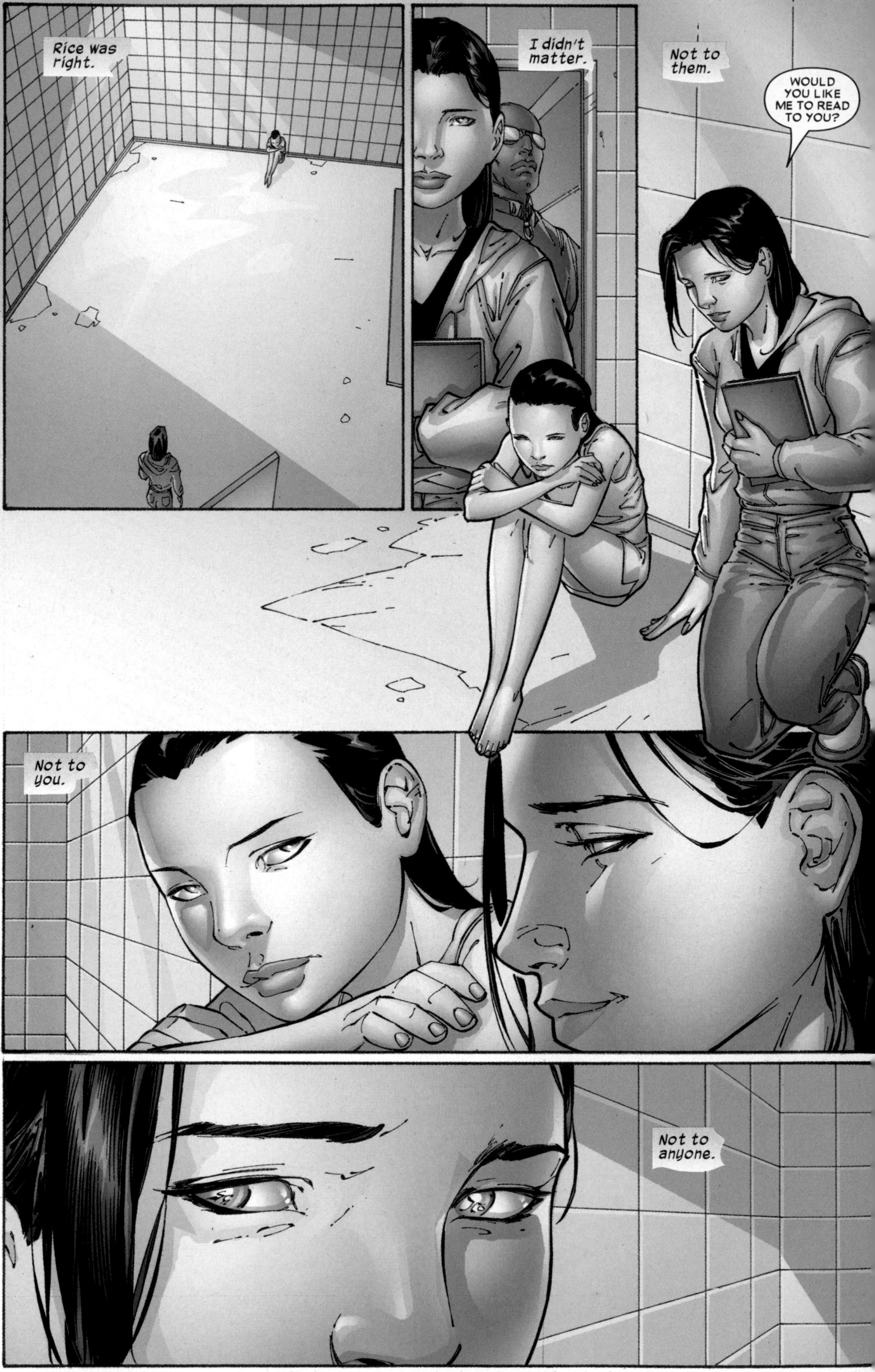
Rice was right.
I didn't matter.
Not to them.
WOULD YOU LIKE ME TO READ TO YOU?
Not to you.
Not to anyone.

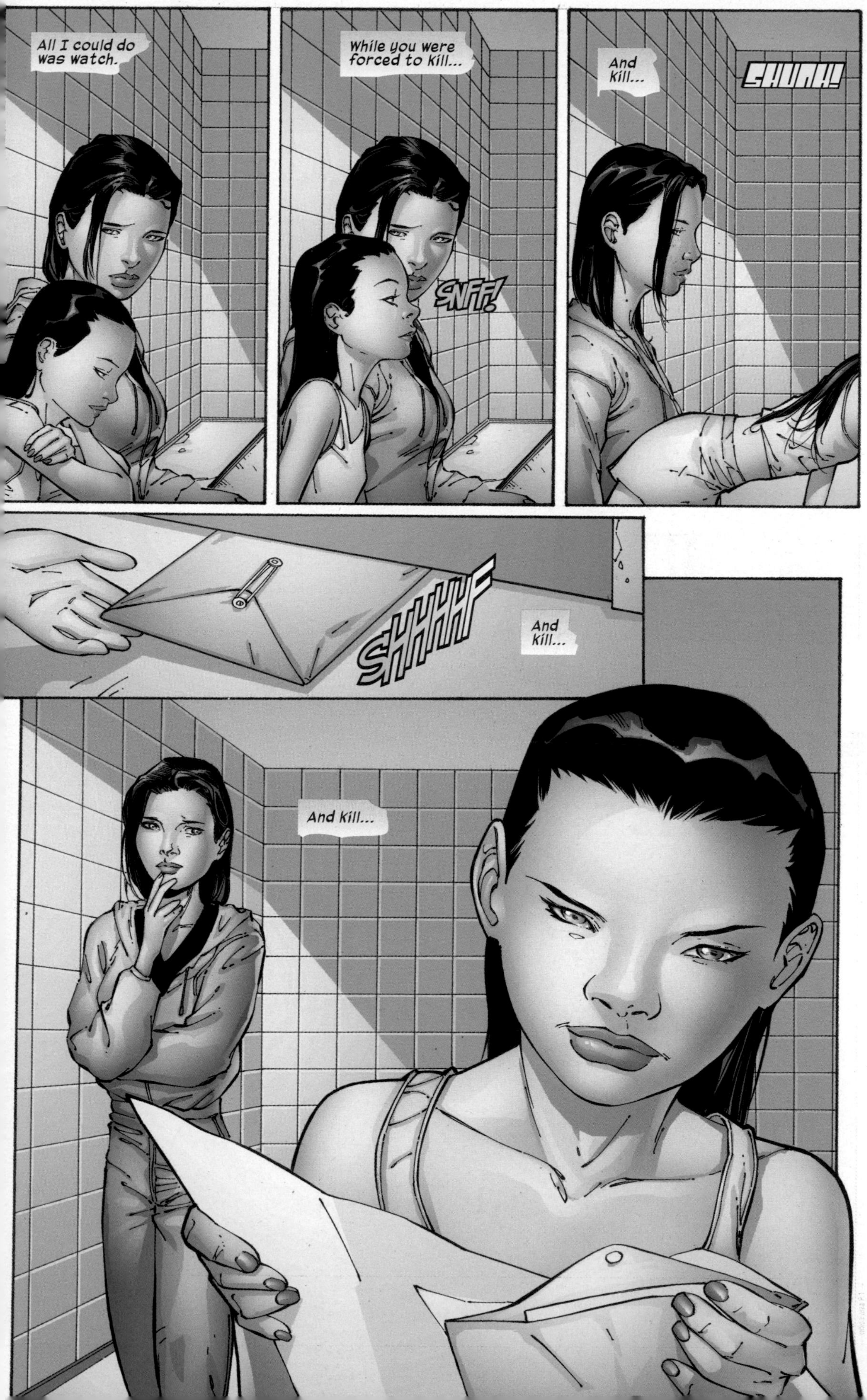
All I could do was watch.
While you were forced to kill...
SNFF!
And kill...
SHUNK!
SHHHF
And kill...
And kill...

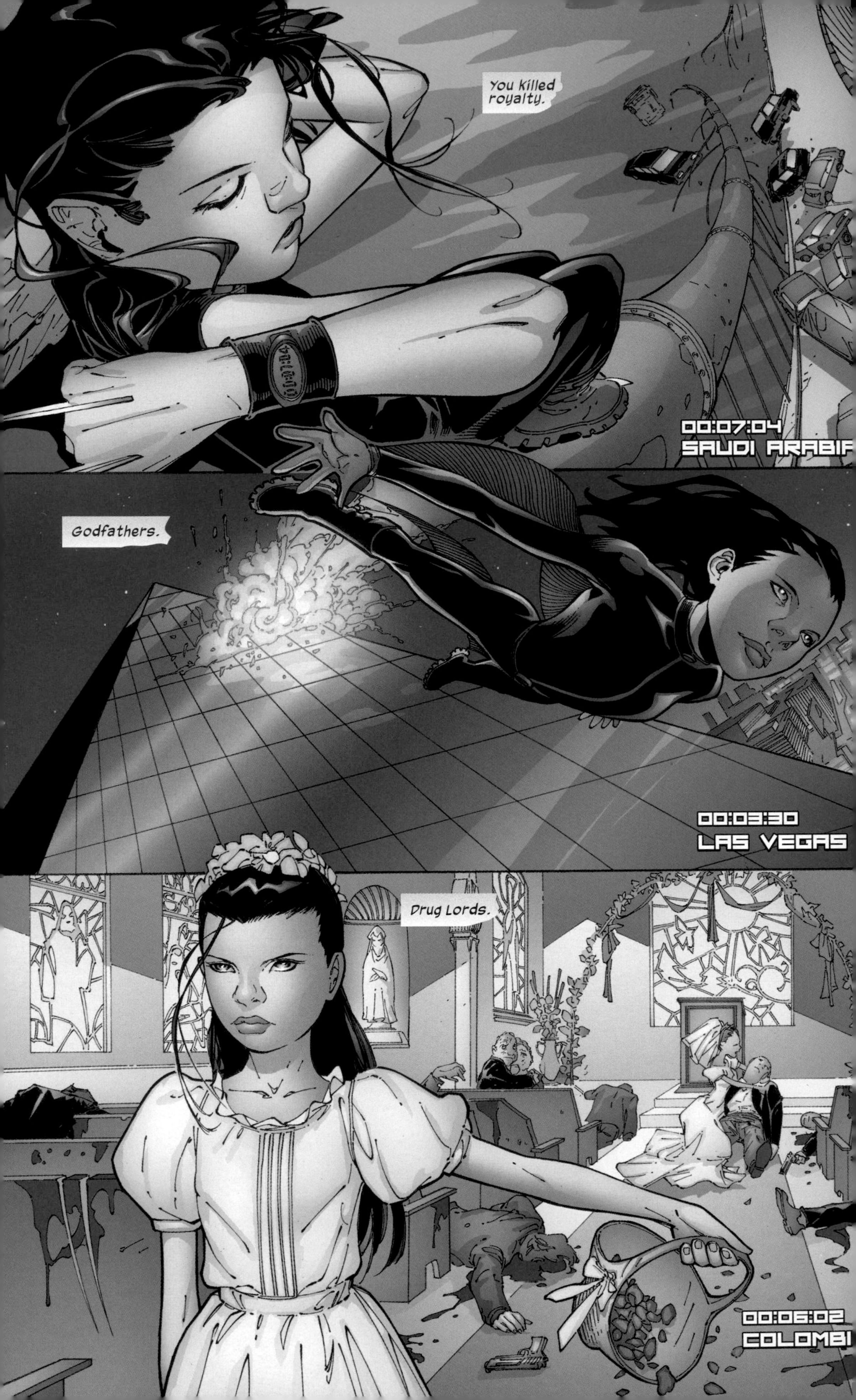
You killed royalty.
00:07:04
SAUDI ARABIA
Godfathers.
00:03:30
LAS VEGAS
Drug Lords.
00:06:02
COLOMBI

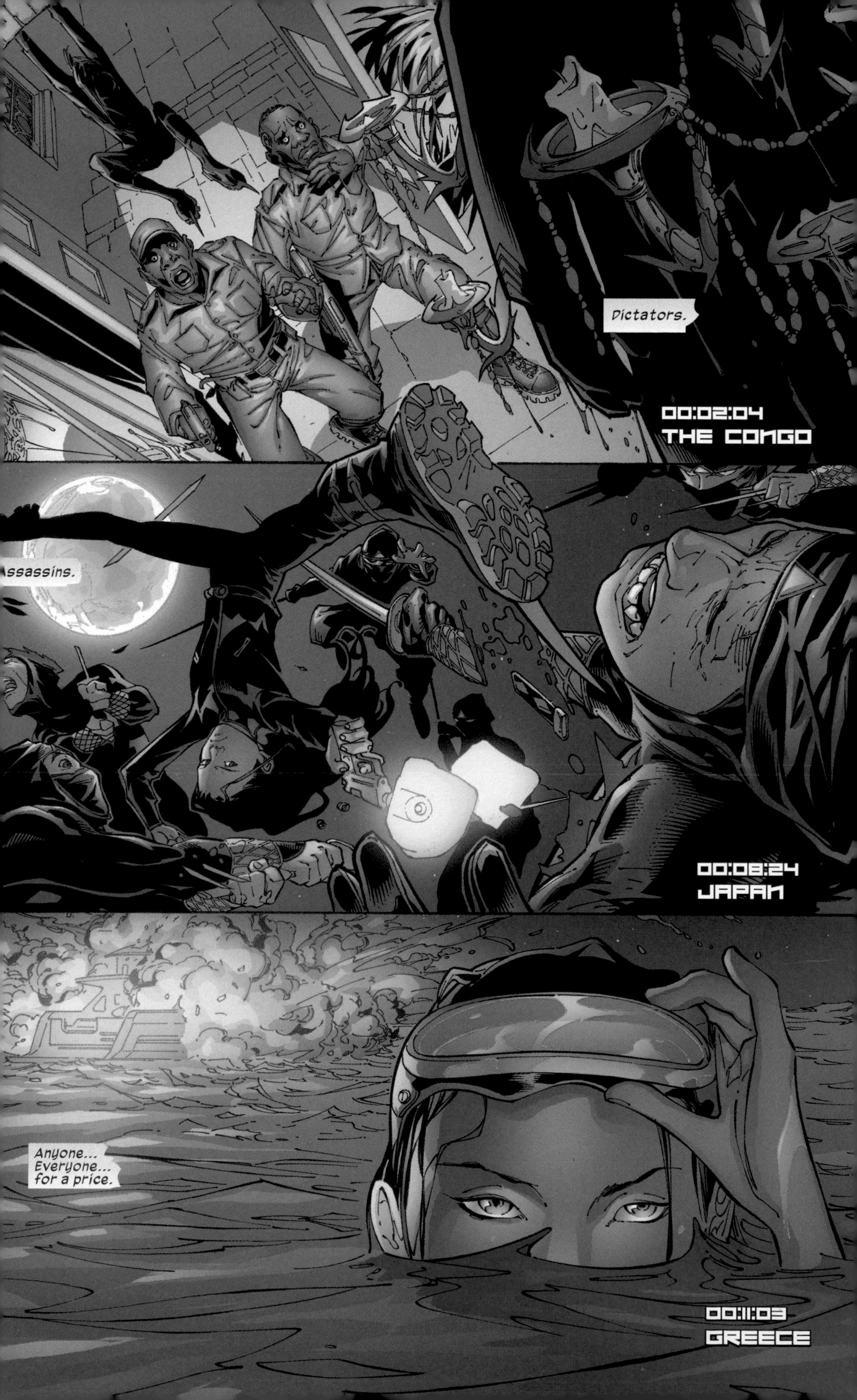
Dictators.
00:02:04
THE CONGO
ssassins.
00:08:24
JAPAN
Anyone... Everyone... for a price.
00:11:03
GREECE

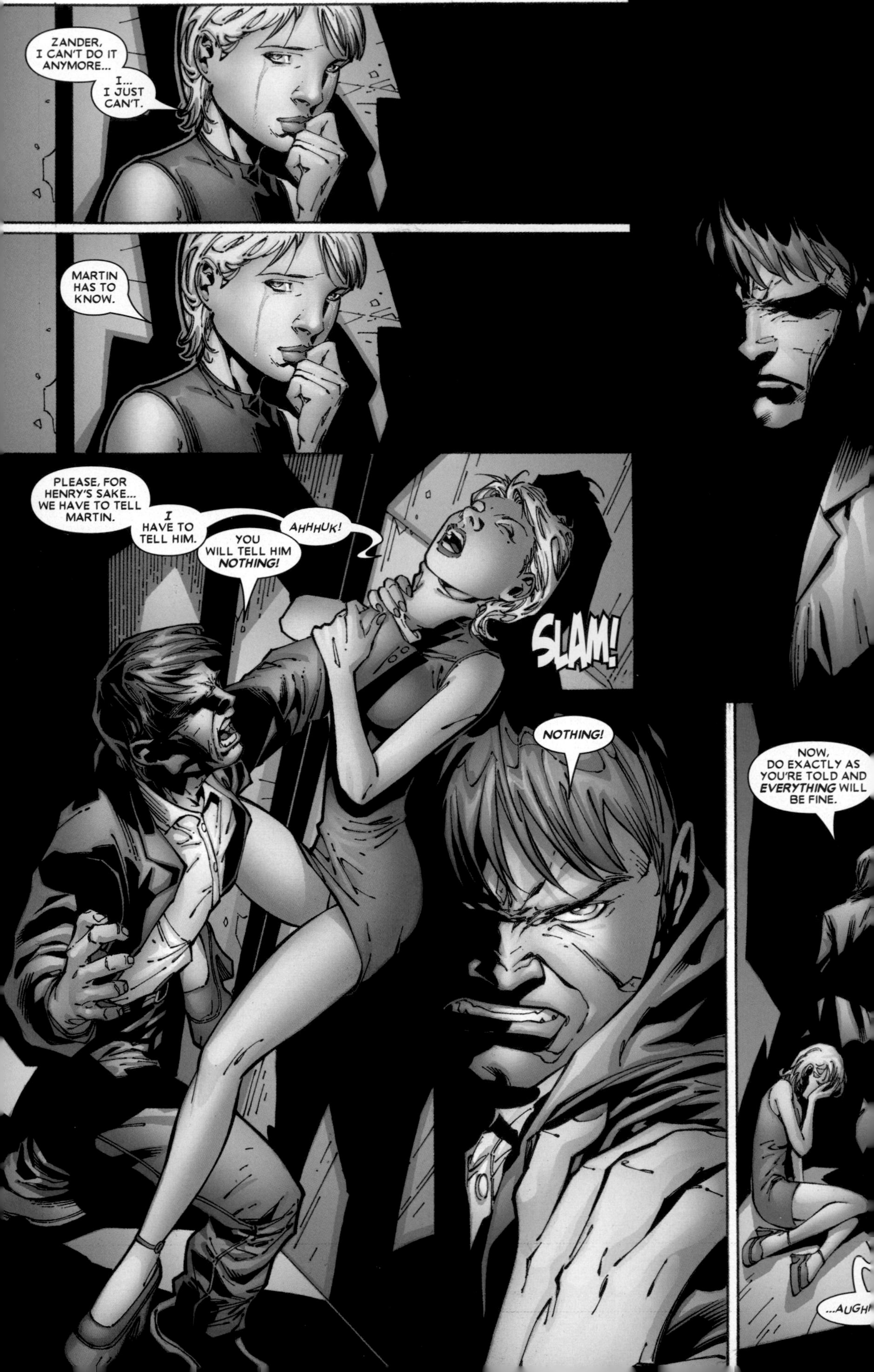

ZANDER, I CAN'T DO IT ANYMORE...
I... I JUST CAN'T.
MARTIN HAS TO KNOW.
PLEASE, FOR HENRY'S SAKE... WE HAVE TO TELL MARTIN.
I HAVE TO TELL HIM.
AHHHUK!
YOU WILL TELL HIM NOTHING!
SLAM!
NOTHING!
NOW, DO EXACTLY AS YOU'RE TOLD AND EVERYTHING WILL BE FINE.
...AUGH

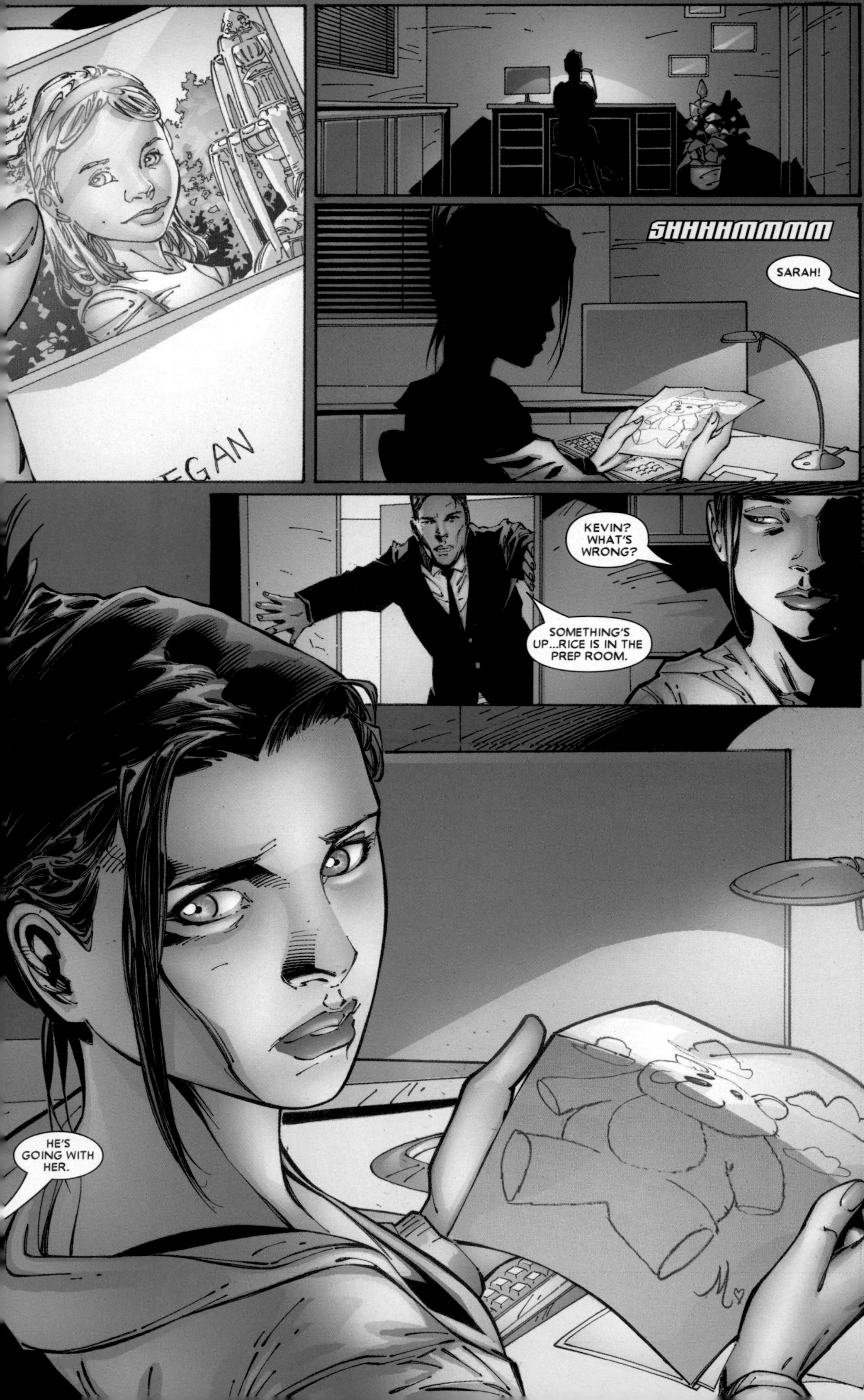

EGAN
SHHHHMMMM
SARAH!
KEVIN? WHAT'S WRONG?
SOMETHING'S UP...RICE IS IN THE PREP ROOM.
HE'S GOING WITH HER.

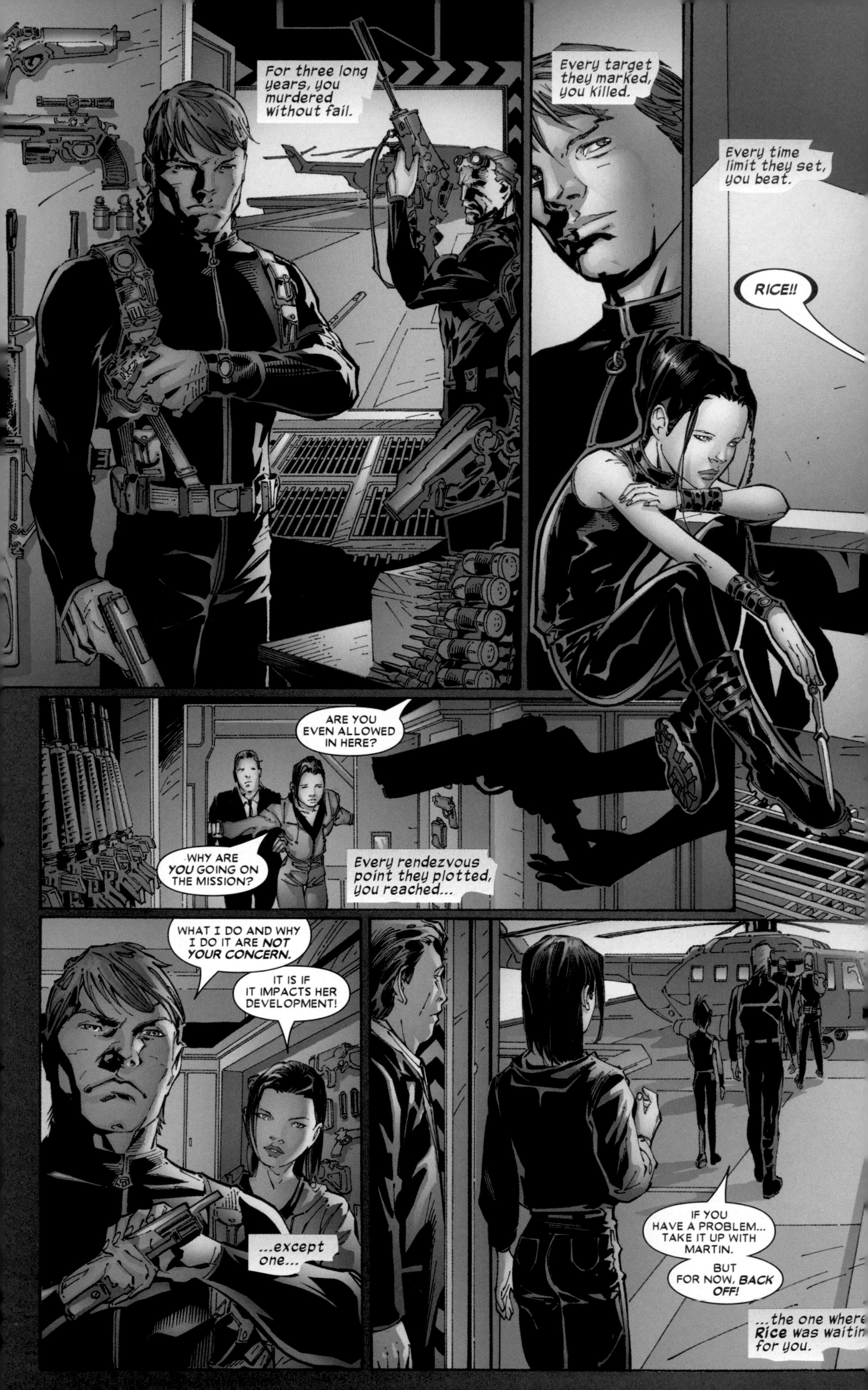
For three long years, you murdered without fail.
Every target they marked, you killed.
Every time limit they set, you beat.
RICE!!
ARE YOU EVEN ALLOWED IN HERE?
WHY ARE YOU GOING ON THE MISSION?
Every rendezvous point they plotted, you reached...
WHAT I DO AND WHY I DO IT ARE NOT YOUR CONCERN.
IT IS IF IT IMPACTS HER DEVELOPMENT!
...except one...
IF YOU HAVE A PROBLEM... TAKE IT UP WITH MARTIN.
BUT FOR NOW, BACK OFF!
...the one where Rice was waitin
for you.

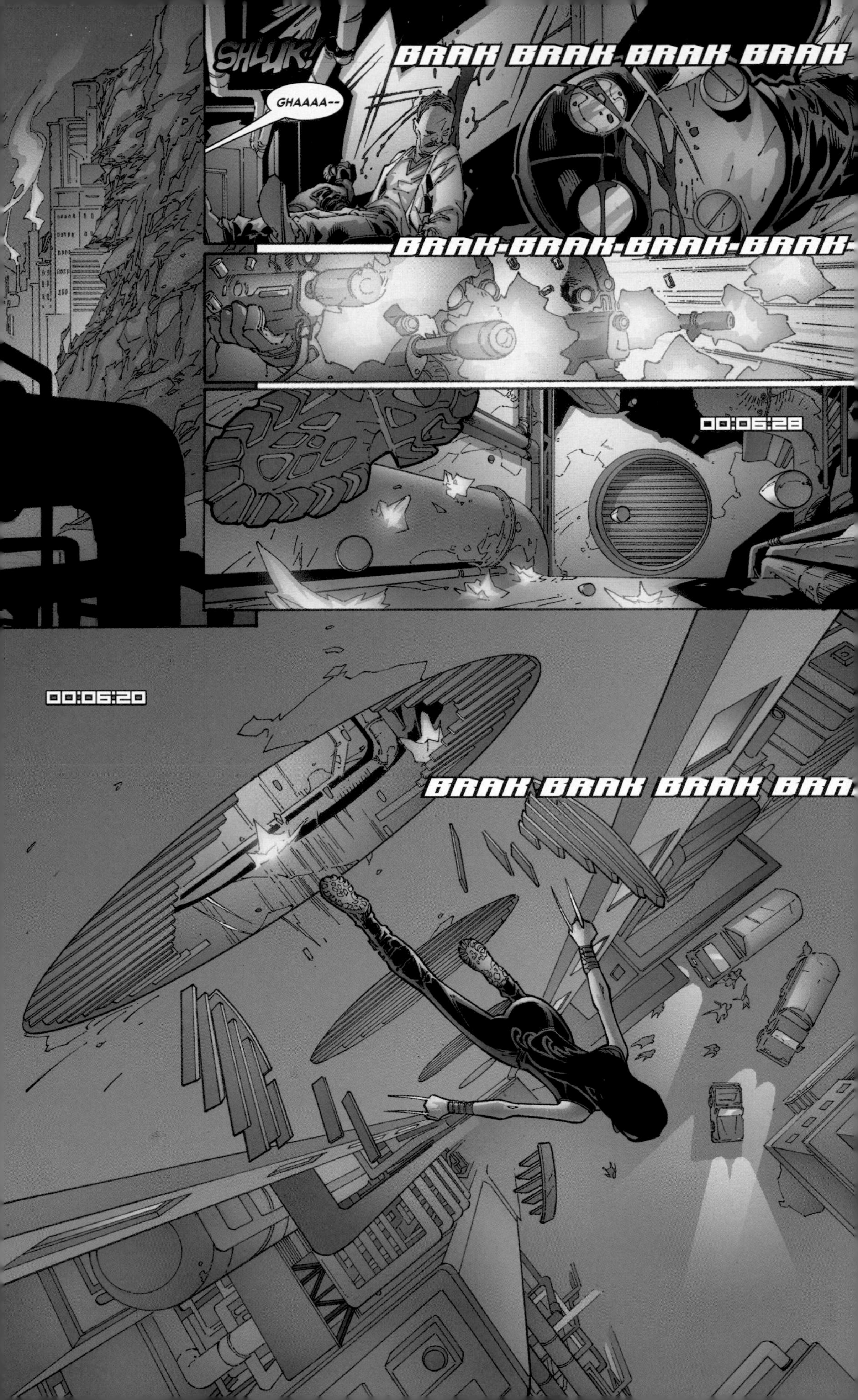
SHLUK!
BRAK BRAK BRAK BRAK
GHAAAA--
BRAK-BRAK-BRAK-BRAK-
00:06:28
00:06:20
BRAK BRAK BRAK BRA

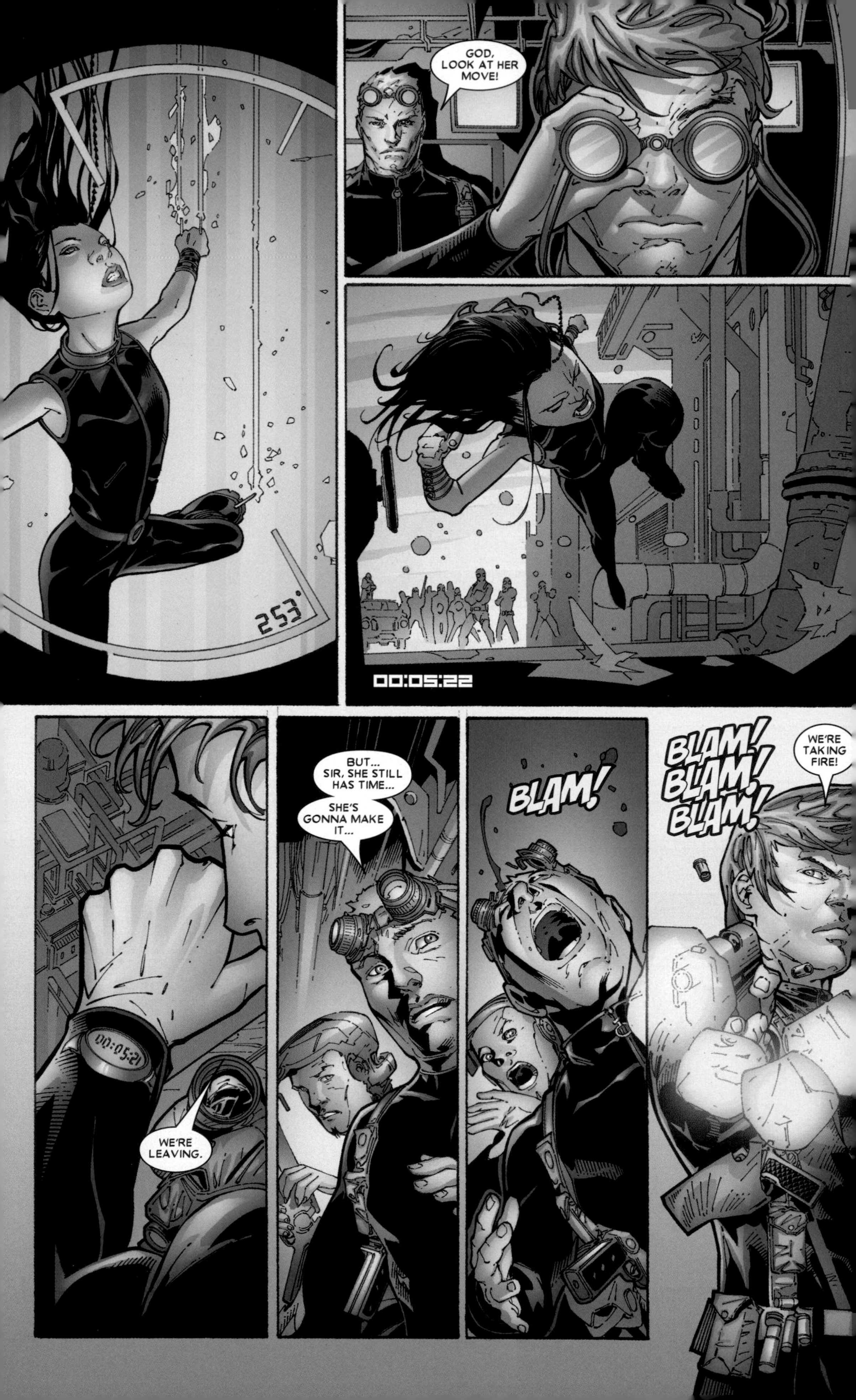
253°
GOD, LOOK AT HER MOVE!
00:05:22
WE'RE LEAVING.
BUT... SIR, SHE STILL HAS TIME...
SHE'S GONNA MAKE IT...
BLAM!
BLAM! BLAM! BLAM!
WE'RE TAKING FIRE!

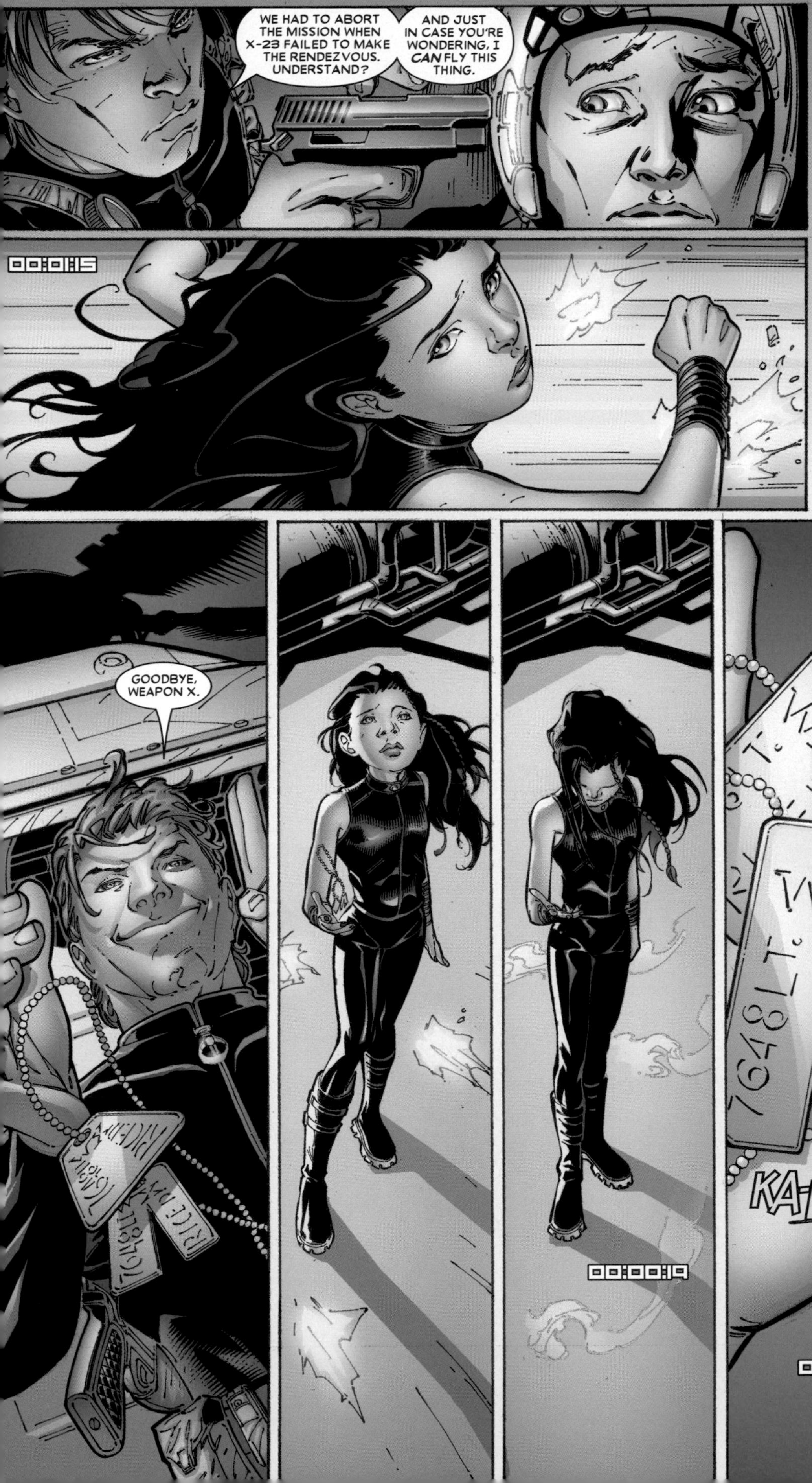

WE HAD TO ABORT THE MISSION WHEN X-23 FAILED TO MAKE THE RENDEZVOUS. UNDERSTAND?
AND JUST IN CASE YOU'RE WONDERING, I *CAN* FLY THIS THING.
00:01:15
GOODBYE, WEAPON X.
00:00:19
KA-KLAK!
00:00:09

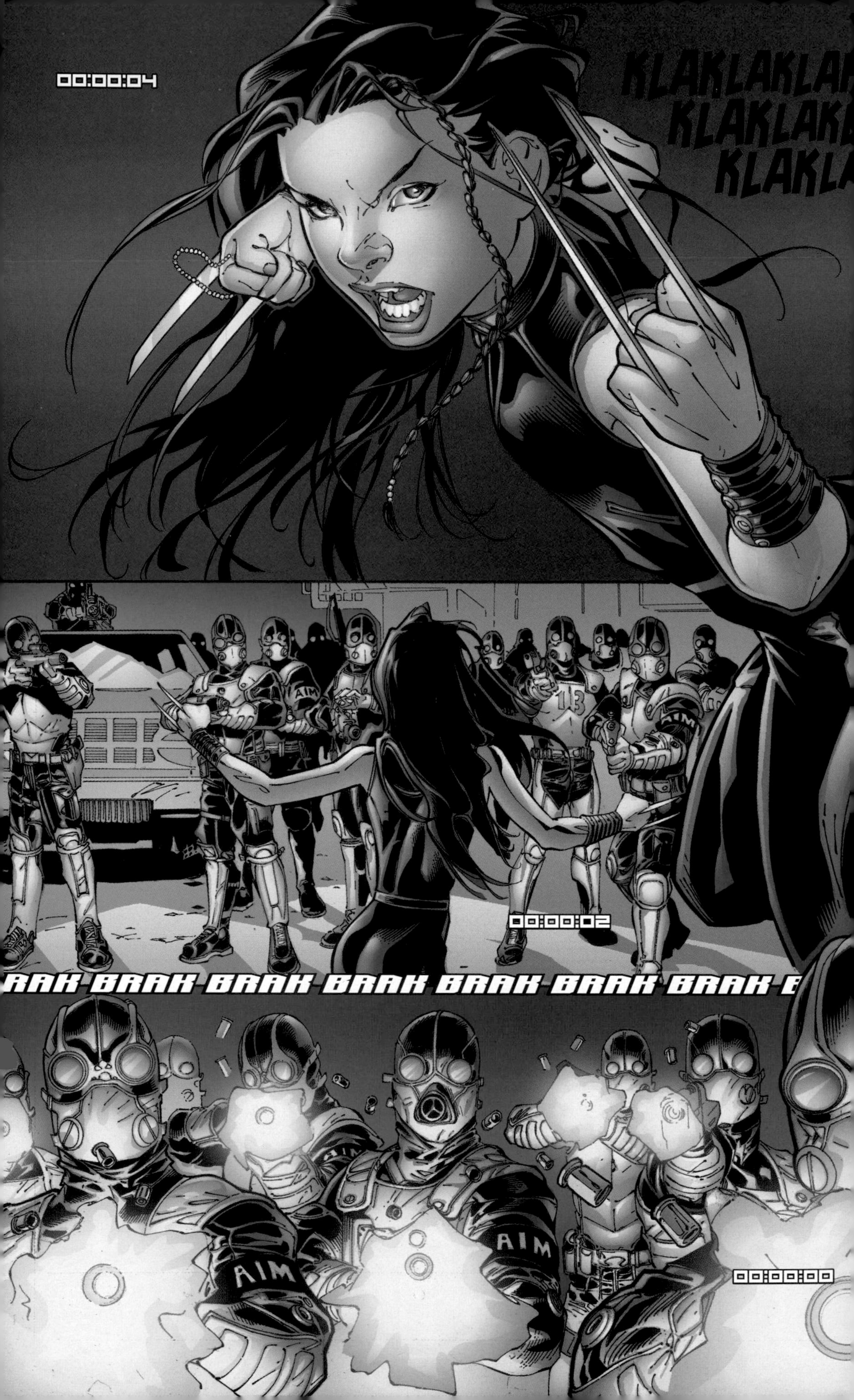

00:00:04
KLAKLAKLAK
KLAKLAK
KLAKL
00:00:02
RAK BRAK BRAK BRAK BRAK BRAK BRAK
AIM
13
AIM
AIM
AIM
00:00:00

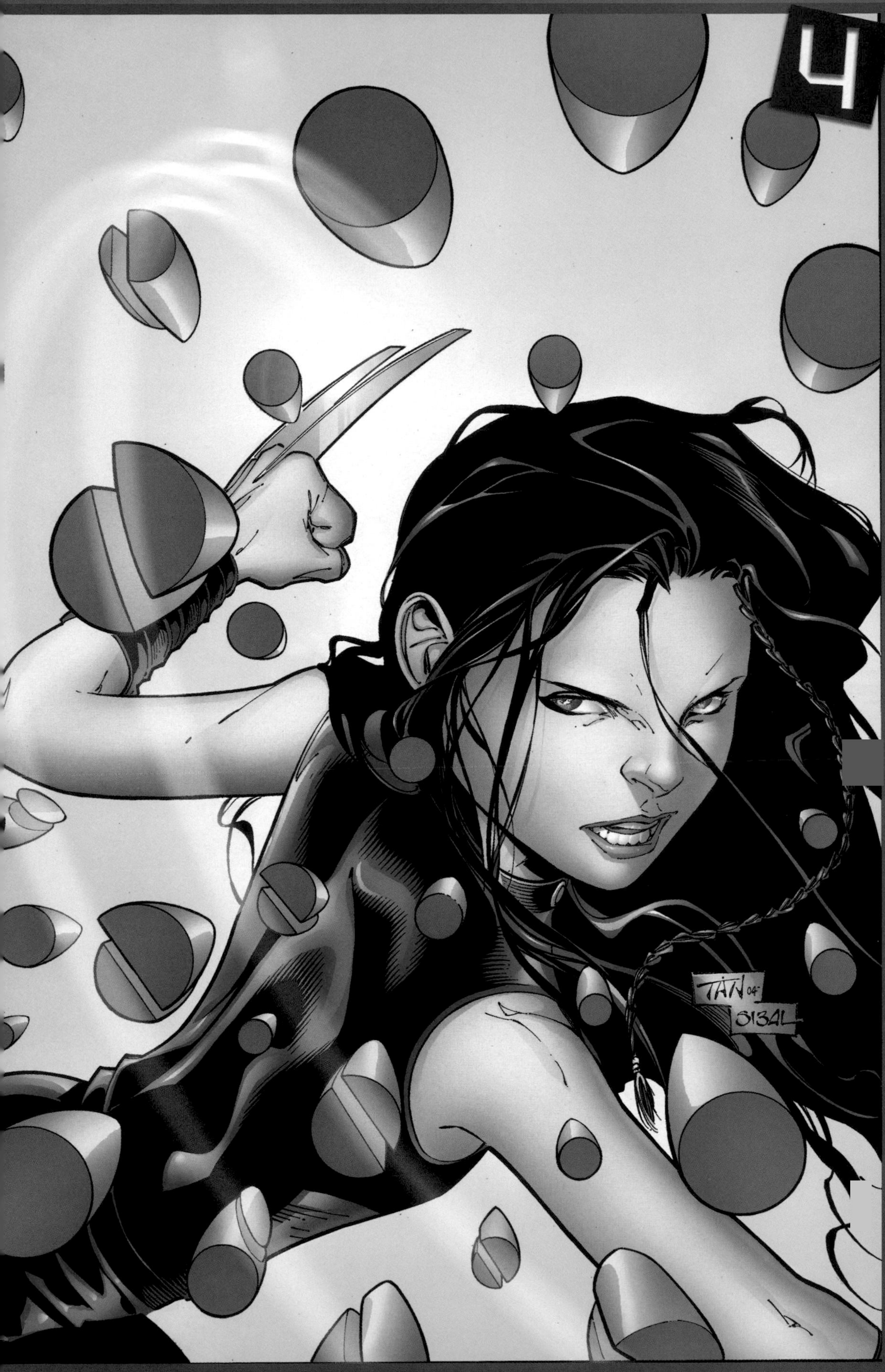
4
TAN 04
SIBAL

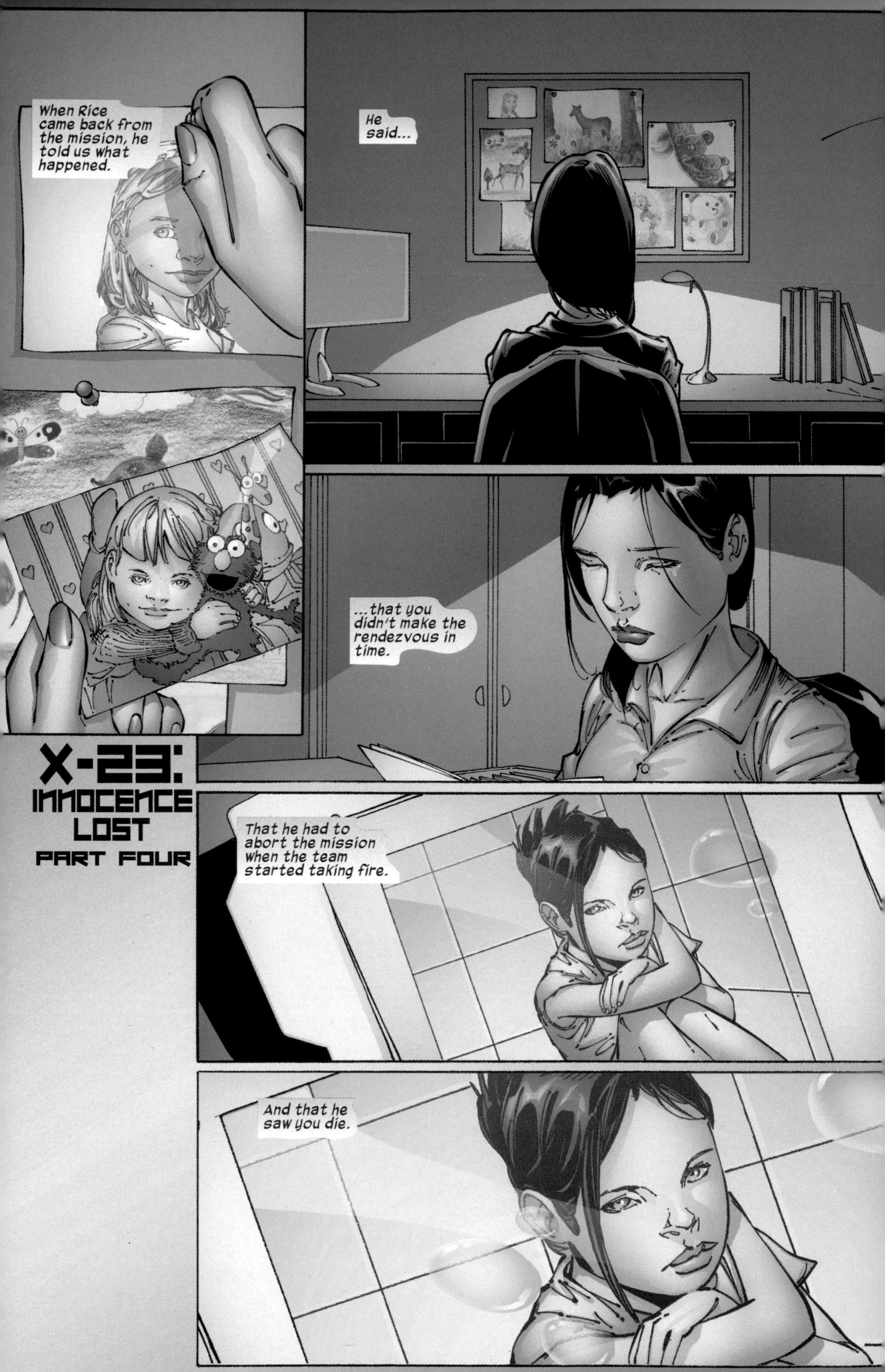
When Rice came back from the mission, he told us what happened.
He said...
...that you didn't make the rendezvous in time.
X-23: INNOCENCE LOST
PART FOUR
That he had to abort the mission when the team started taking fire.
And that he saw you die.

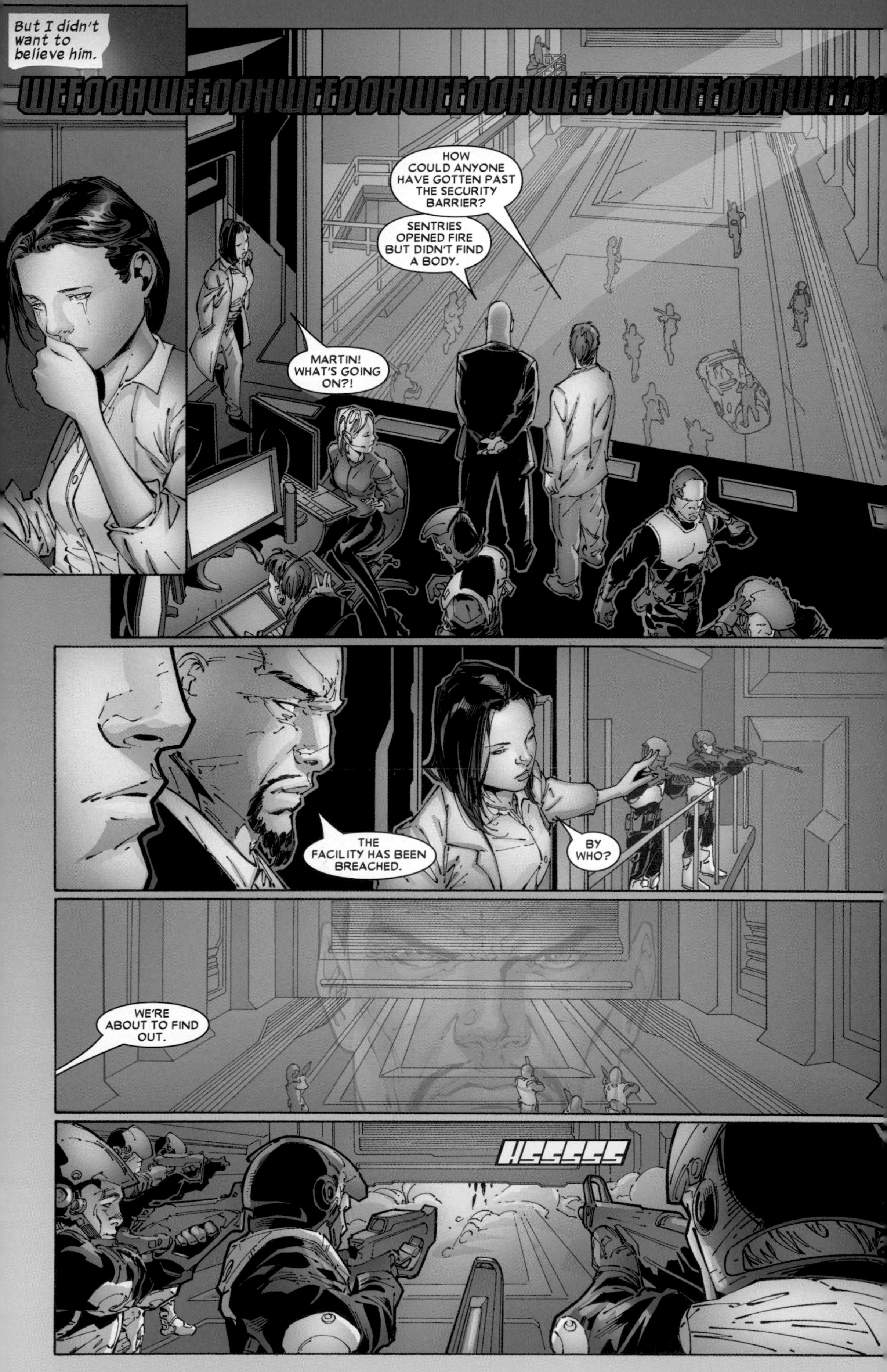
But I didn't want to believe him.
WEEOOHWEEOOHWEEOOHWEEOOHWEEOOHWEEOOHWEEO
HOW COULD ANYONE HAVE GOTTEN PAST THE SECURITY BARRIER?
SENTRIES OPENED FIRE BUT DIDN'T FIND A BODY.
MARTIN! WHAT'S GOING ON?!
THE FACILITY HAS BEEN BREACHED.
BY WHO?
WE'RE ABOUT TO FIND OUT.
HSSSSS

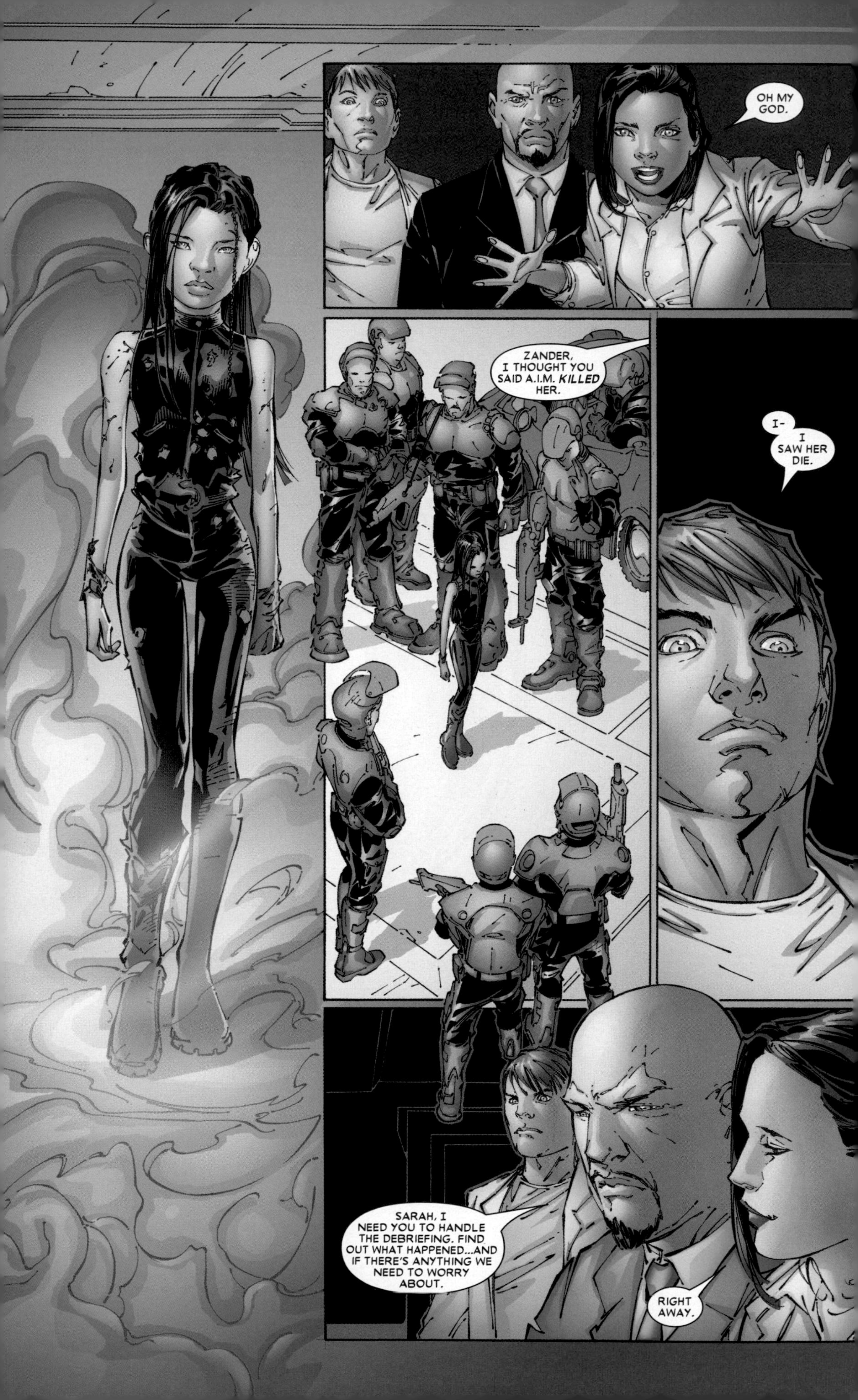
OH MY GOD.
ZANDER, I THOUGHT YOU SAID A.I.M. KILLED HER.
I-
I SAW HER DIE.
SARAH, I NEED YOU TO HANDLE THE DEBRIEFING. FIND OUT WHAT HAPPENED...AND IF THERE'S ANYTHING WE NEED TO WORRY ABOUT.
RIGHT AWAY.

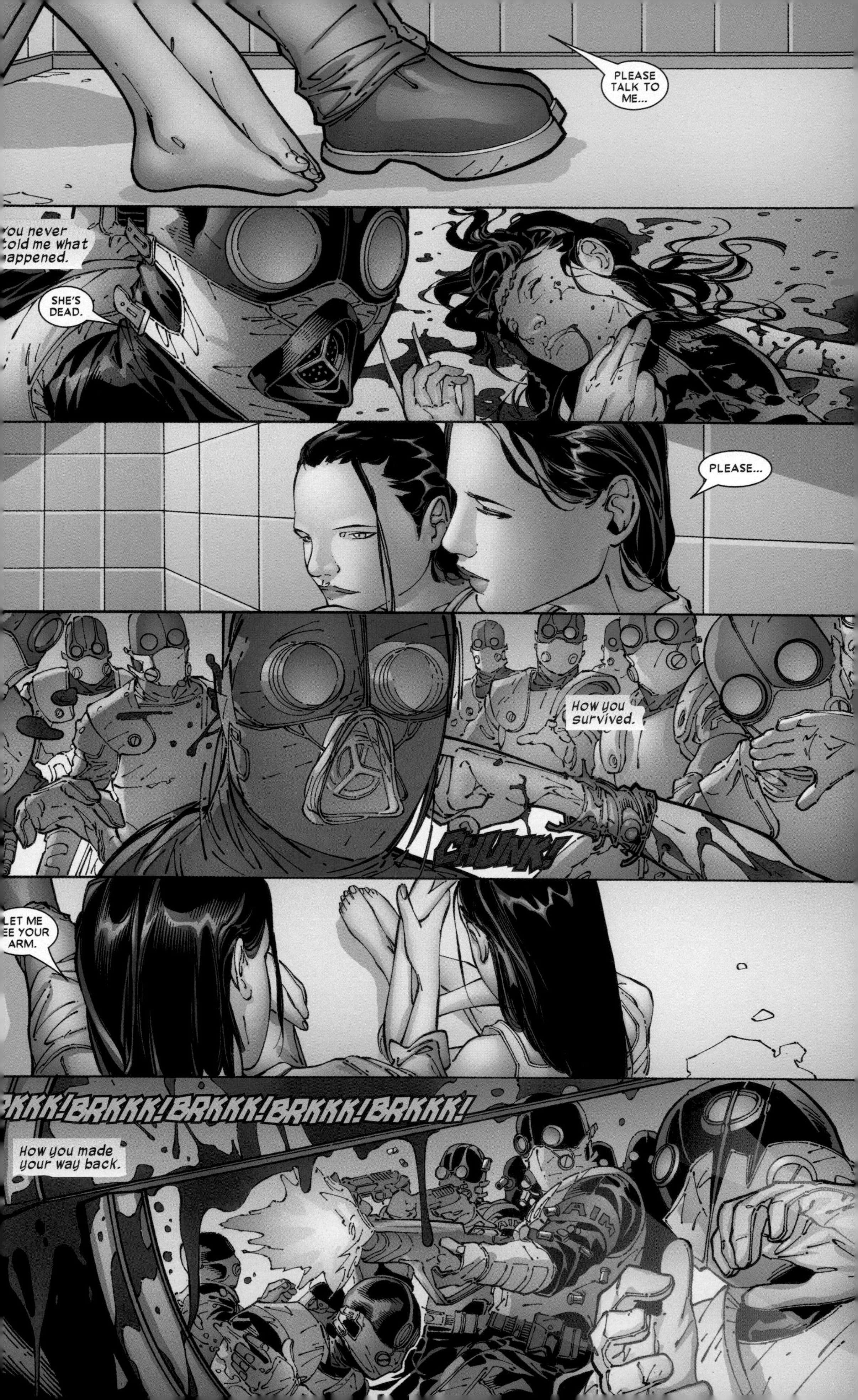

PLEASE TALK TO ME...
You never told me what happened.
SHE'S DEAD.
PLEASE...
How you survived.
CHUNK!
LET ME SEE YOUR ARM.
BRKKK! BRKKK! BRKKK! BRKKK! BRKKK!
How you made your way back.
AIM

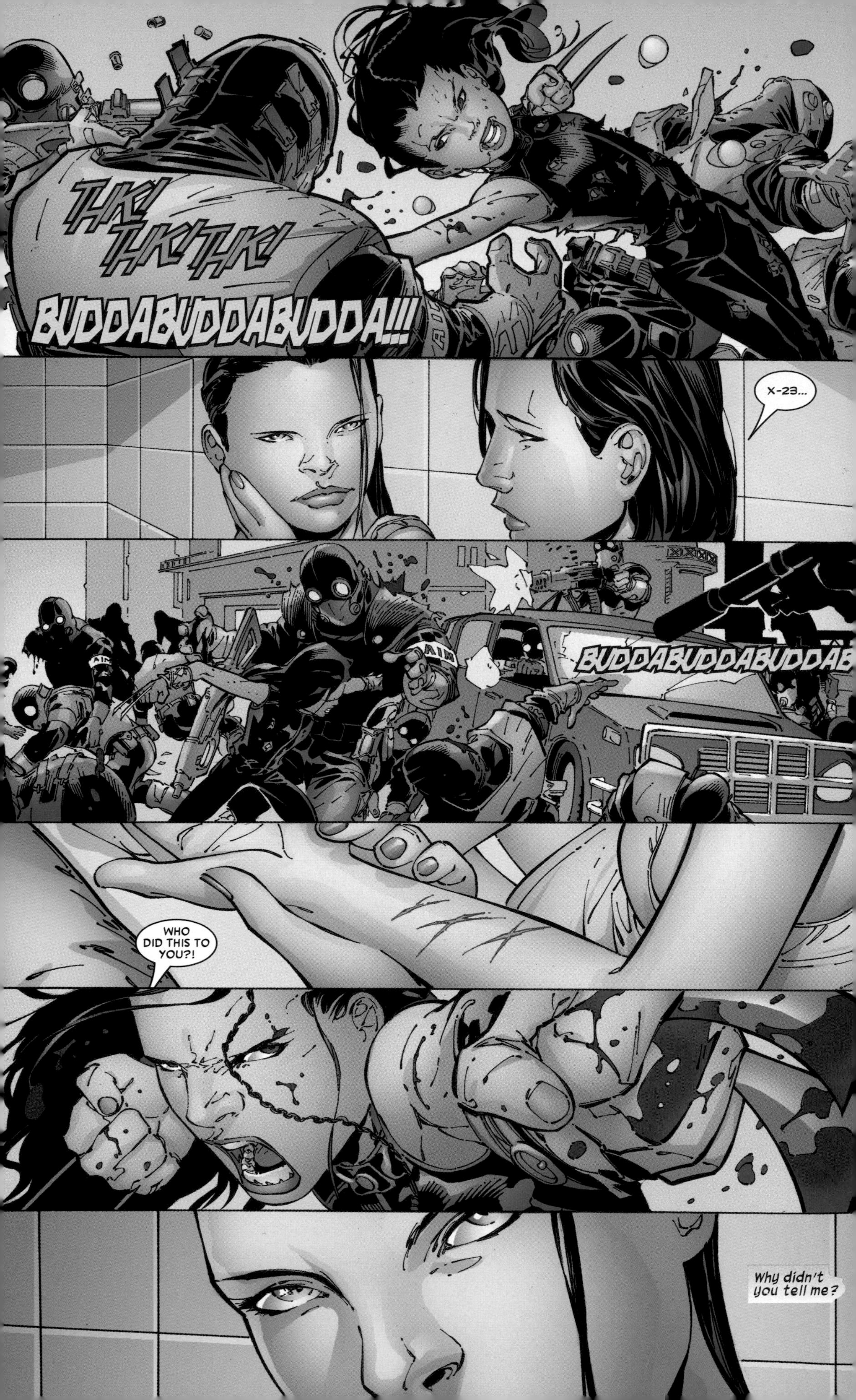
THK! THK! THK!
BUDDABUDDABUDDA!!!
X-23...
BUDDABUDDABUDDAB
WHO DID THIS TO YOU?!
Why didn't you tell me?

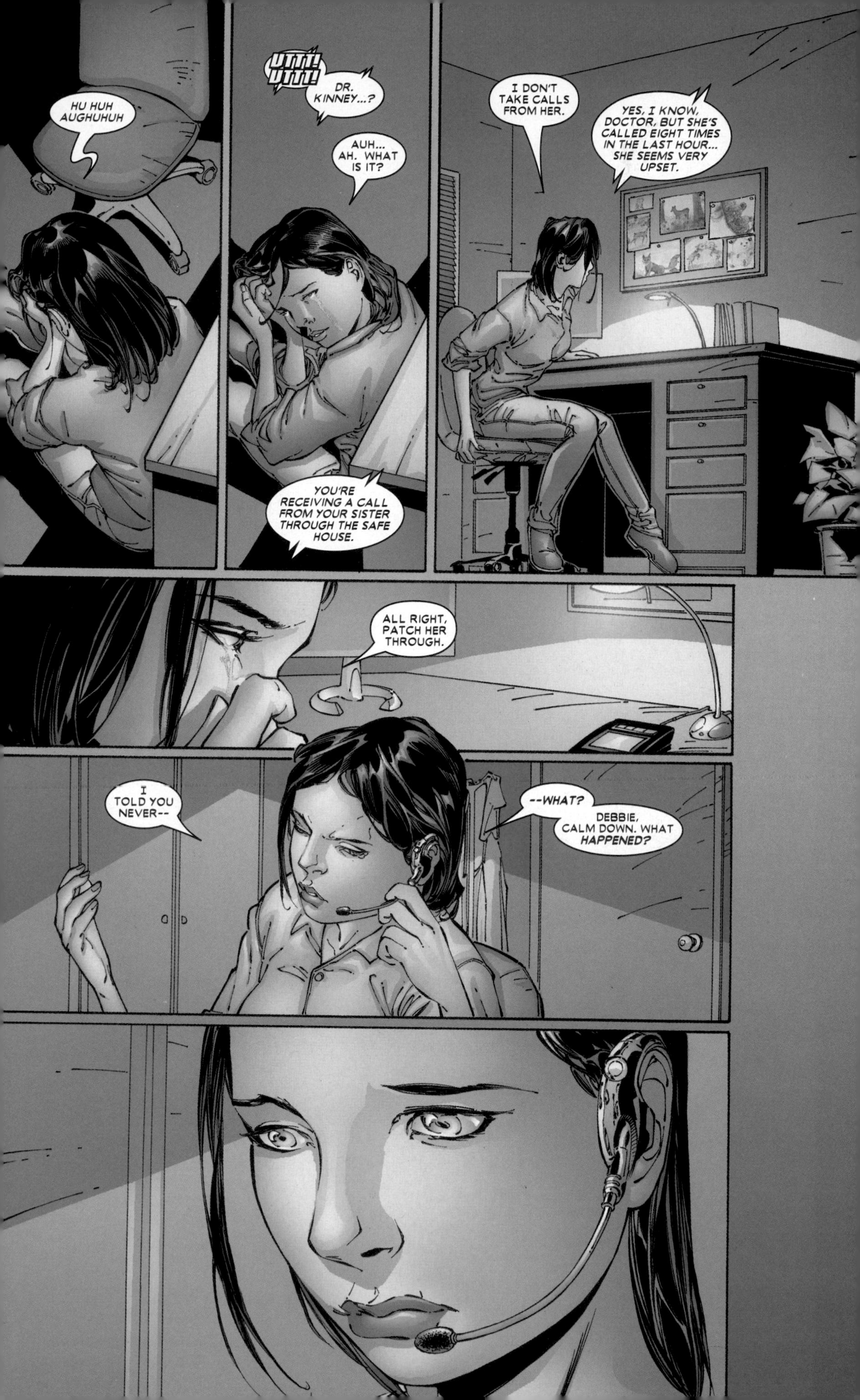
HU HUH AUGHUHUH
UTTT! UTTT!
DR. KINNEY...?
AUH... AH. WHAT IS IT?
YOU'RE RECEIVING A CALL FROM YOUR SISTER THROUGH THE SAFE HOUSE.
I DON'T TAKE CALLS FROM HER.
YES, I KNOW, DOCTOR, BUT SHE'S CALLED EIGHT TIMES IN THE LAST HOUR... SHE SEEMS VERY UPSET.
ALL RIGHT, PATCH HER THROUGH.
I TOLD YOU NEVER--
--WHAT?
DEBBIE, CALM DOWN. WHAT HAPPENED?

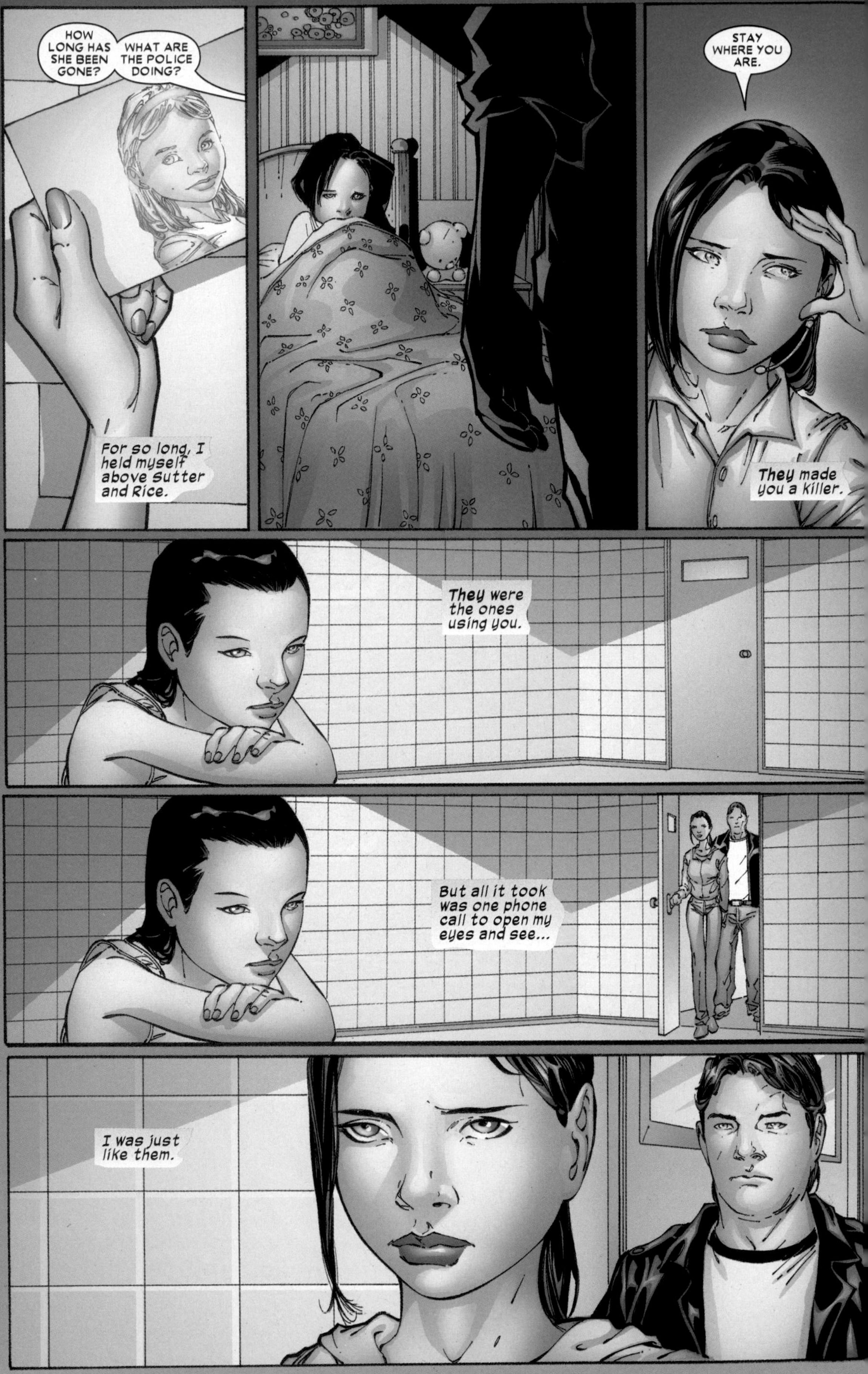
HOW LONG HAS SHE BEEN GONE?
WHAT ARE THE POLICE DOING?
For so long, I held myself above Sutter and Rice.
STAY WHERE YOU ARE.
They made you a killer.
They were the ones using you.
But all it took was one phone call to open my eyes and see...
I was just like them.

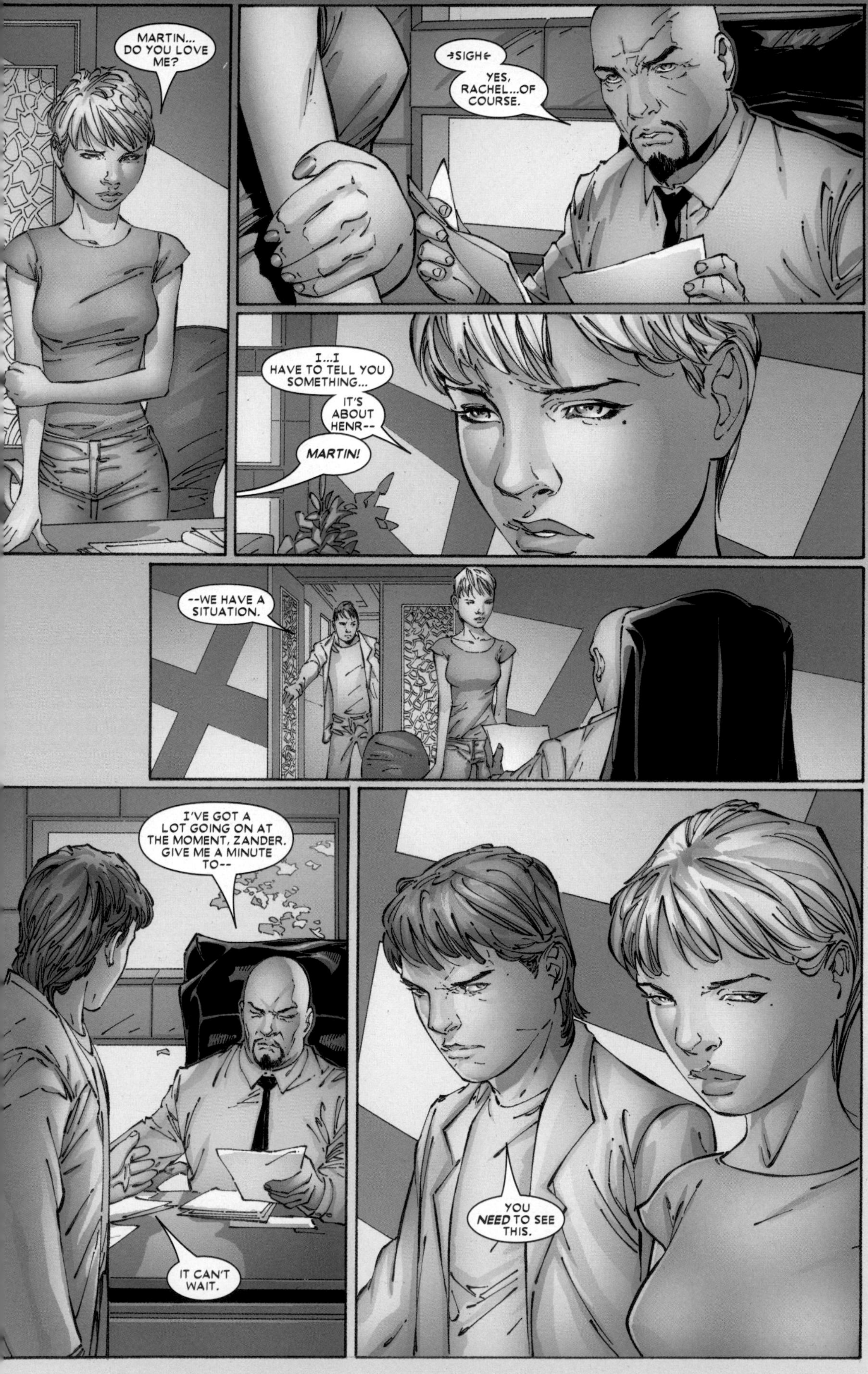
MARTIN... DO YOU LOVE ME?
SIGH
YES, RACHEL...OF COURSE.
I...I HAVE TO TELL YOU SOMETHING...
IT'S ABOUT HENR--
MARTIN!
--WE HAVE A SITUATION.
I'VE GOT A LOT GOING ON AT THE MOMENT, ZANDER. GIVE ME A MINUTE TO--
IT CAN'T WAIT.
YOU NEED TO SEE THIS.

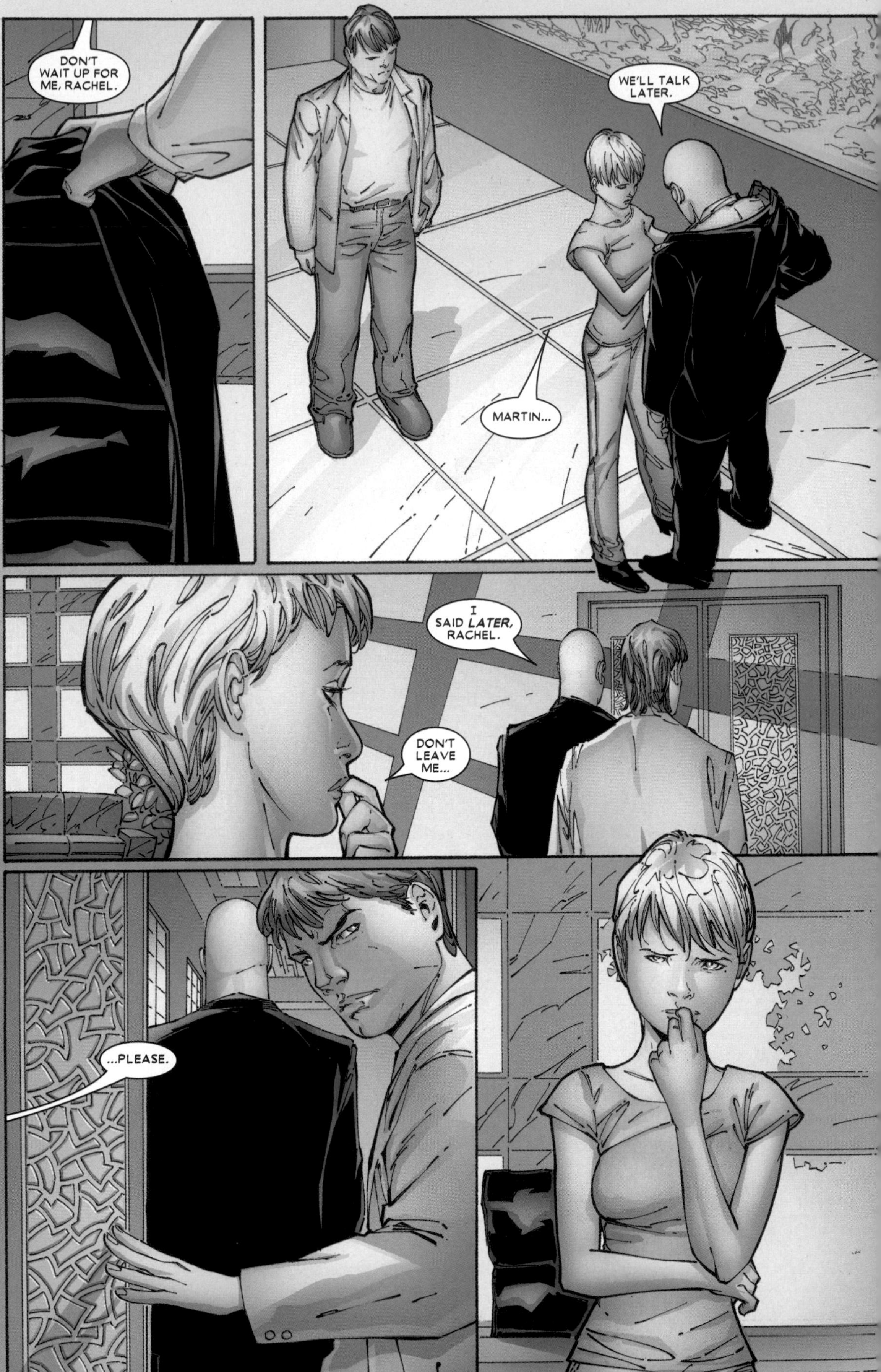
DON'T WAIT UP FOR ME, RACHEL.
WE'LL TALK LATER.
MARTIN...
I SAID LATER, RACHEL.
DON'T LEAVE ME...
...PLEASE.

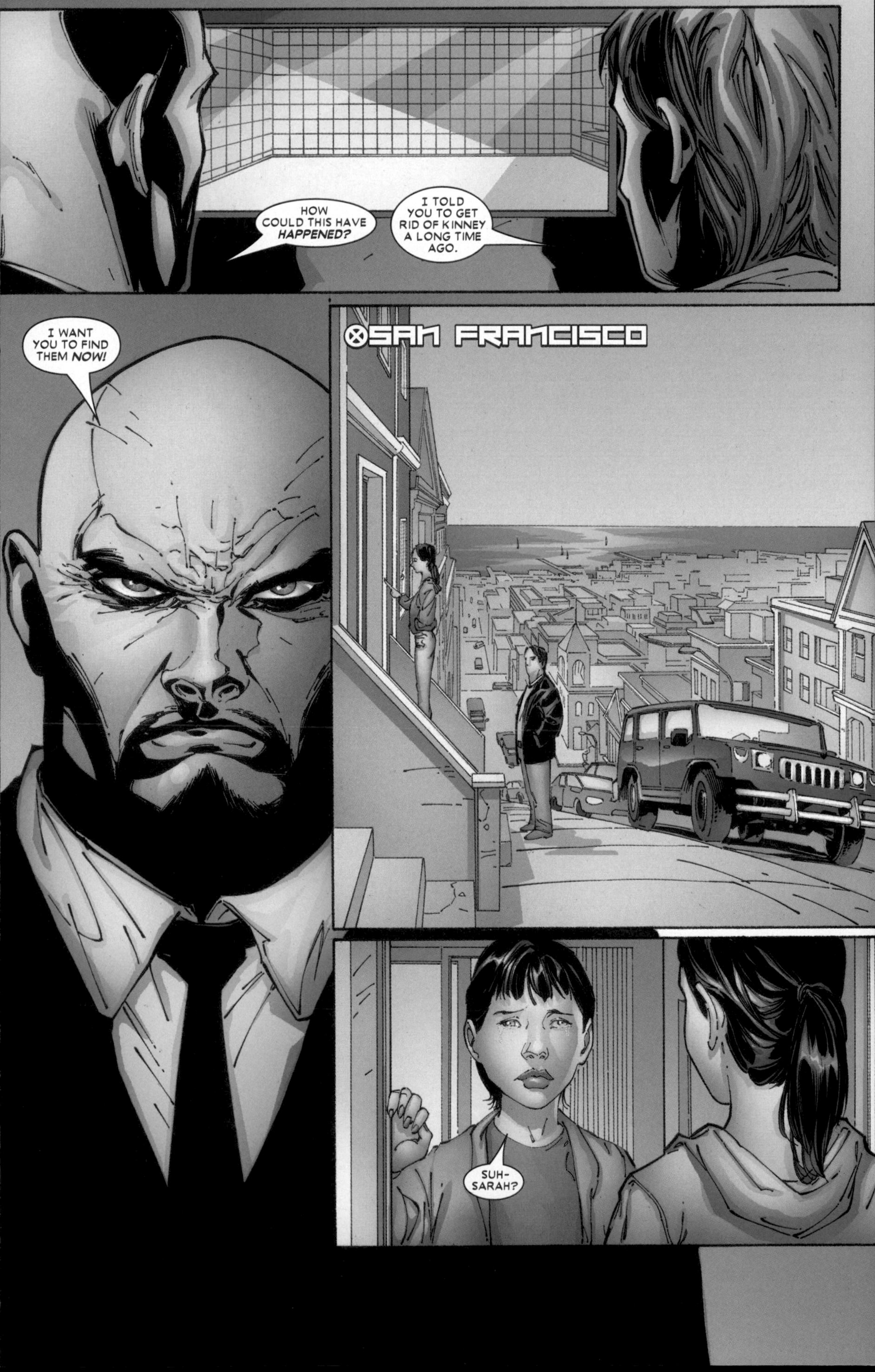
HOW COULD THIS HAVE HAPPENED?
I TOLD YOU TO GET RID OF KINNEY A LONG TIME AGO.
I WANT YOU TO FIND THEM NOW!
SAN FRANCISCO
SUH-SARAH?

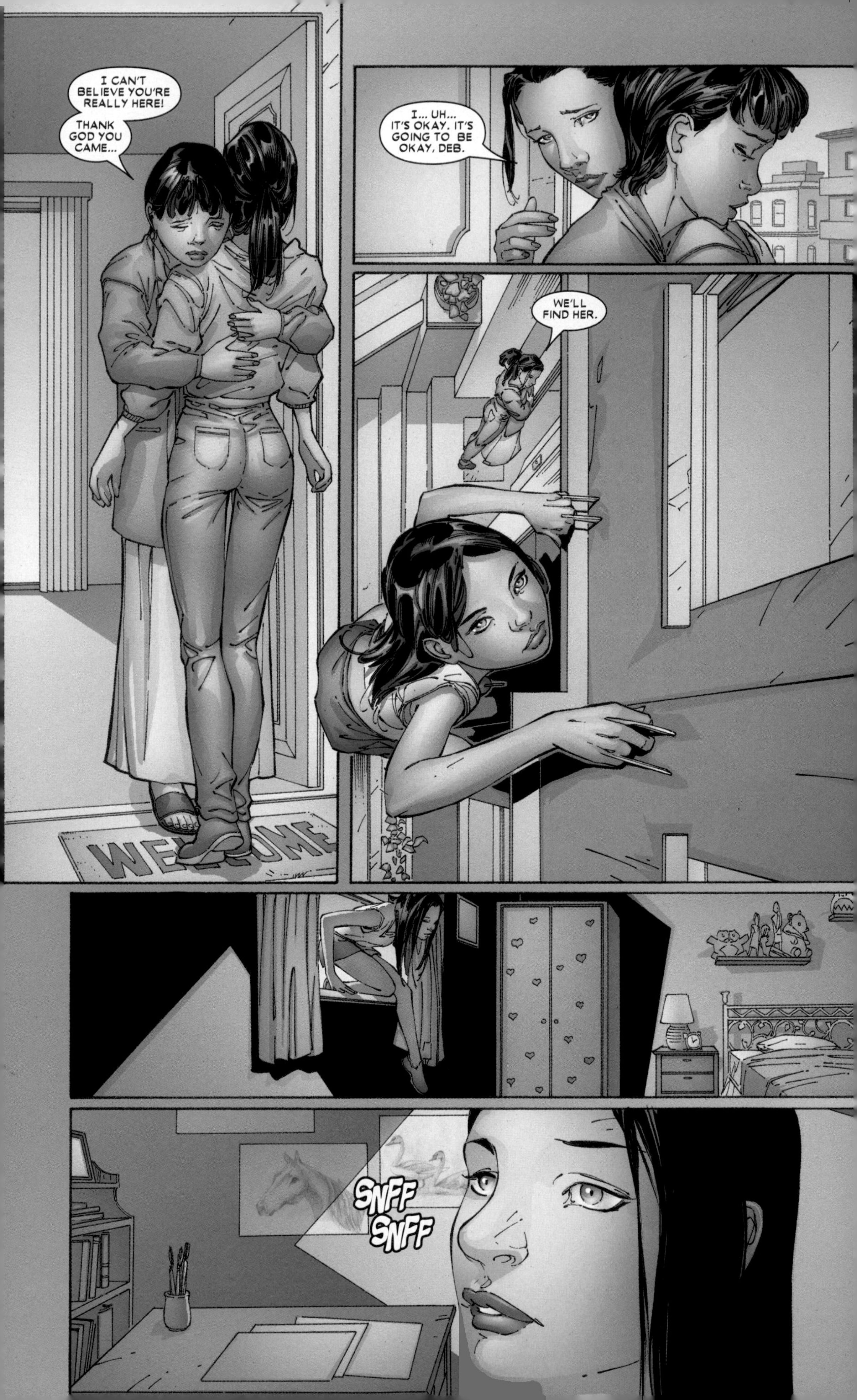

I CAN'T BELIEVE YOU'RE REALLY HERE!
THANK GOD YOU CAME...
I... UH... IT'S OKAY. IT'S GOING TO BE OKAY, DEB.
WE'LL FIND HER.
WELCOME
SNFF
SNFF

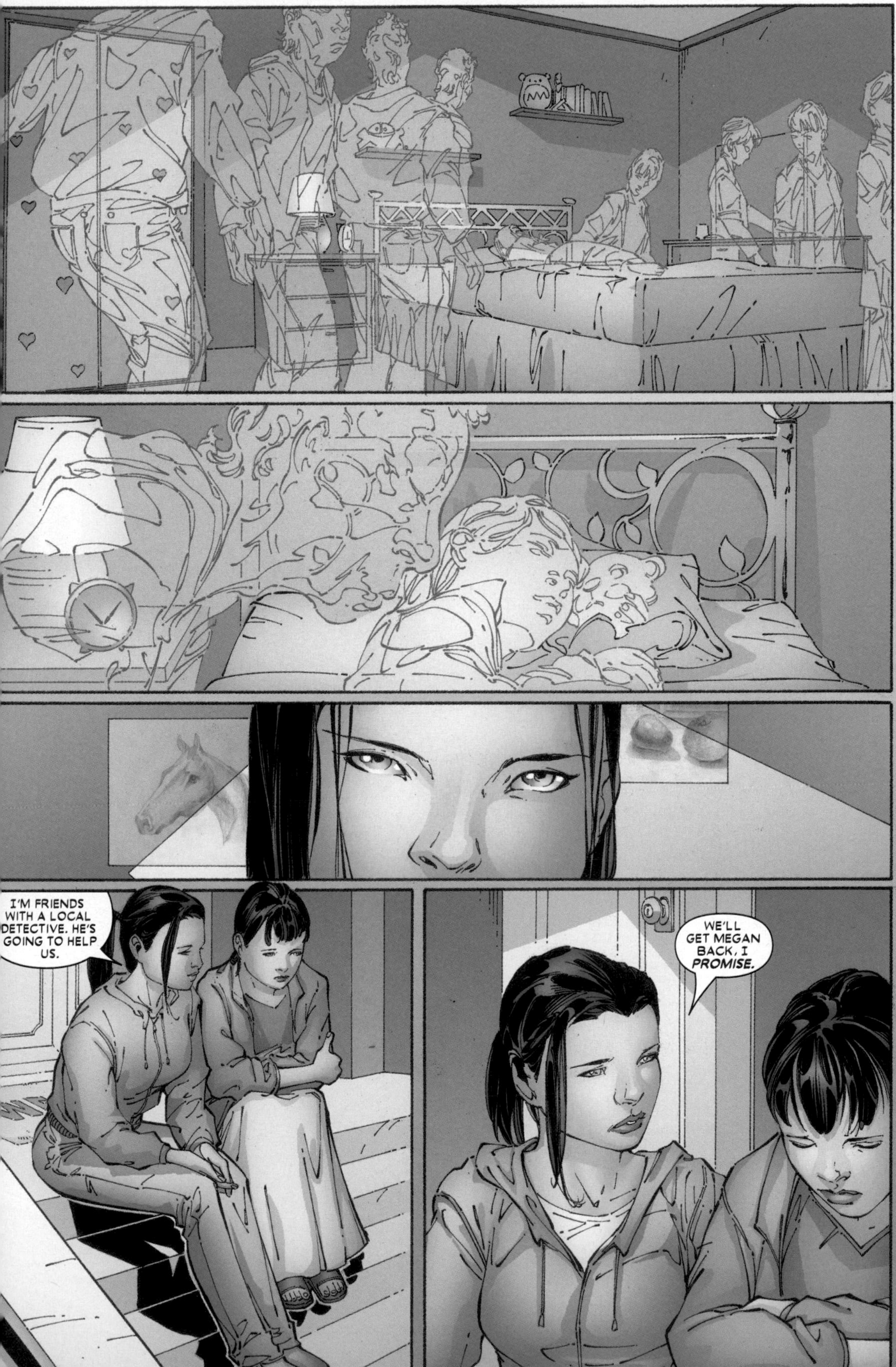
I'M FRIENDS WITH A LOCAL DETECTIVE. HE'S GOING TO HELP US.
WE'LL GET MEGAN BACK, I *PROMISE.*

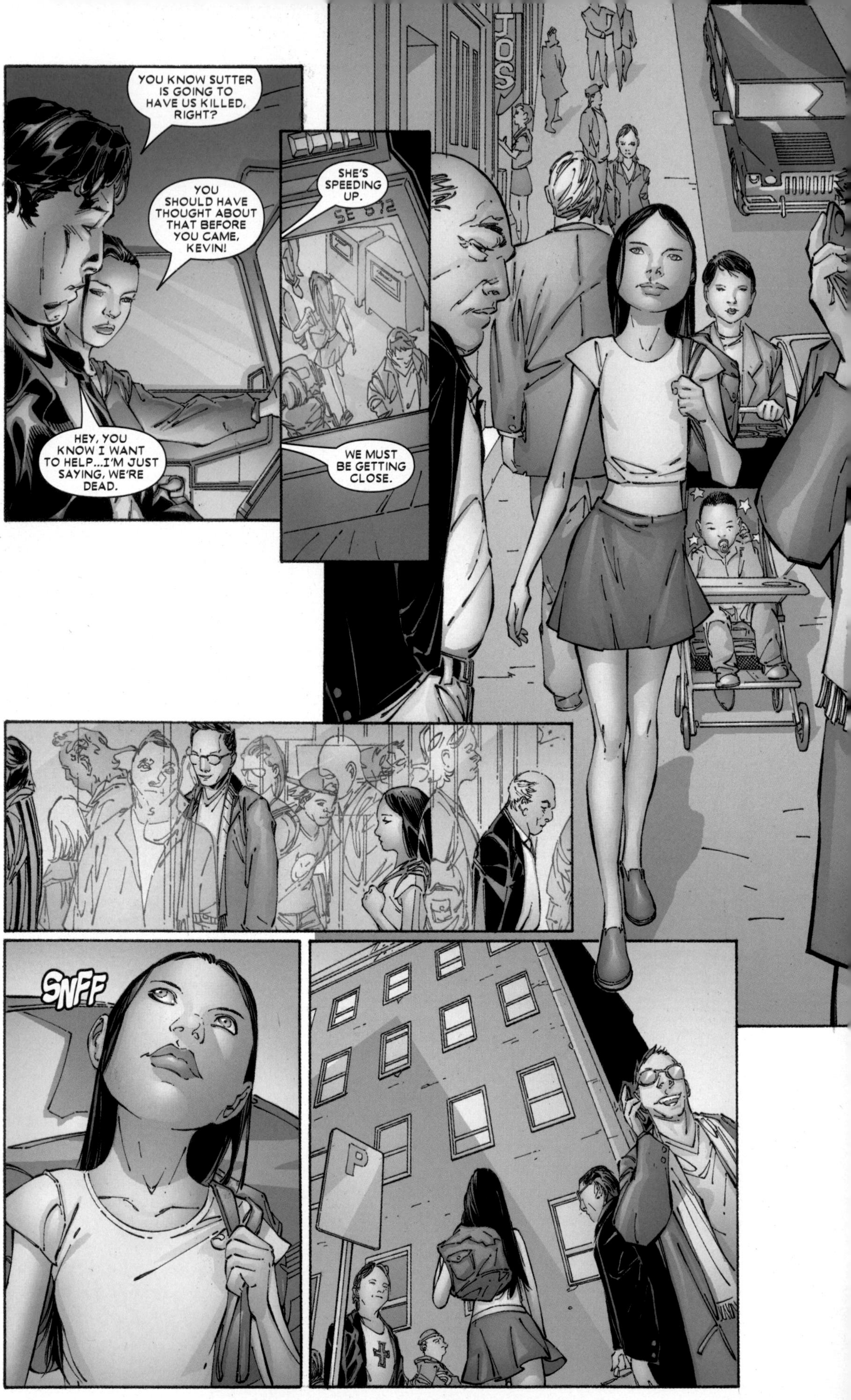
YOU KNOW SUTTER IS GOING TO HAVE US KILLED, RIGHT?
YOU SHOULD HAVE THOUGHT ABOUT THAT BEFORE YOU CAME, KEVIN!
HEY, YOU KNOW I WANT TO HELP...I'M JUST SAYING, WE'RE DEAD.
SHE'S SPEEDING UP.
WE MUST BE GETTING CLOSE.
SNFF
P

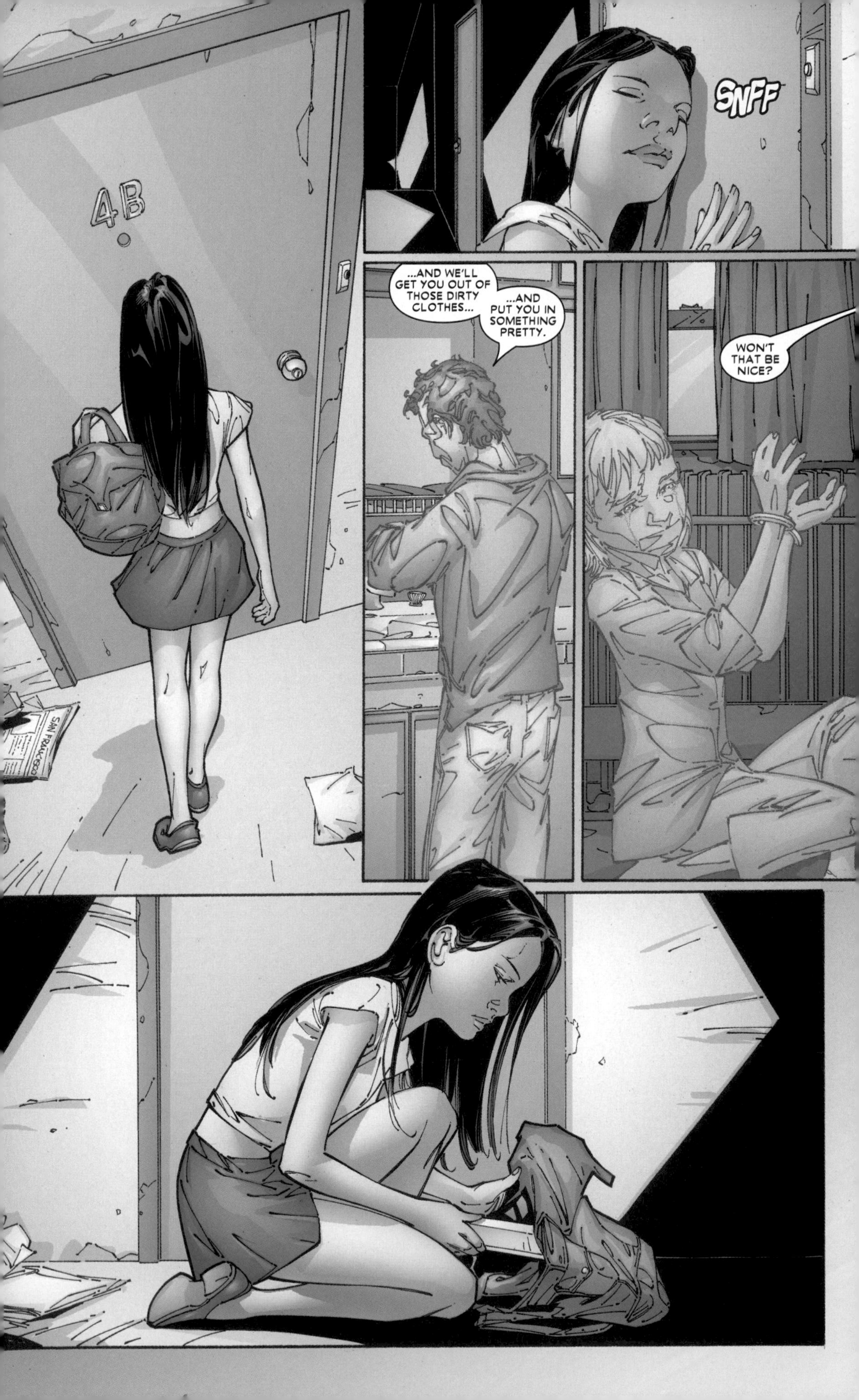
4B
SNFF
...AND WE'LL GET YOU OUT OF THOSE DIRTY CLOTHES...
...AND PUT YOU IN SOMETHING PRETTY.
WON'T THAT BE NICE?

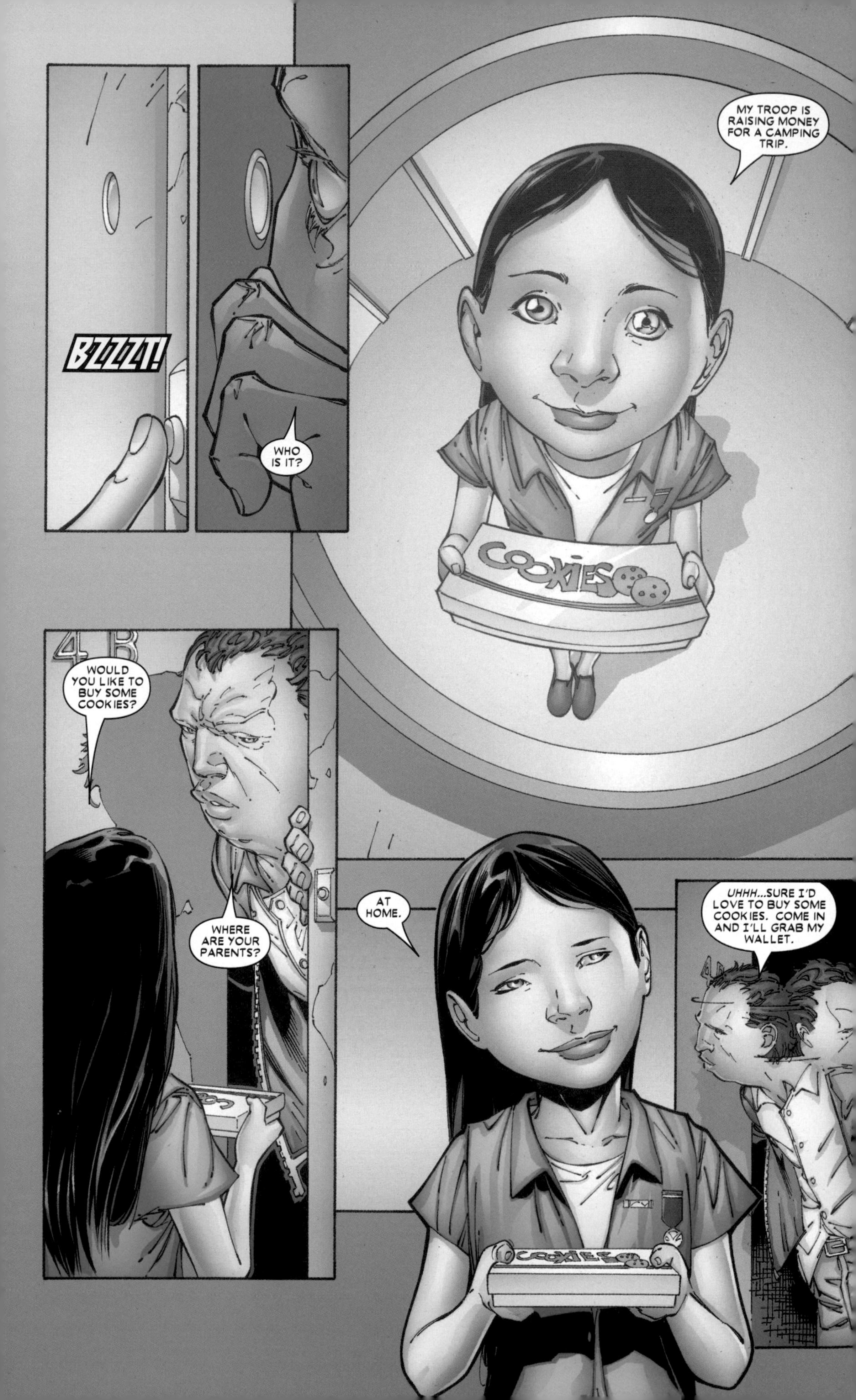
BZZZT!
WHO IS IT?
MY TROOP IS RAISING MONEY FOR A CAMPING TRIP.
COOKIES
WOULD YOU LIKE TO BUY SOME COOKIES?
WHERE ARE YOUR PARENTS?
AT HOME.
UHHH...SURE I'D LOVE TO BUY SOME COOKIES. COME IN AND I'LL GRAB MY WALLET.

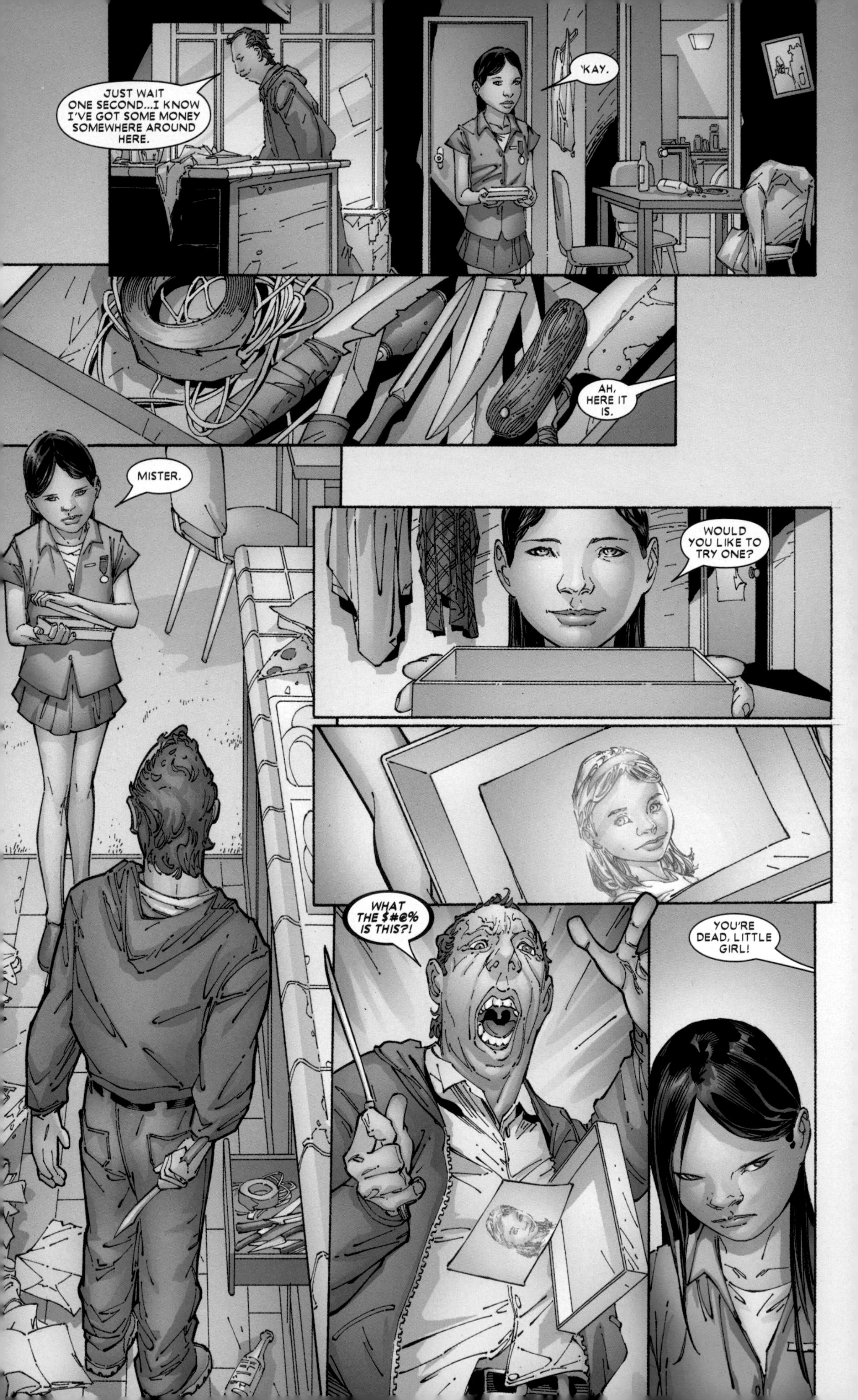
JUST WAIT ONE SECOND...I KNOW I'VE GOT SOME MONEY SOMEWHERE AROUND HERE.
'KAY.
AH, HERE IT IS.
MISTER.
WOULD YOU LIKE TO TRY ONE?
WHAT THE $#@% IS THIS?!
YOU'RE DEAD, LITTLE GIRL!

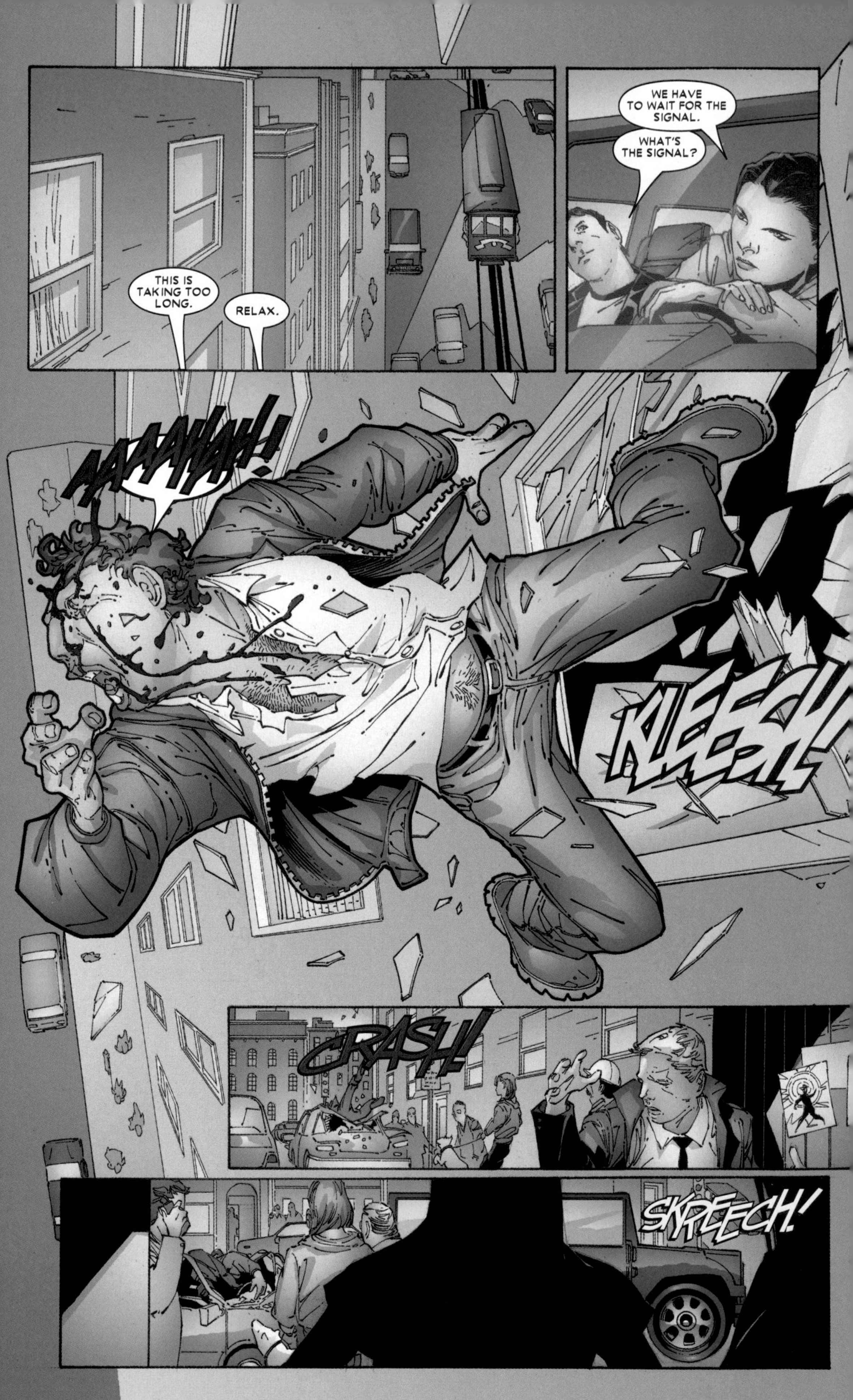
THIS IS TAKING TOO LONG.
RELAX.
WE HAVE TO WAIT FOR THE SIGNAL.
WHAT'S THE SIGNAL?
AAAAAAH!
KLEESH!
CRASH!
SKREECH!

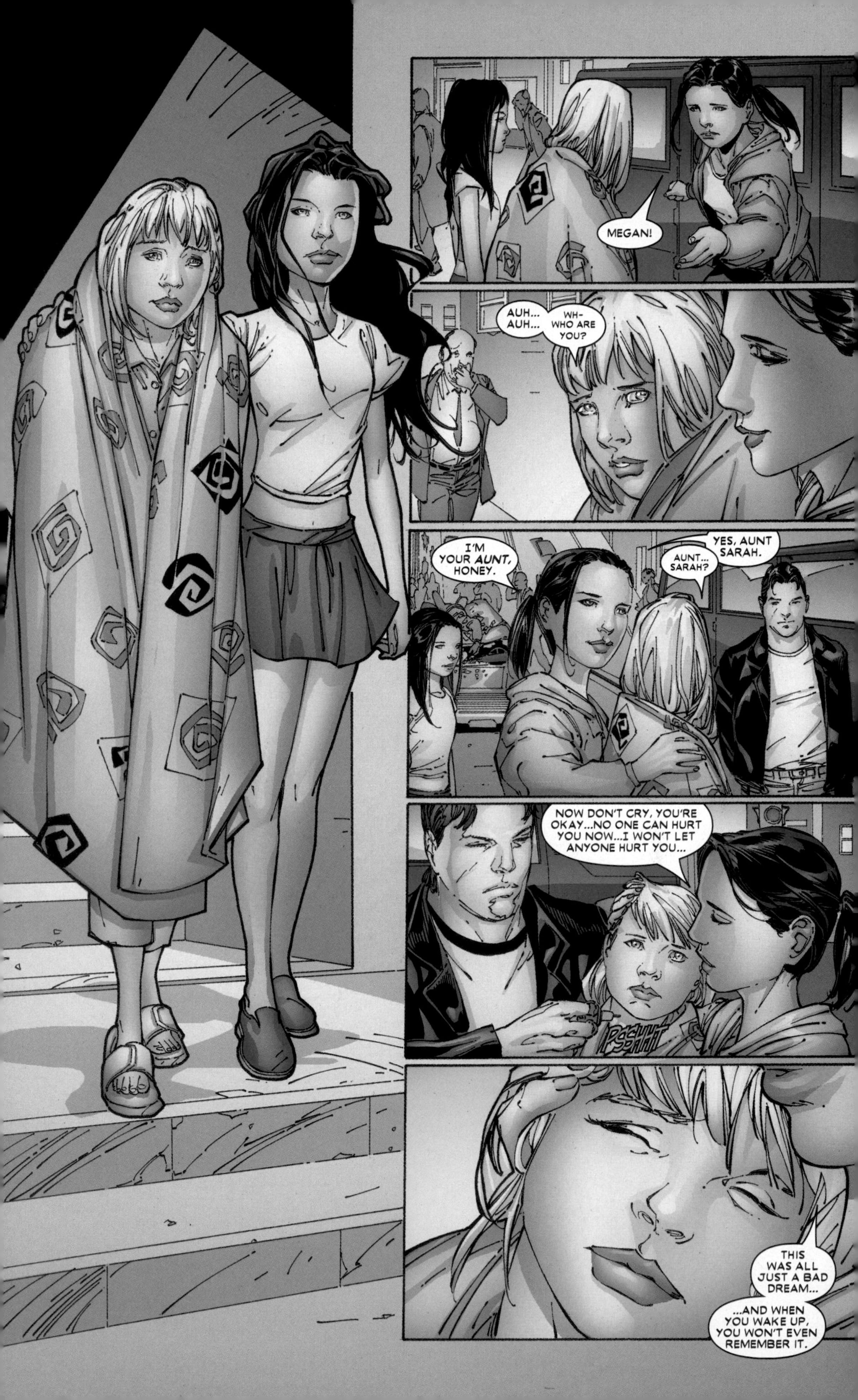
MEGAN!
AUH... AUH...
WH- WHO ARE YOU?
I'M YOUR AUNT, HONEY.
AUNT... SARAH?
YES, AUNT SARAH.
NOW DON'T CRY, YOU'RE OKAY...NO ONE CAN HURT YOU NOW...I WON'T LET ANYONE HURT YOU...
PSSHHT
THIS WAS ALL JUST A BAD DREAM...
...AND WHEN YOU WAKE UP, YOU WON'T EVEN REMEMBER IT.

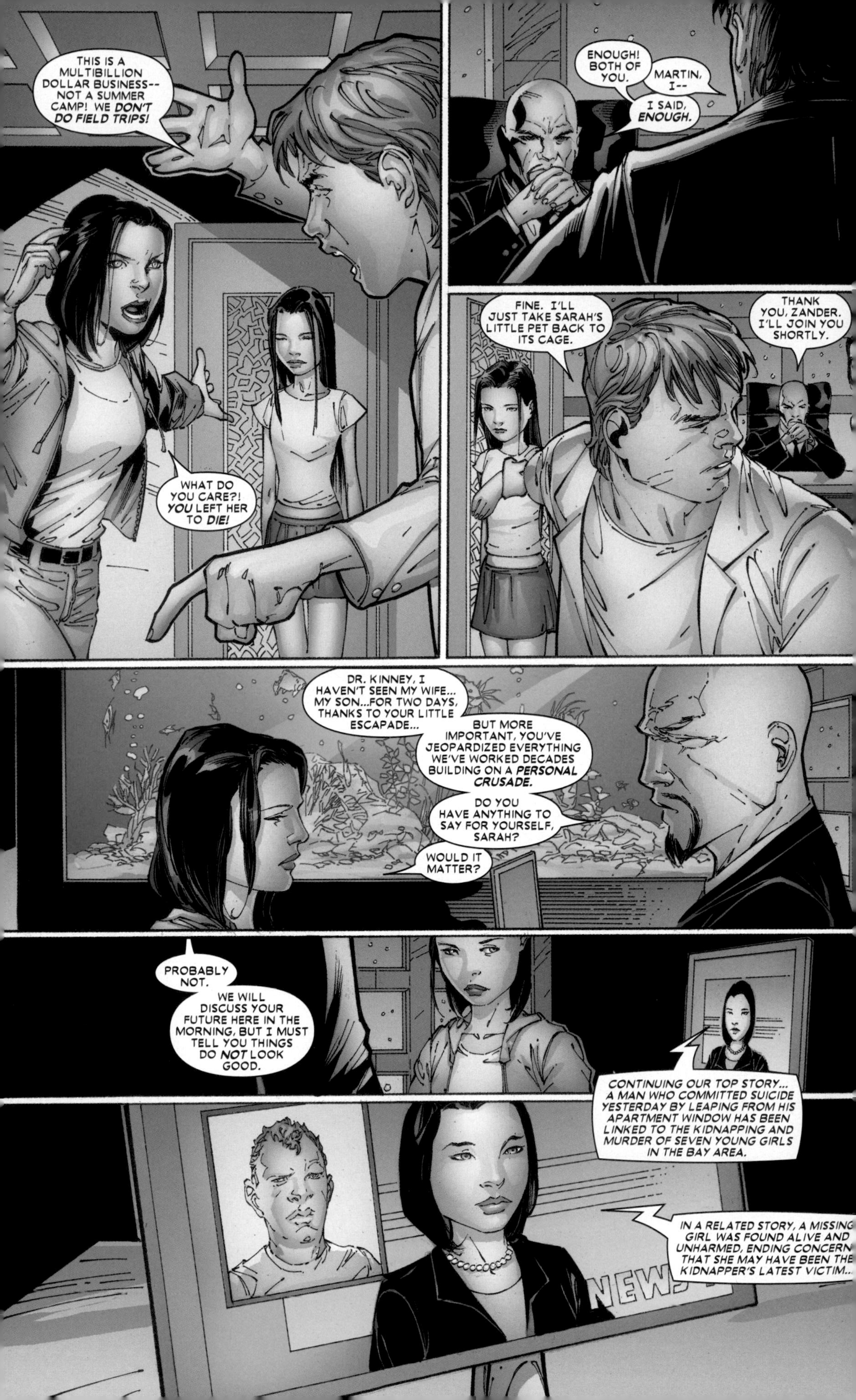
THIS IS A MULTIBILLION DOLLAR BUSINESS-- NOT A SUMMER CAMP! WE DON'T DO FIELD TRIPS!
WHAT DO YOU CARE?! YOU LEFT HER TO DIE!
ENOUGH! BOTH OF YOU.
MARTIN, I--
I SAID, ENOUGH.
FINE. I'LL JUST TAKE SARAH'S LITTLE PET BACK TO ITS CAGE.
THANK YOU, ZANDER. I'LL JOIN YOU SHORTLY.
DR. KINNEY, I HAVEN'T SEEN MY WIFE... MY SON...FOR TWO DAYS, THANKS TO YOUR LITTLE ESCAPADE...
BUT MORE IMPORTANT, YOU'VE JEOPARDIZED EVERYTHING WE'VE WORKED DECADES BUILDING ON A PERSONAL CRUSADE.
DO YOU HAVE ANYTHING TO SAY FOR YOURSELF, SARAH?
WOULD IT MATTER?
PROBABLY NOT.
WE WILL DISCUSS YOUR FUTURE HERE IN THE MORNING, BUT I MUST TELL YOU THINGS DO NOT LOOK GOOD.
CONTINUING OUR TOP STORY... A MAN WHO COMMITTED SUICIDE YESTERDAY BY LEAPING FROM HIS APARTMENT WINDOW HAS BEEN LINKED TO THE KIDNAPPING AND MURDER OF SEVEN YOUNG GIRLS IN THE BAY AREA.
IN A RELATED STORY, A MISSING GIRL WAS FOUND ALIVE AND UNHARMED, ENDING CONCERN THAT SHE MAY HAVE BEEN THE KIDNAPPER'S LATEST VICTIM...

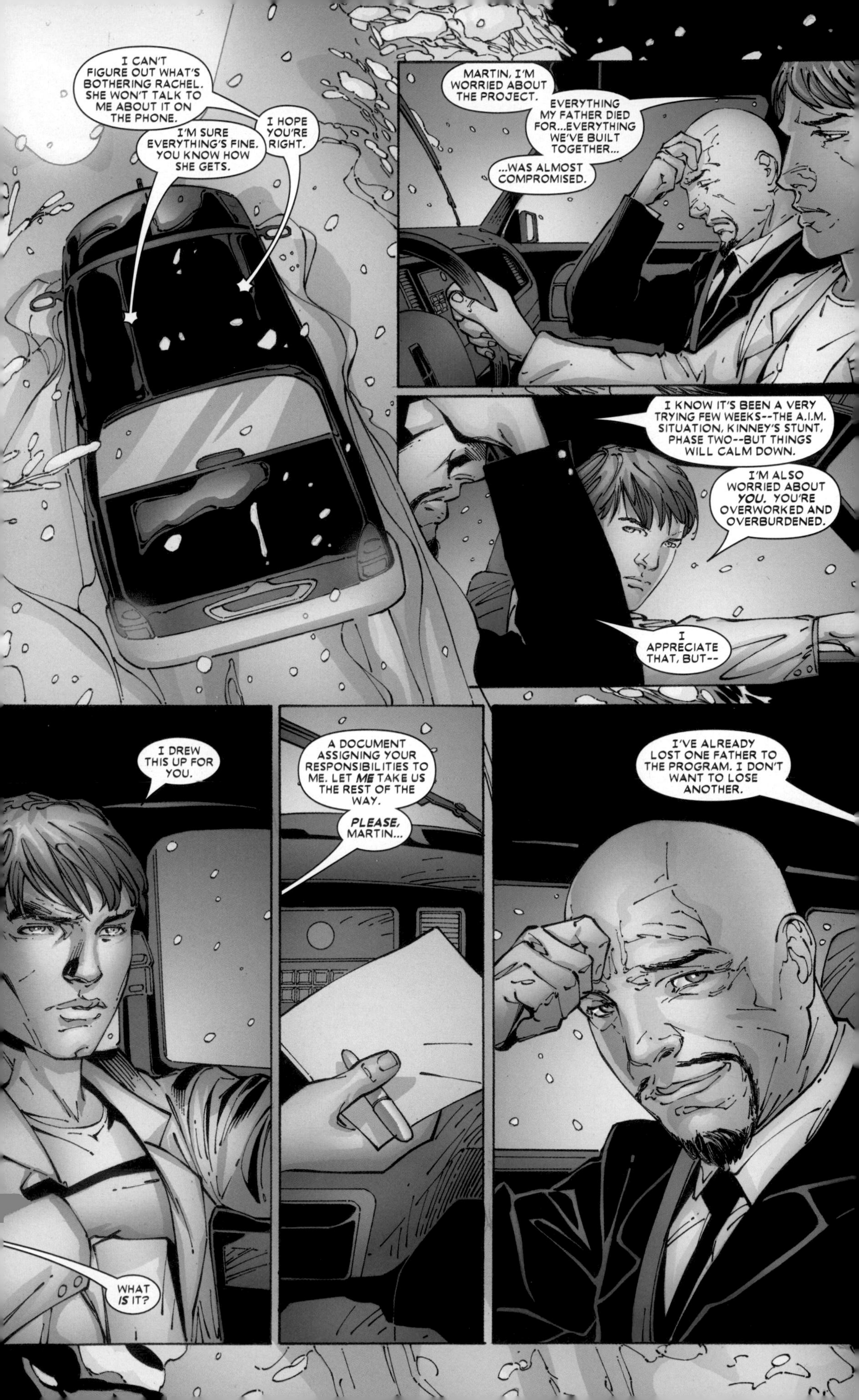
I CAN'T FIGURE OUT WHAT'S BOTHERING RACHEL. SHE WON'T TALK TO ME ABOUT IT ON THE PHONE.
I'M SURE EVERYTHING'S FINE. YOU KNOW HOW SHE GETS.
I HOPE YOU'RE RIGHT.
MARTIN, I'M WORRIED ABOUT THE PROJECT.
EVERYTHING MY FATHER DIED FOR...EVERYTHING WE'VE BUILT TOGETHER...
...WAS ALMOST COMPROMISED.
I KNOW IT'S BEEN A VERY TRYING FEW WEEKS--THE A.I.M. SITUATION, KINNEY'S STUNT, PHASE TWO--BUT THINGS WILL CALM DOWN.
I'M ALSO WORRIED ABOUT *YOU.* YOU'RE OVERWORKED AND OVERBURDENED.
I APPRECIATE THAT, BUT--
I DREW THIS UP FOR YOU.
WHAT *IS* IT?
A DOCUMENT ASSIGNING YOUR RESPONSIBILITIES TO ME. LET *ME* TAKE US THE REST OF THE WAY.
PLEASE, MARTIN...
I'VE ALREADY LOST ONE FATHER TO THE PROGRAM. I DON'T WANT TO LOSE ANOTHER.

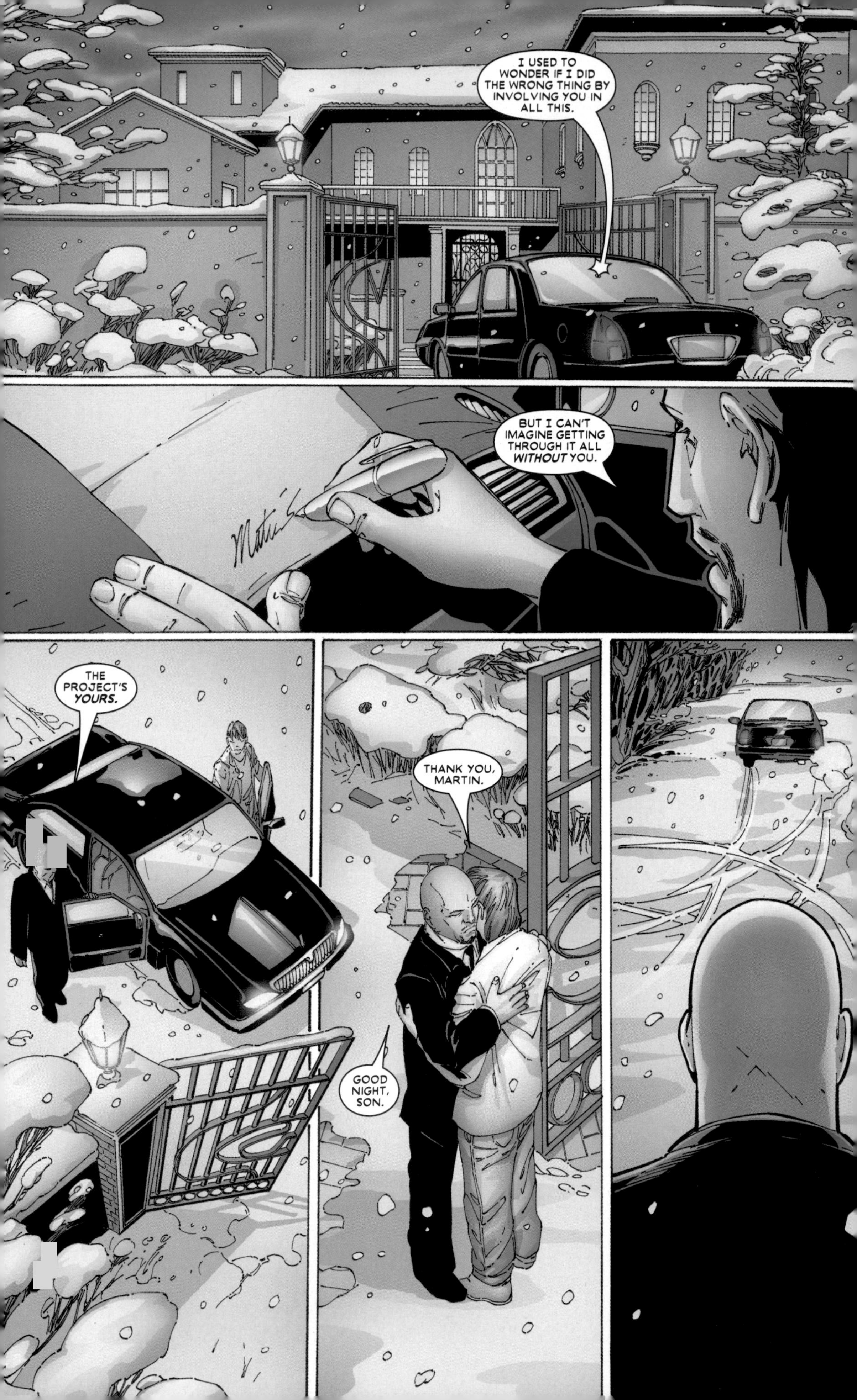
I USED TO WONDER IF I DID THE WRONG THING BY INVOLVING YOU IN ALL THIS.
BUT I CAN'T IMAGINE GETTING THROUGH IT ALL *WITHOUT* YOU.
THE PROJECT'S *YOURS.*
THANK YOU, MARTIN.
GOOD NIGHT, SON.

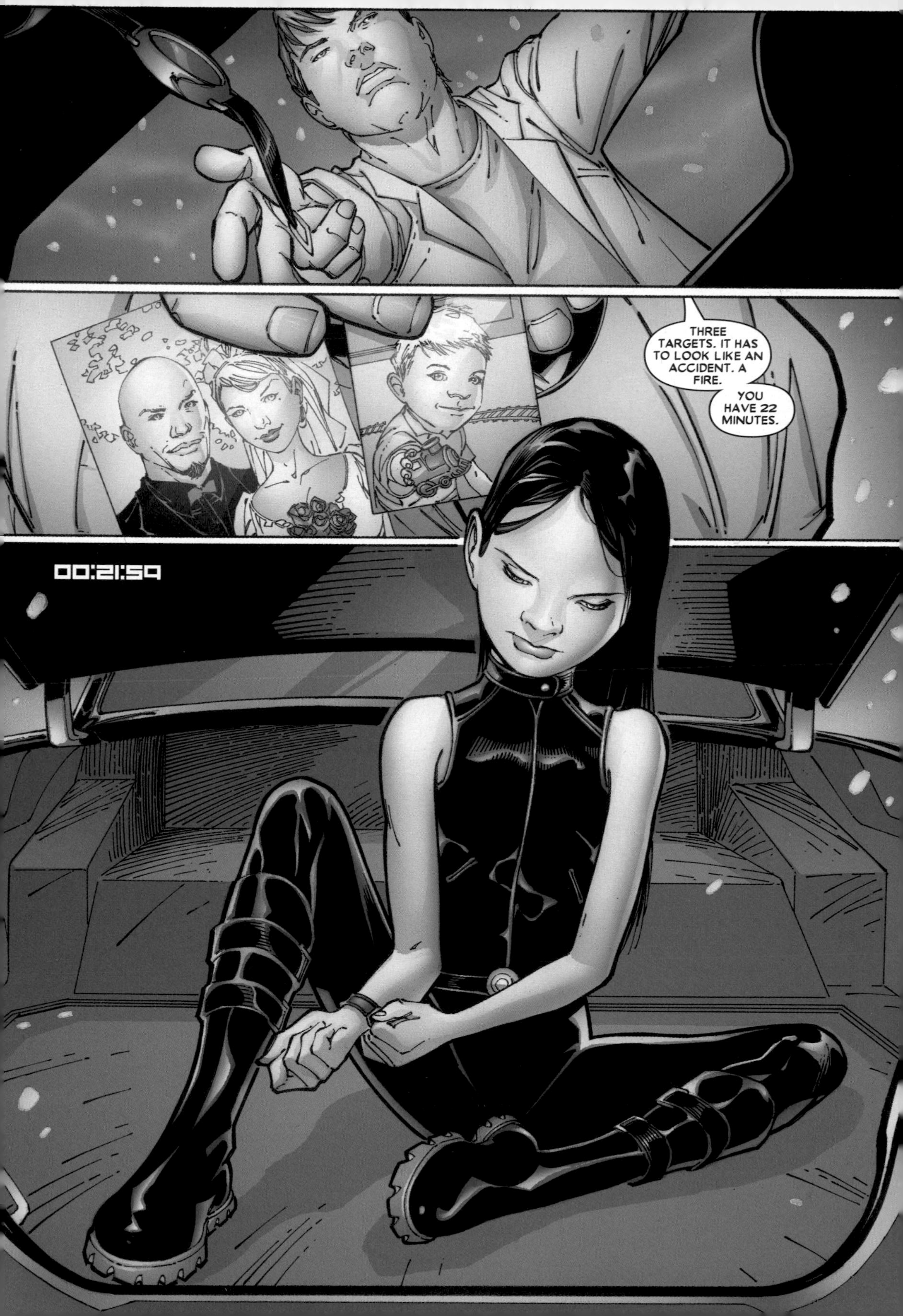
THREE TARGETS. IT HAS TO LOOK LIKE AN ACCIDENT. A FIRE.
YOU HAVE 22 MINUTES.
00:21:59

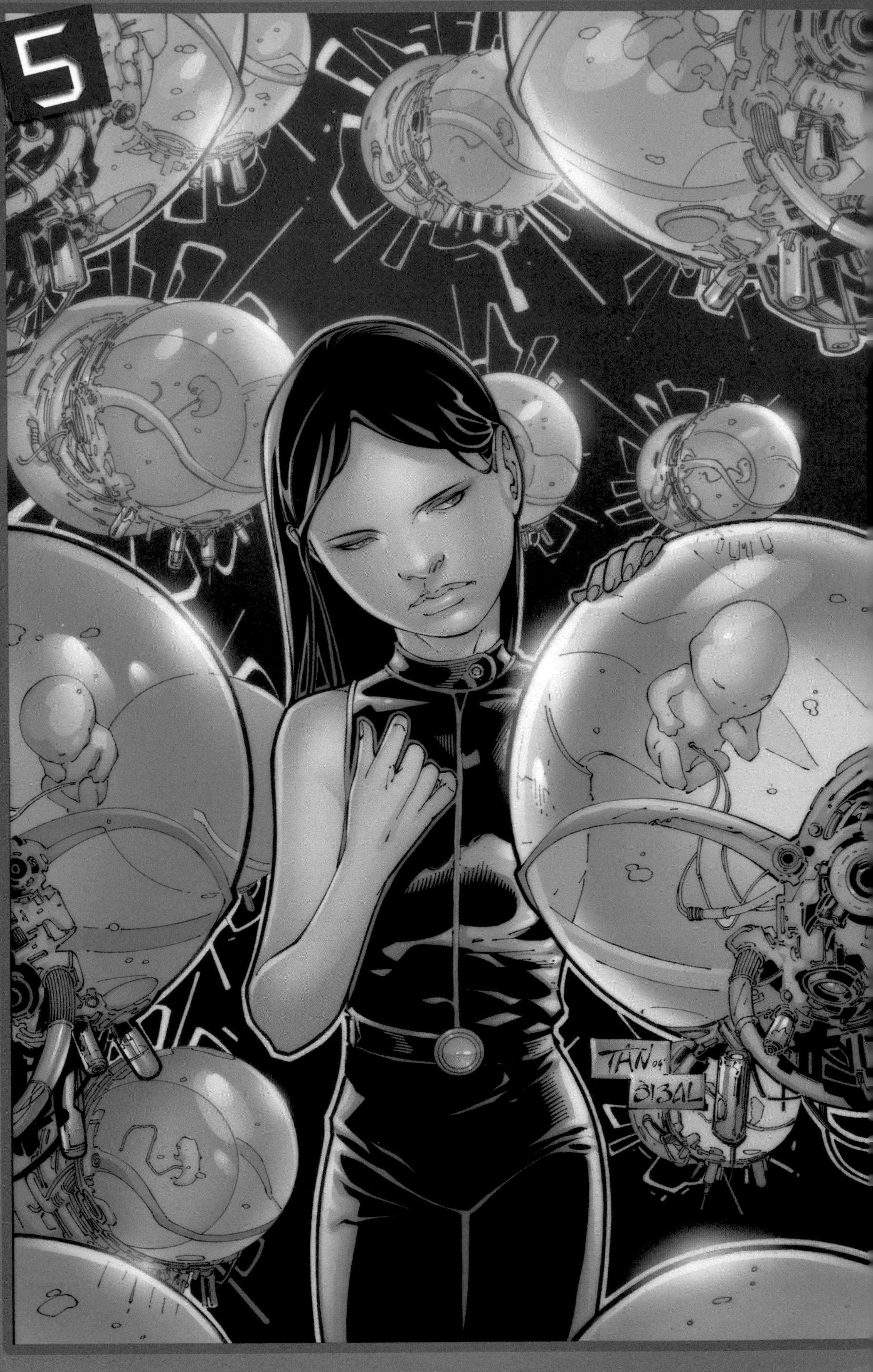
5
TAN 04'
SIBAL

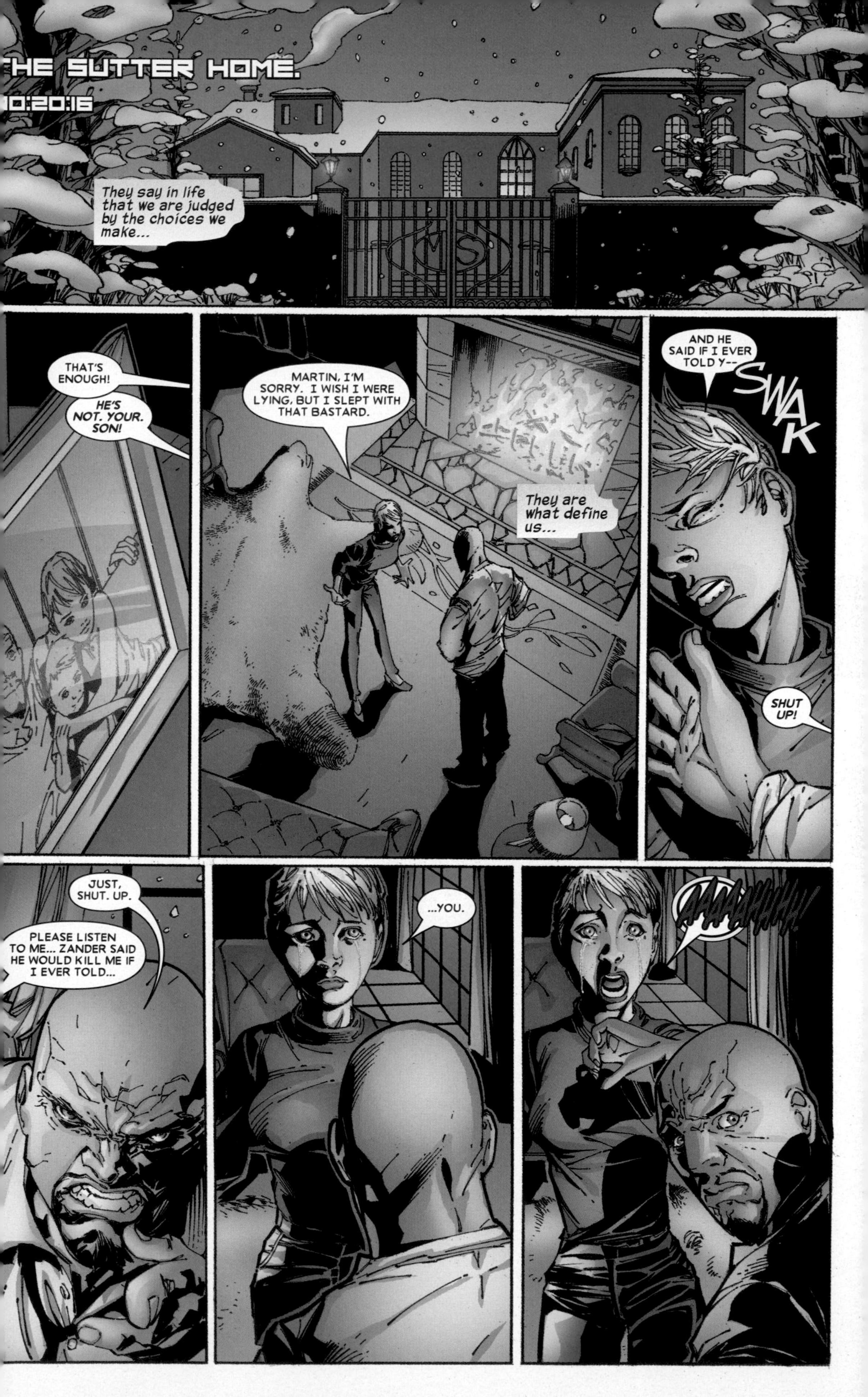
THE SUTTER HOME.
0:20:16
They say in life that we are judged by the choices we make...
THAT'S ENOUGH!
HE'S NOT. YOUR. SON!
MARTIN, I'M SORRY. I WISH I WERE LYING, BUT I SLEPT WITH THAT BASTARD.
They are what define us...
AND HE SAID IF I EVER TOLD Y--
SWAK
SHUT UP!
JUST, SHUT. UP.
PLEASE LISTEN TO ME... ZANDER SAID HE WOULD KILL ME IF I EVER TOLD...
...YOU.
AAAAHHHH!

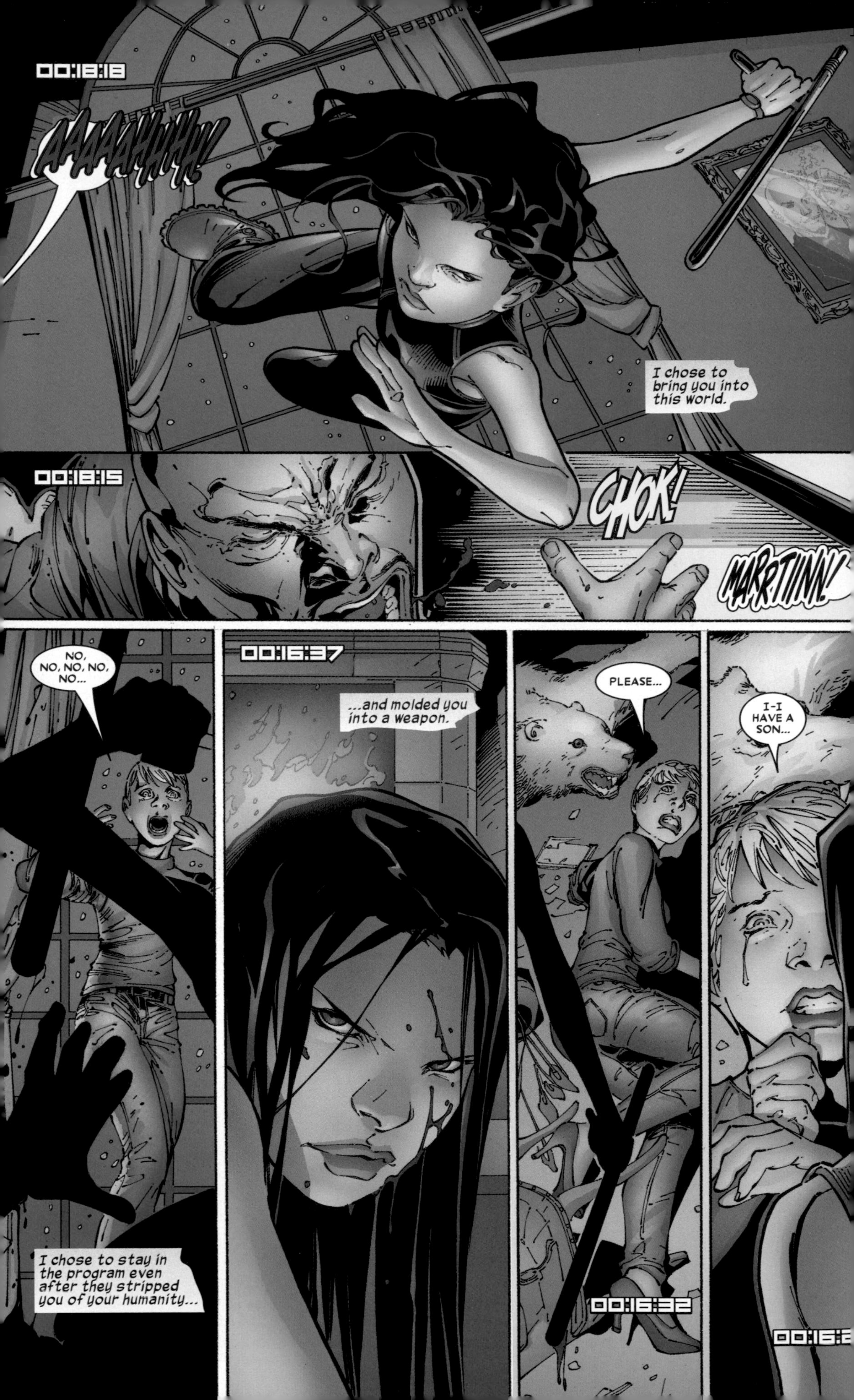
00:18:18
AAAAAHHHH!
I chose to bring you into this world.
00:18:15
CHOK!
MARRTINN!
NO, NO, NO, NO, NO...
I chose to stay in the program even after they stripped you of your humanity...
00:16:37
...and molded you into a weapon.
PLEASE...
00:16:32
I-I HAVE A SON...

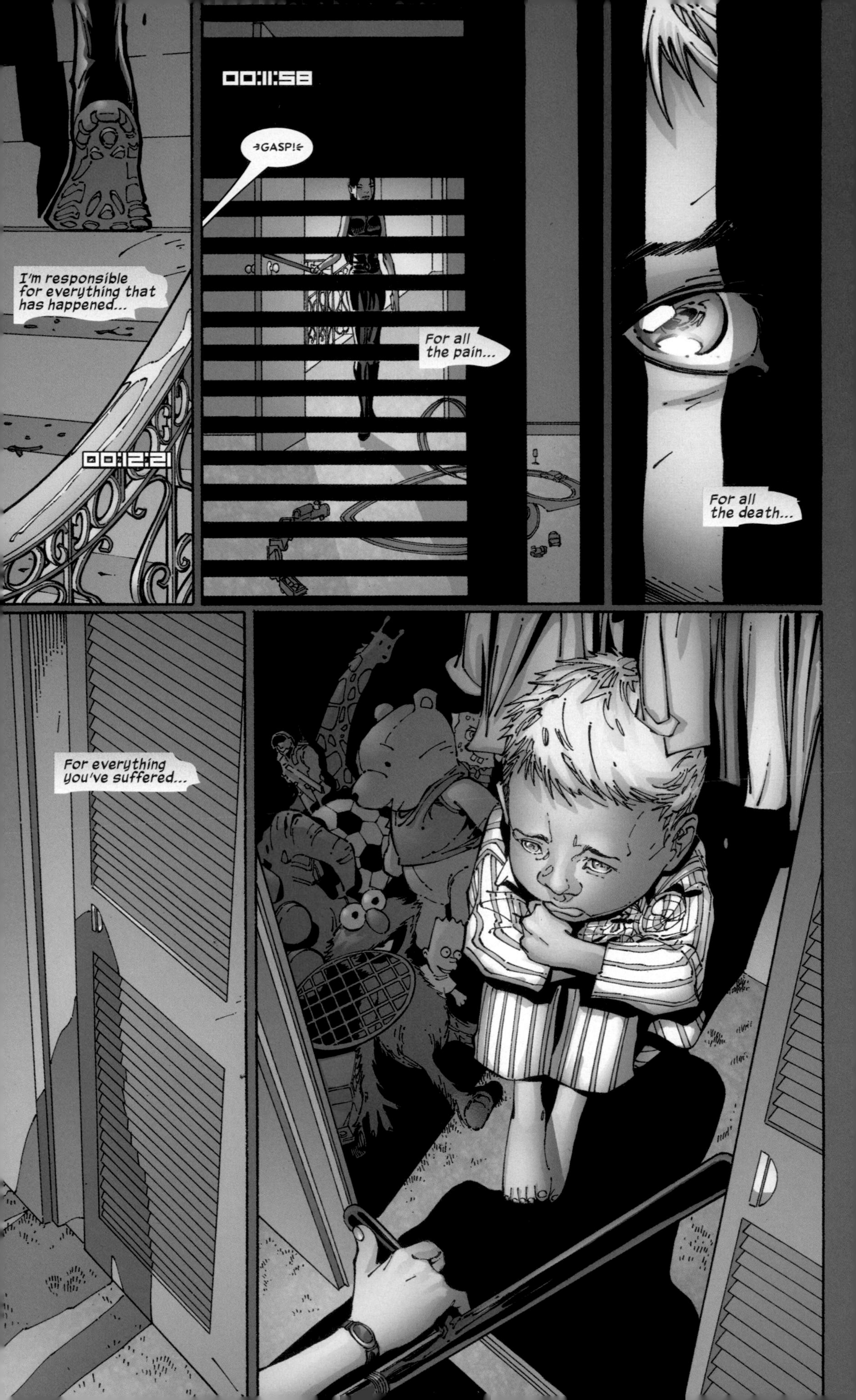

00:11:58
GASP!
I'm responsible for everything that has happened...
00:12:21
For all the pain...
For all the death...
For everything you've suffered...

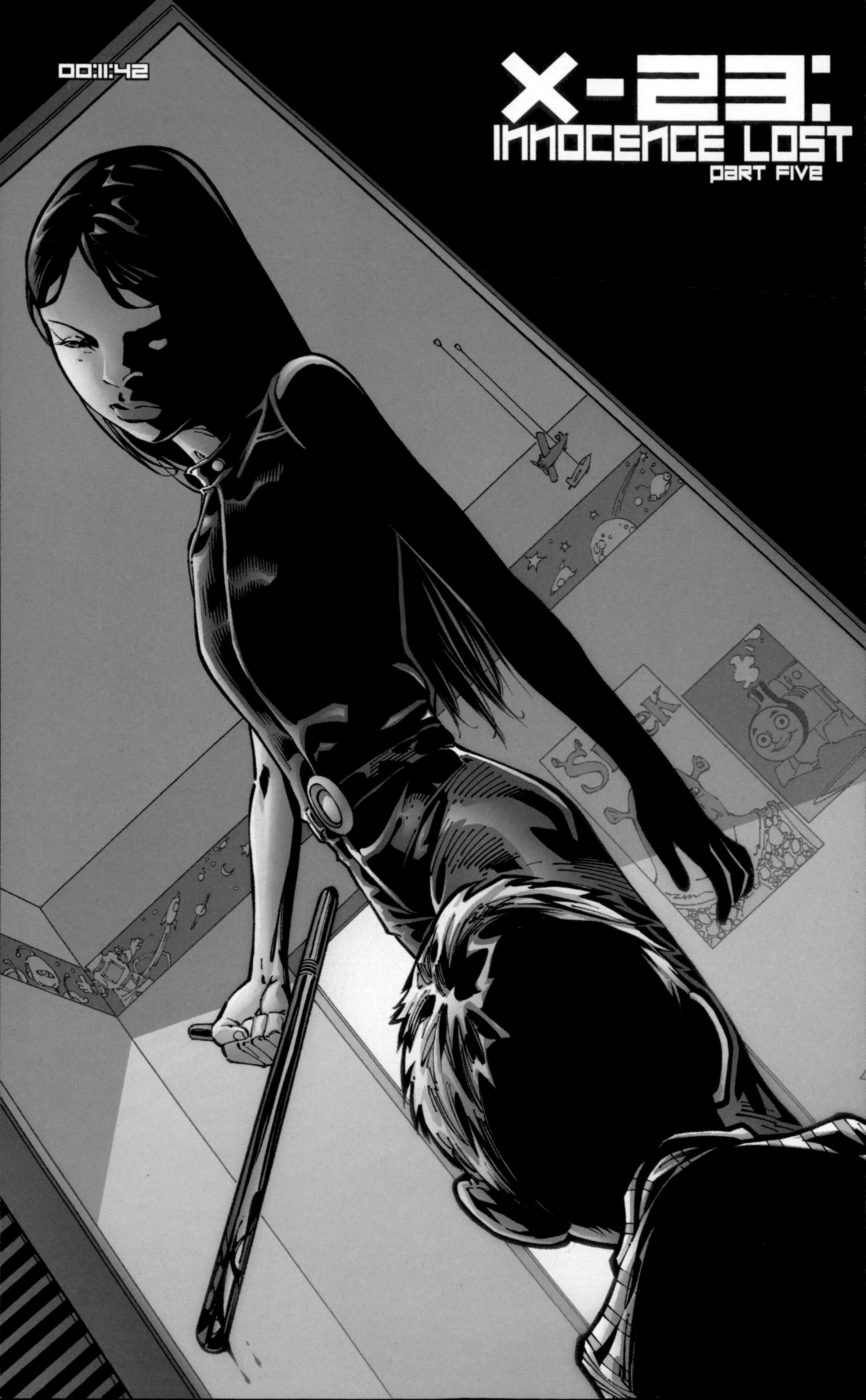
00:11:42
X-23:
INNOCENCE LOST
PART FIVE

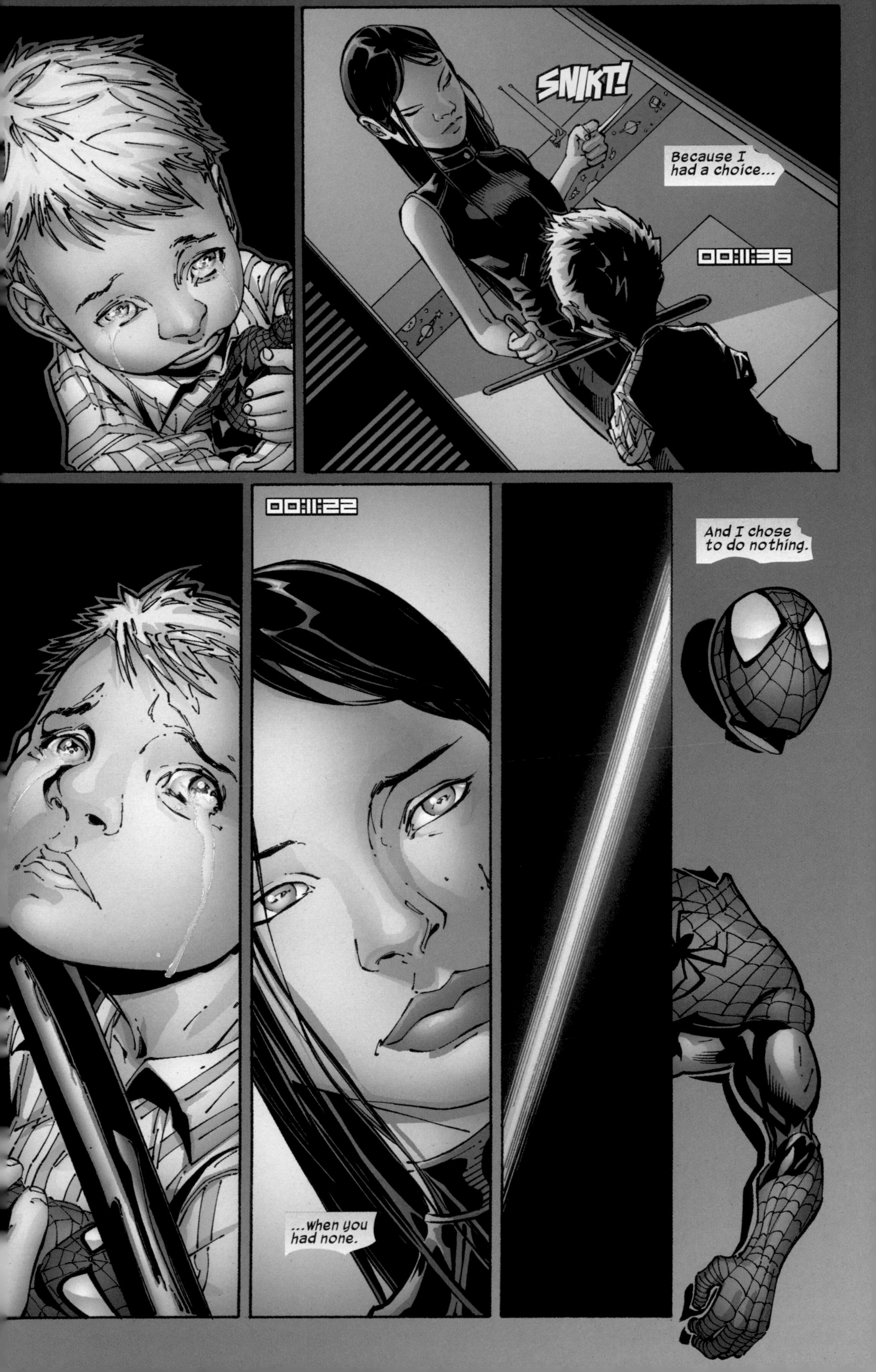
SNIKT!
Because I had a choice...
00:11:36
00:11:22
...when you had none.
And I chose to do nothing.

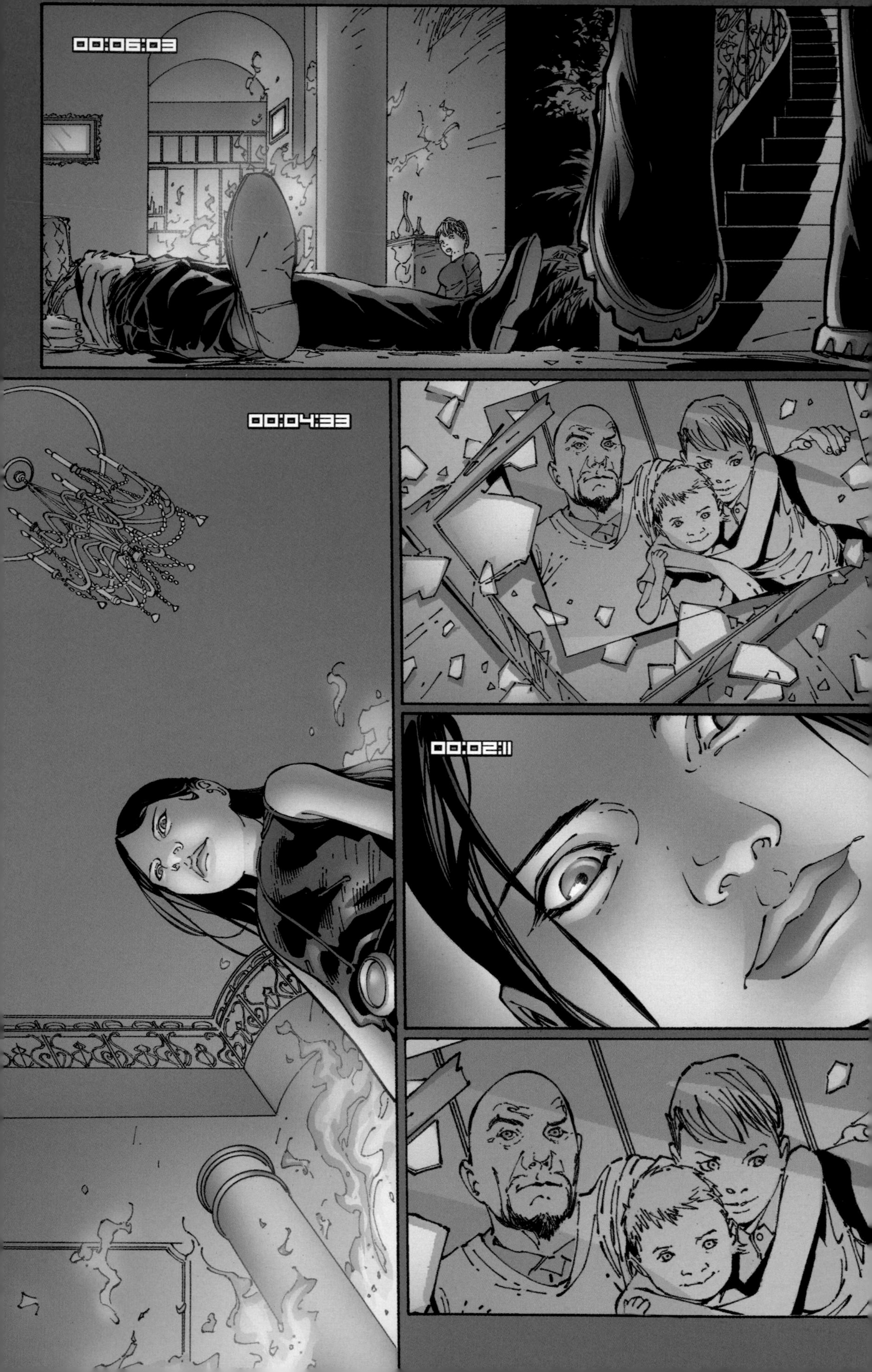
00:06:03
00:04:33
00:02:11

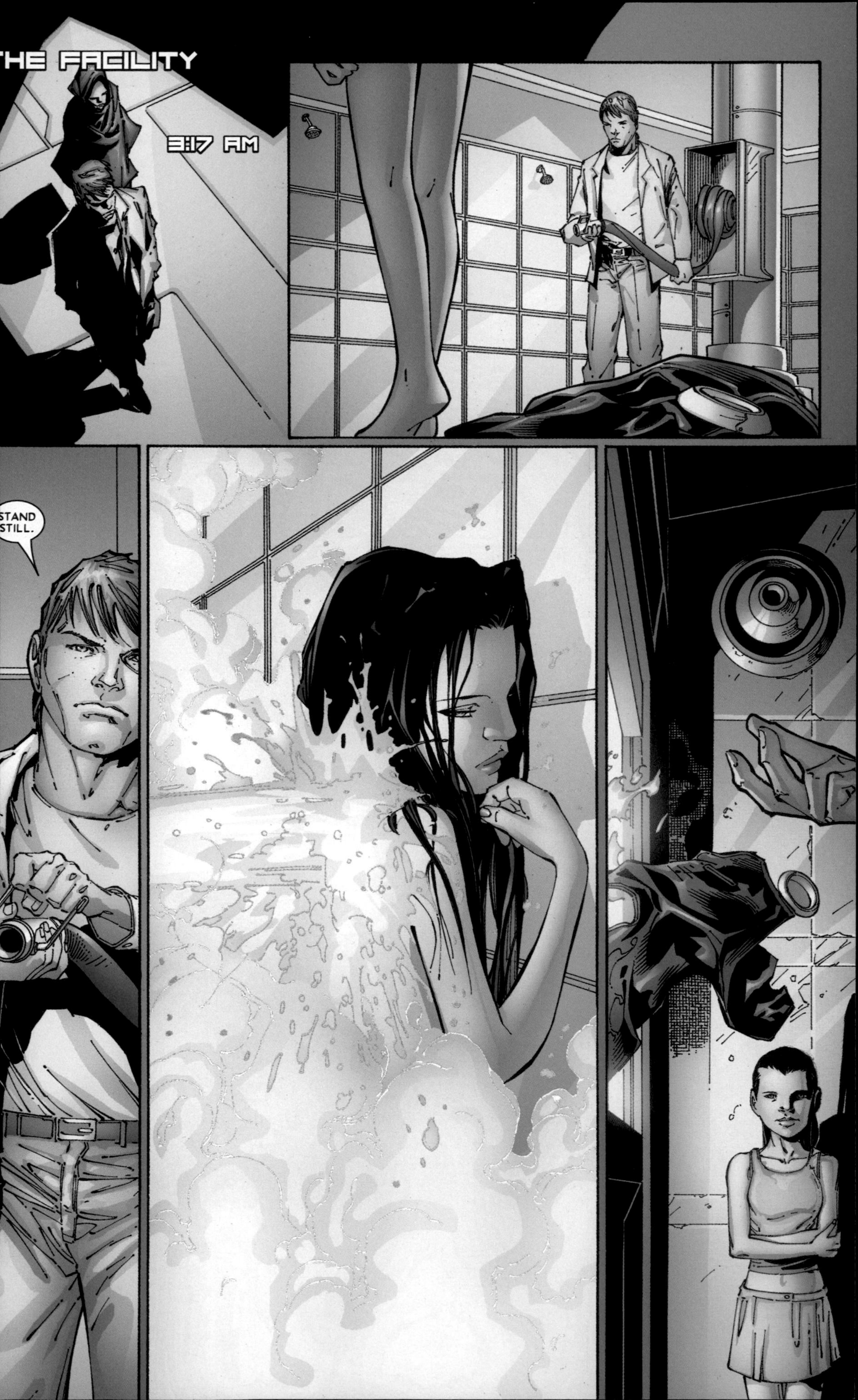
THE FACILITY
3:17 AM
STAND STILL.

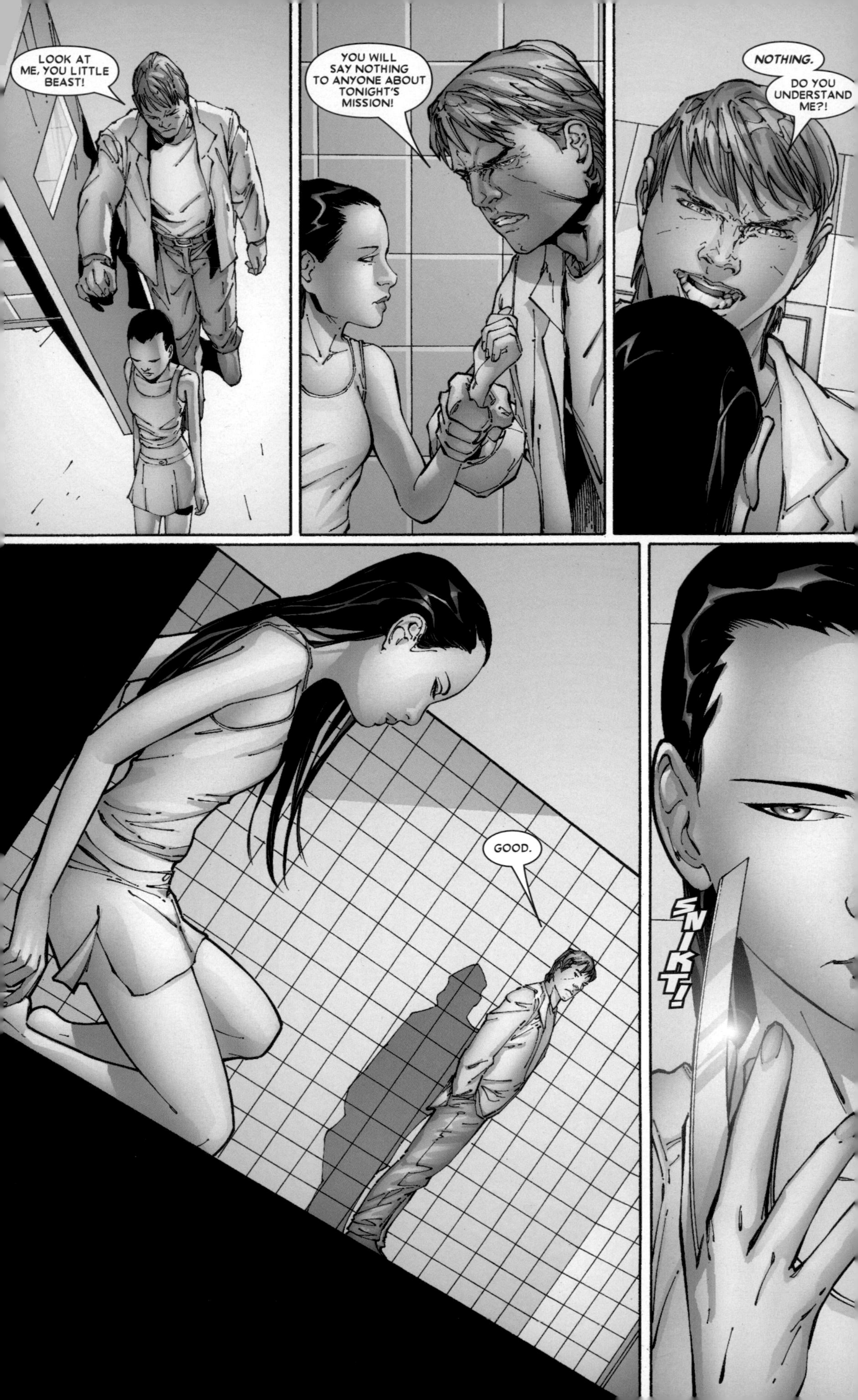
LOOK AT ME, YOU LITTLE BEAST!
YOU WILL SAY NOTHING TO ANYONE ABOUT TONIGHT'S MISSION!
NOTHING.
DO YOU UNDERSTAND ME?!
GOOD.
SNIKT!

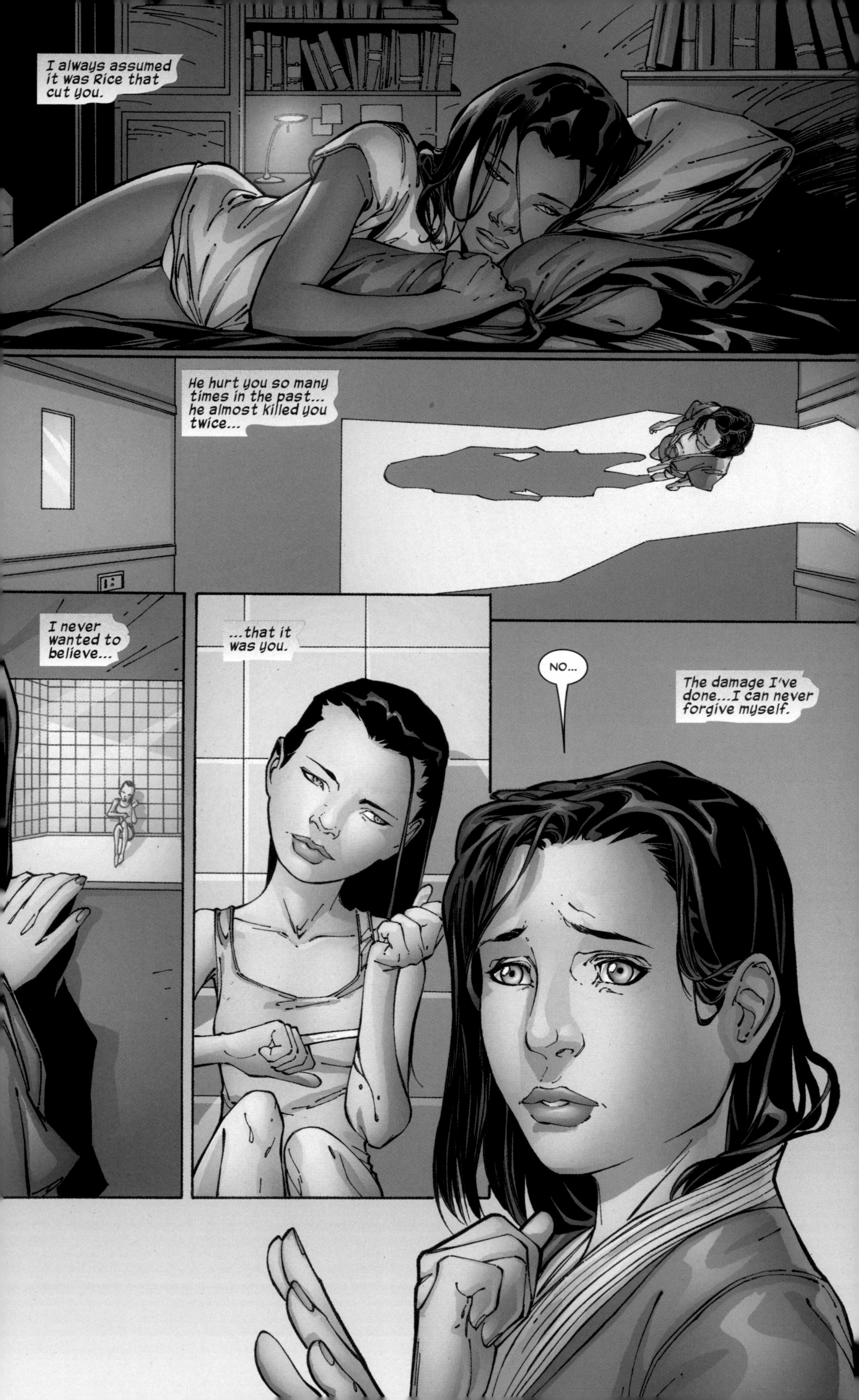
I always assumed it was Rice that cut you.
He hurt you so many times in the past... he almost killed you twice...
I never wanted to believe...
...that it was you.
NO...
The damage I've done...I can never forgive myself.

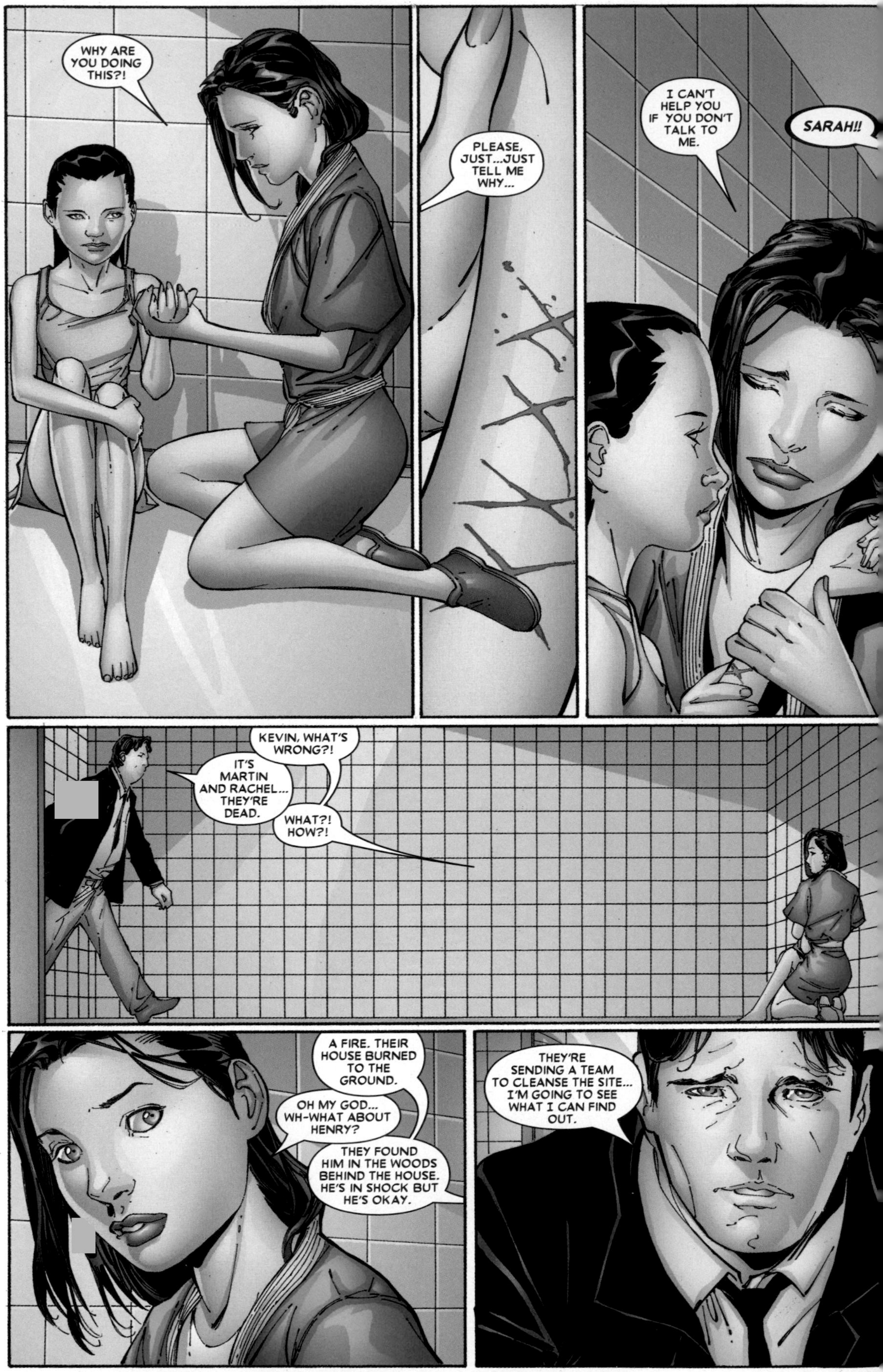
WHY ARE YOU DOING THIS?!
PLEASE, JUST...JUST TELL ME WHY...
I CAN'T HELP YOU IF YOU DON'T TALK TO ME.
SARAH!!
KEVIN, WHAT'S WRONG?!
IT'S MARTIN AND RACHEL... THEY'RE DEAD.
WHAT?! HOW?!
A FIRE. THEIR HOUSE BURNED TO THE GROUND.
OH MY GOD... WH-WHAT ABOUT HENRY?
THEY FOUND HIM IN THE WOODS BEHIND THE HOUSE. HE'S IN SHOCK BUT HE'S OKAY.
THEY'RE SENDING A TEAM TO CLEANSE THE SITE... I'M GOING TO SEE WHAT I CAN FIND OUT.

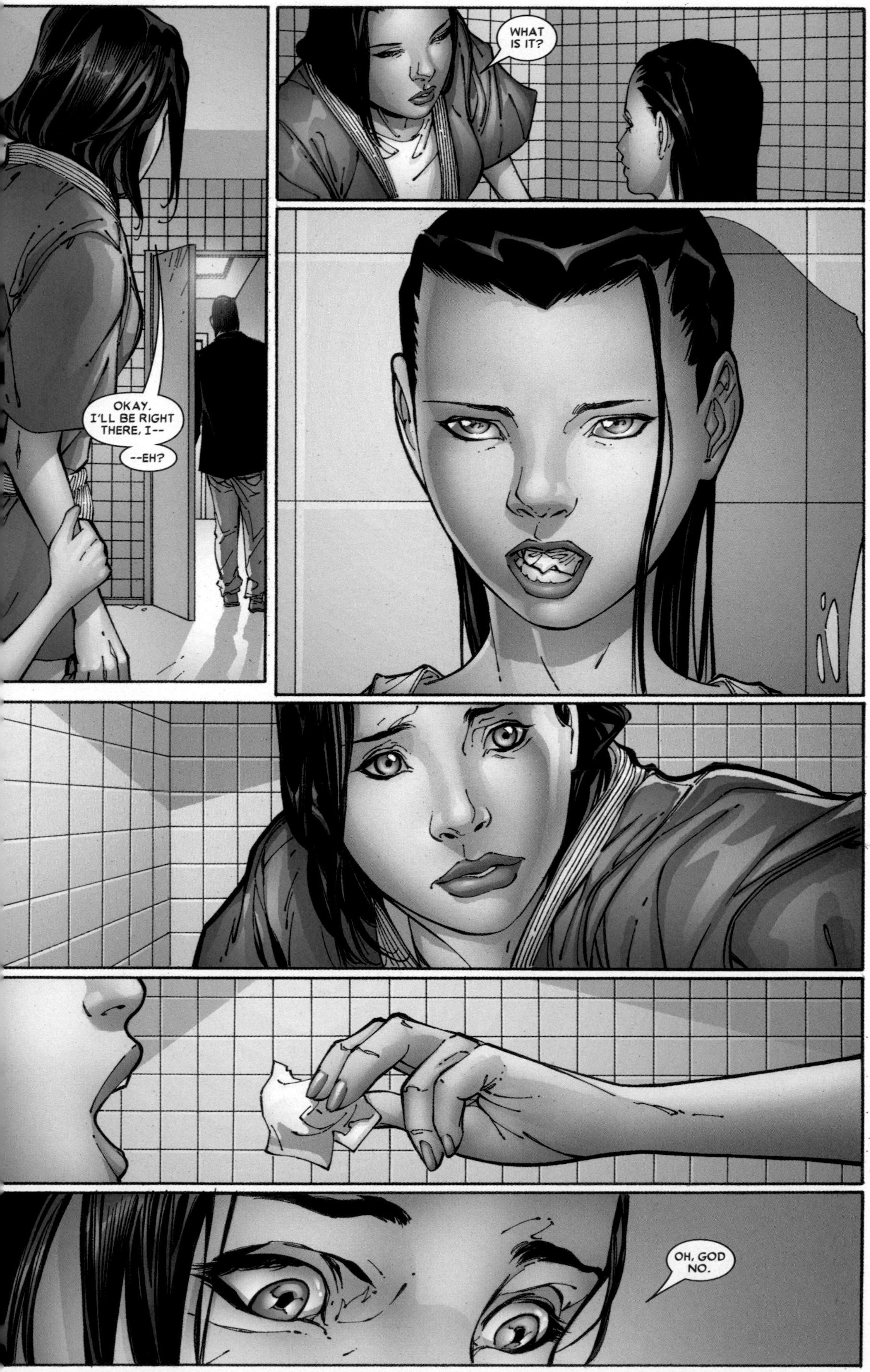
OKAY. I'LL BE RIGHT THERE, I--
--EH?
WHAT IS IT?
OH, GOD NO.

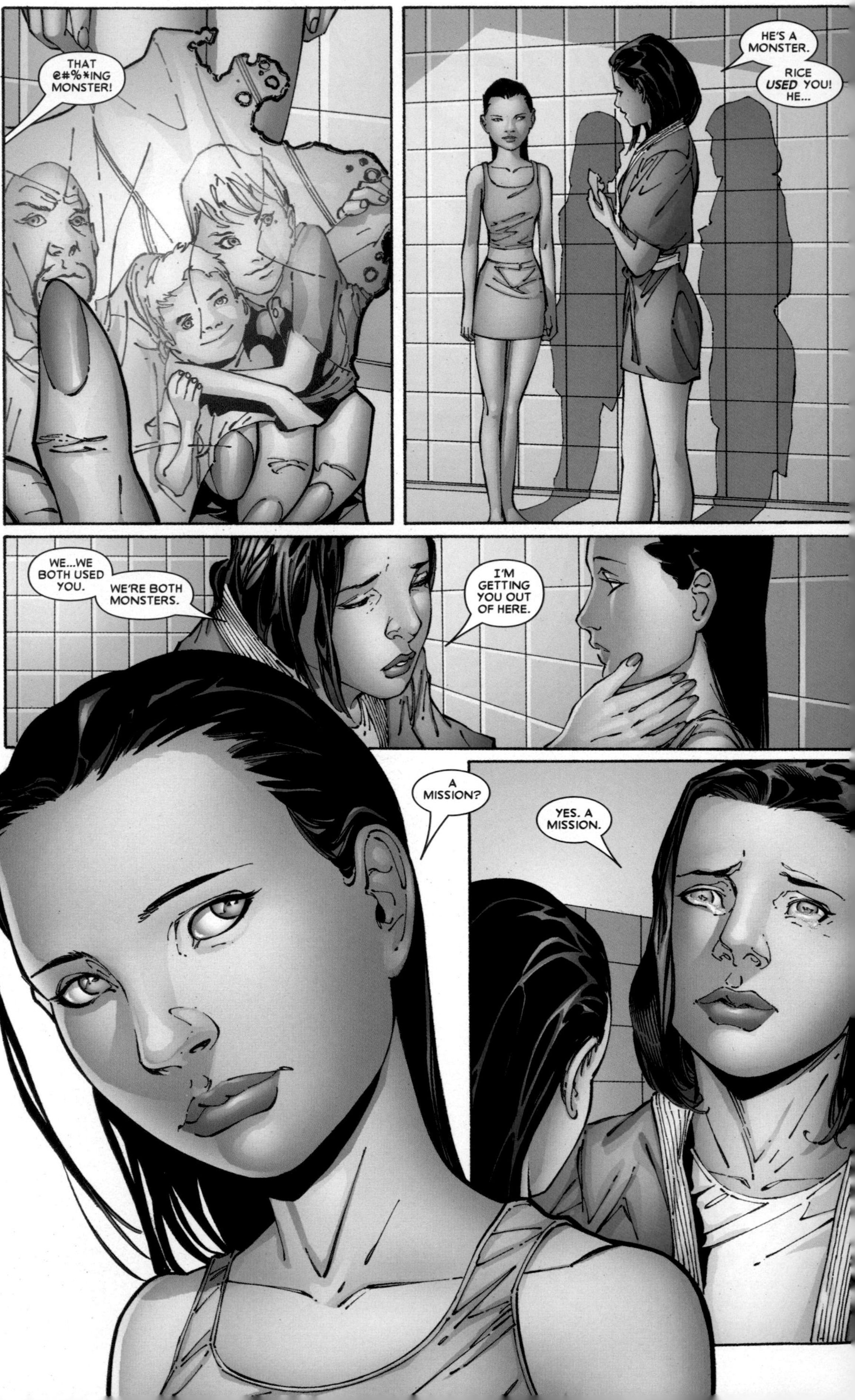
THAT @#%*ING MONSTER!
HE'S A MONSTER.
RICE USED YOU! HE...
WE...WE BOTH USED YOU.
WE'RE BOTH MONSTERS.
I'M GETTING YOU OUT OF HERE.
A MISSION?
YES. A MISSION.

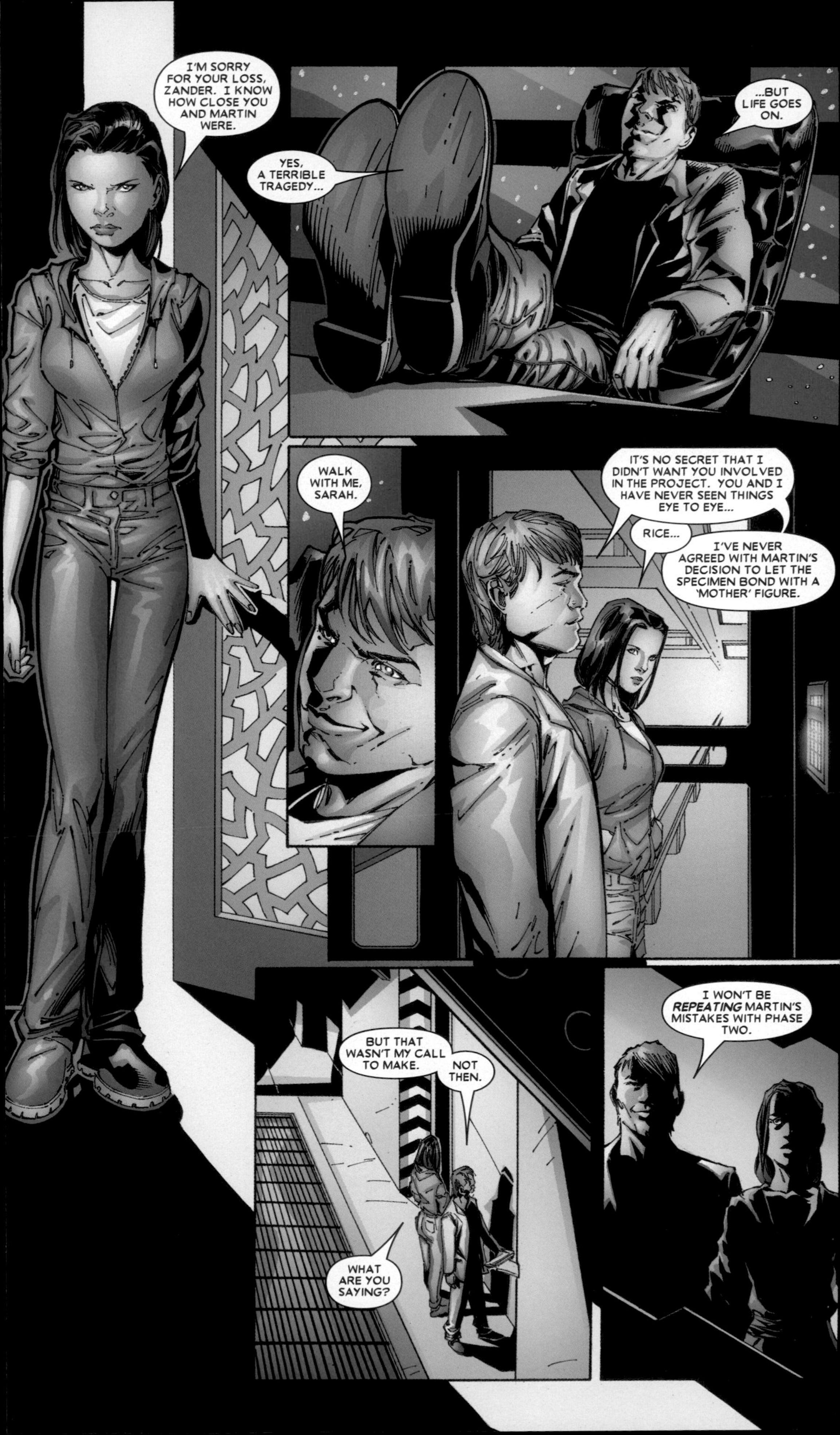

I'M SORRY FOR YOUR LOSS, ZANDER. I KNOW HOW CLOSE YOU AND MARTIN WERE.
YES, A TERRIBLE TRAGEDY...
...BUT LIFE GOES ON.
WALK WITH ME, SARAH.
IT'S NO SECRET THAT I DIDN'T WANT YOU INVOLVED IN THE PROJECT. YOU AND I HAVE NEVER SEEN THINGS EYE TO EYE...
RICE...
I'VE NEVER AGREED WITH MARTIN'S DECISION TO LET THE SPECIMEN BOND WITH A 'MOTHER' FIGURE.
BUT THAT WASN'T MY CALL TO MAKE.
NOT THEN.
WHAT ARE YOU SAYING?
I WON'T BE *REPEATING* MARTIN'S MISTAKES WITH PHASE TWO.

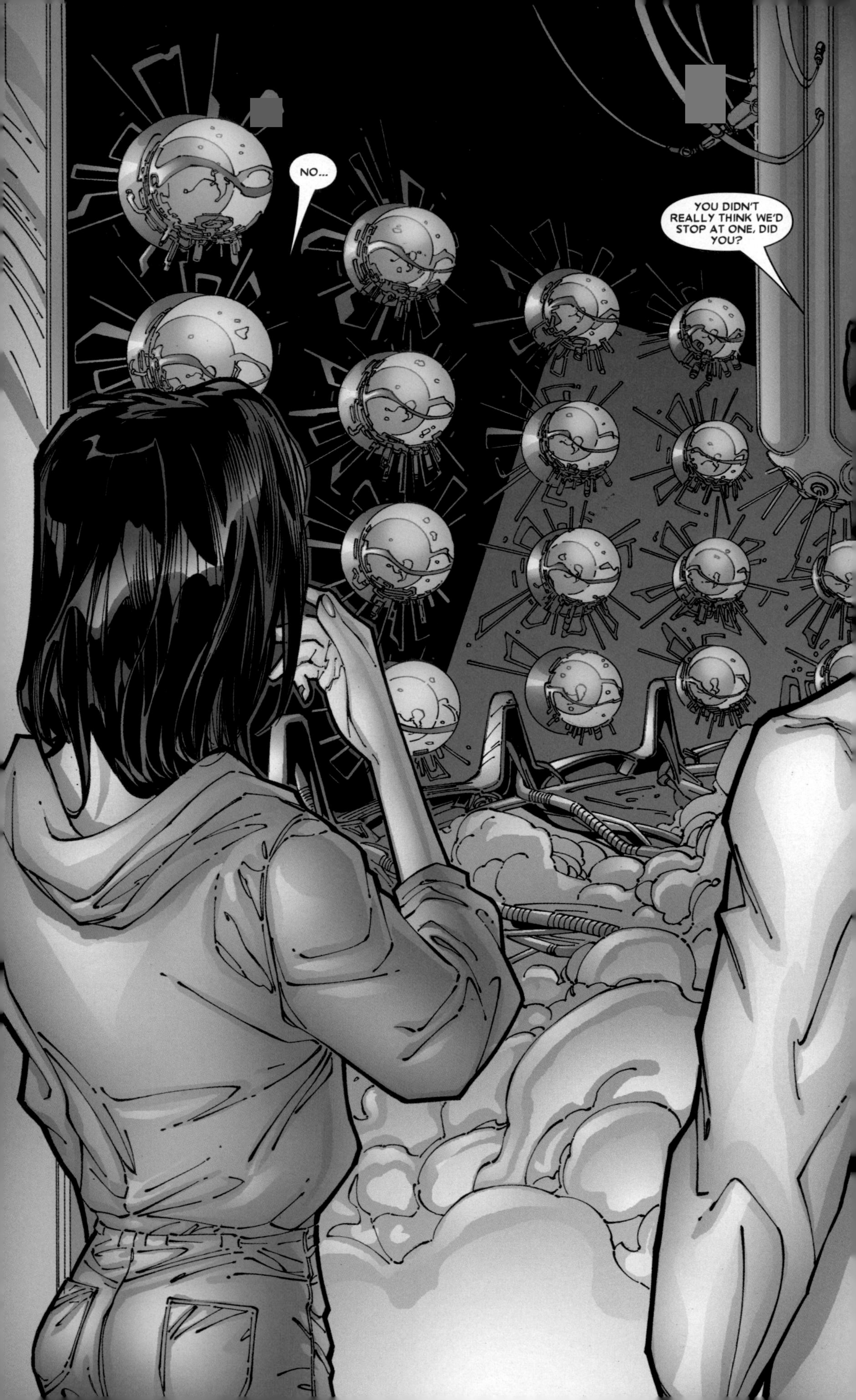
NO...
YOU DIDN'T REALLY THINK WE'D STOP AT ONE, DID YOU?

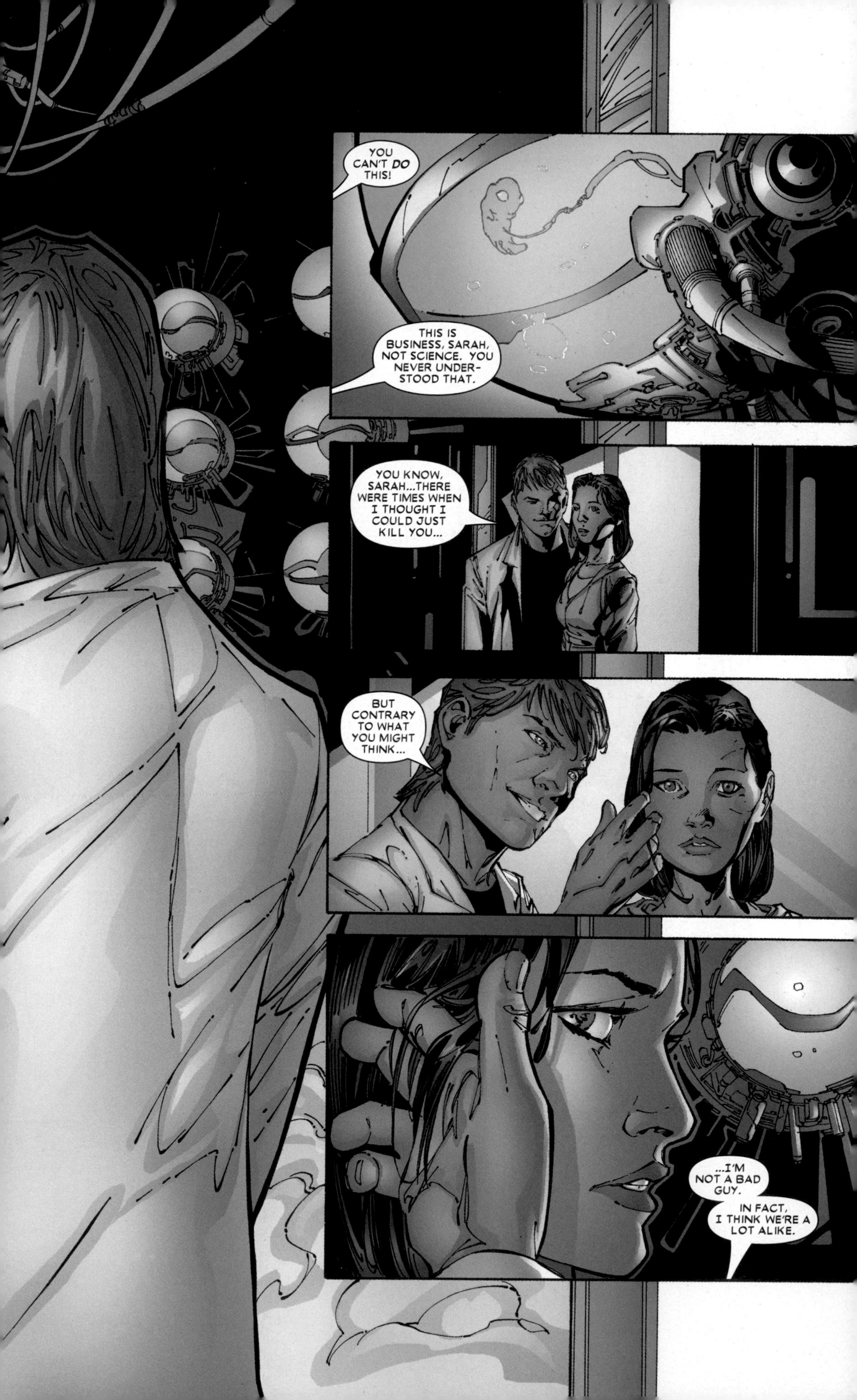
YOU CAN'T *DO* THIS!
THIS IS BUSINESS, SARAH, NOT SCIENCE. YOU NEVER UNDER-STOOD THAT.
YOU KNOW, SARAH...THERE WERE TIMES WHEN I THOUGHT I COULD JUST KILL YOU...
BUT CONTRARY TO WHAT YOU MIGHT THINK...
...I'M NOT A BAD GUY.
IN FACT, I THINK WE'RE A LOT ALIKE.

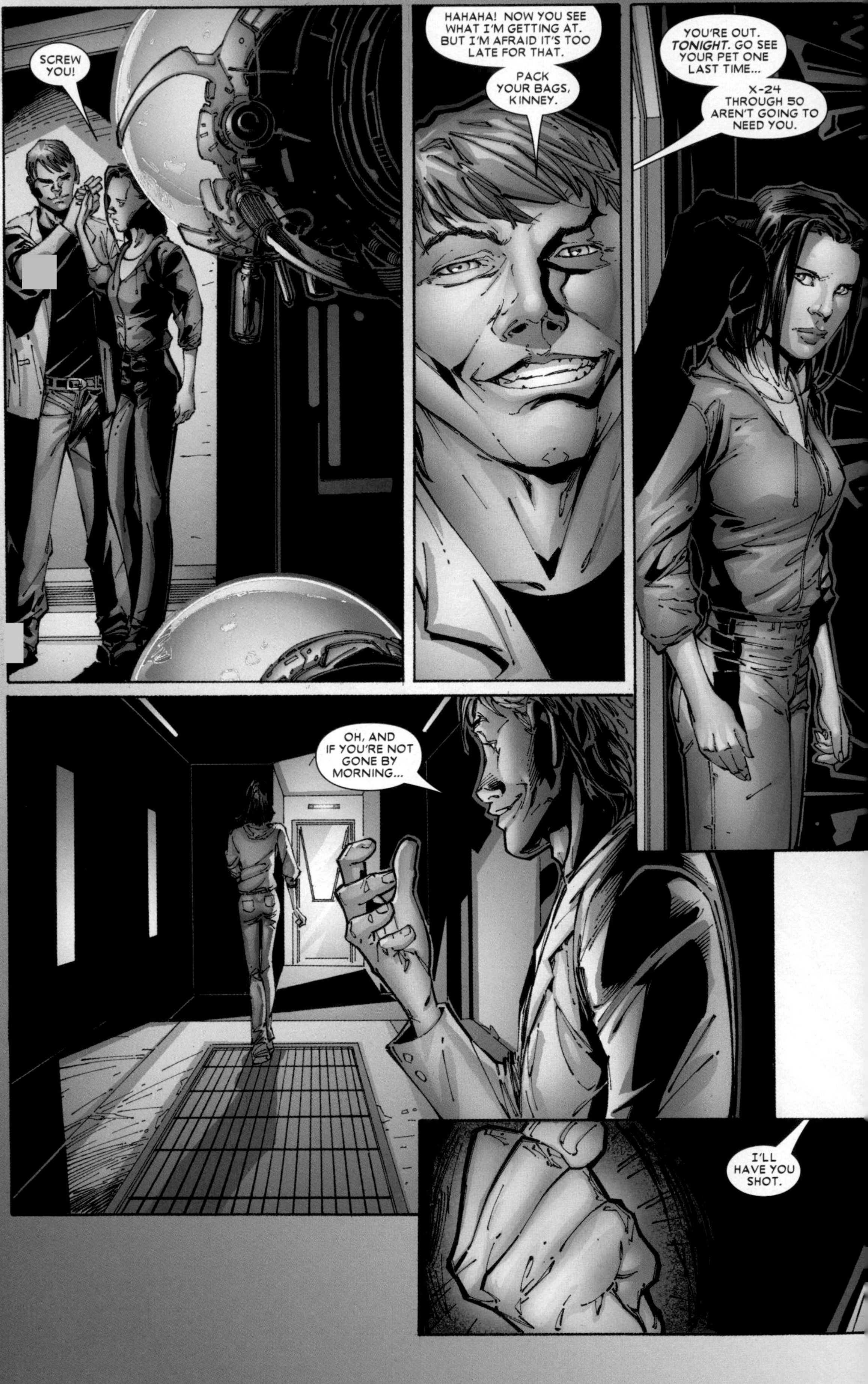
SCREW YOU!
HAHAHA! NOW YOU SEE WHAT I'M GETTING AT. BUT I'M AFRAID IT'S TOO LATE FOR THAT.
PACK YOUR BAGS, KINNEY.
YOU'RE OUT. *TONIGHT.* GO SEE YOUR PET ONE LAST TIME...
X-24 THROUGH 50 AREN'T GOING TO NEED YOU.
OH, AND IF YOU'RE NOT GONE BY MORNING...
I'LL HAVE YOU SHOT.

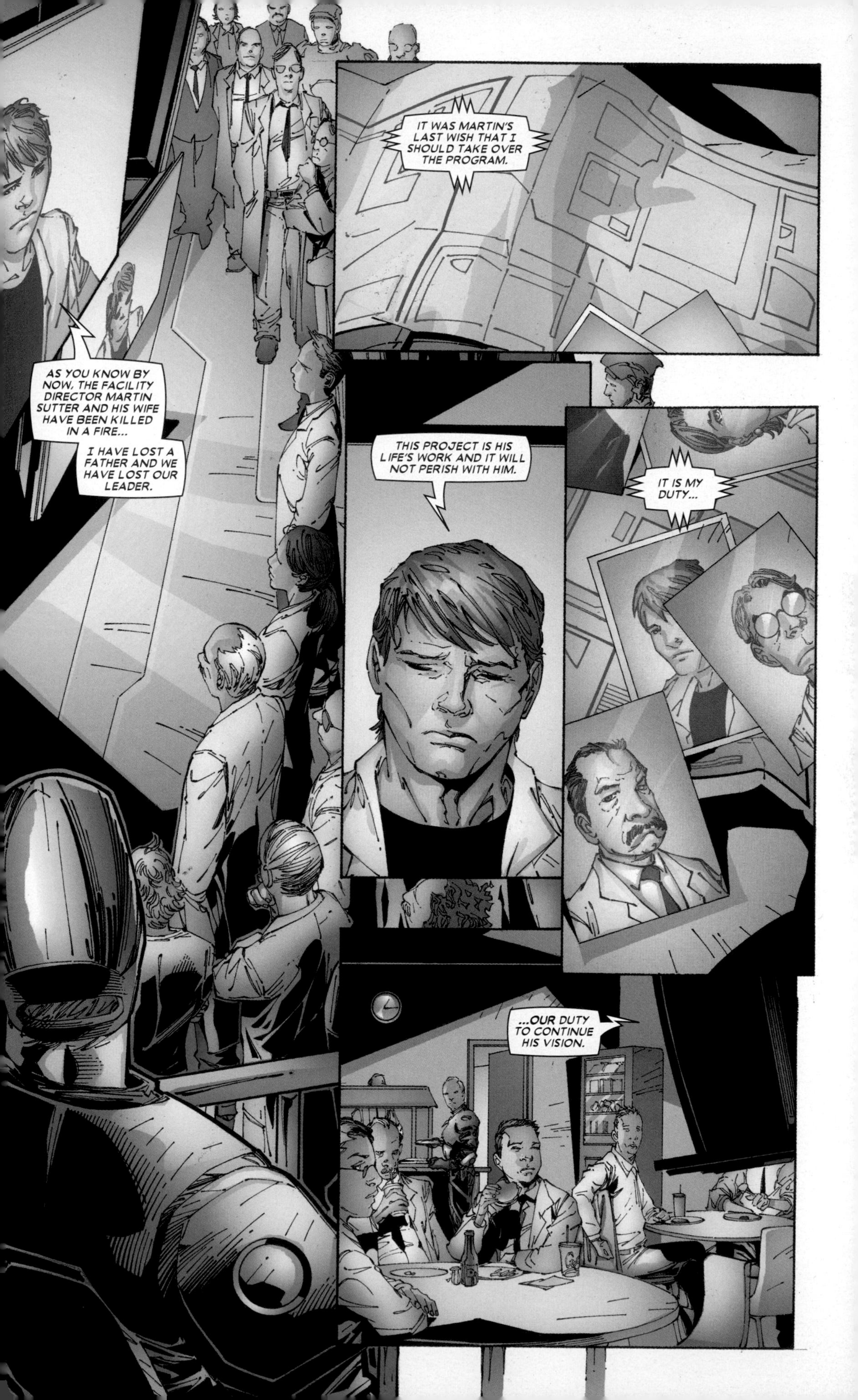
IT WAS MARTIN'S LAST WISH THAT I SHOULD TAKE OVER THE PROGRAM.
AS YOU KNOW BY NOW, THE FACILITY DIRECTOR MARTIN SUTTER AND HIS WIFE HAVE BEEN KILLED IN A FIRE...
I HAVE LOST A FATHER AND WE HAVE LOST OUR LEADER.
THIS PROJECT IS HIS LIFE'S WORK AND IT WILL NOT PERISH WITH HIM.
IT IS MY DUTY...
...OUR DUTY TO CONTINUE HIS VISION.

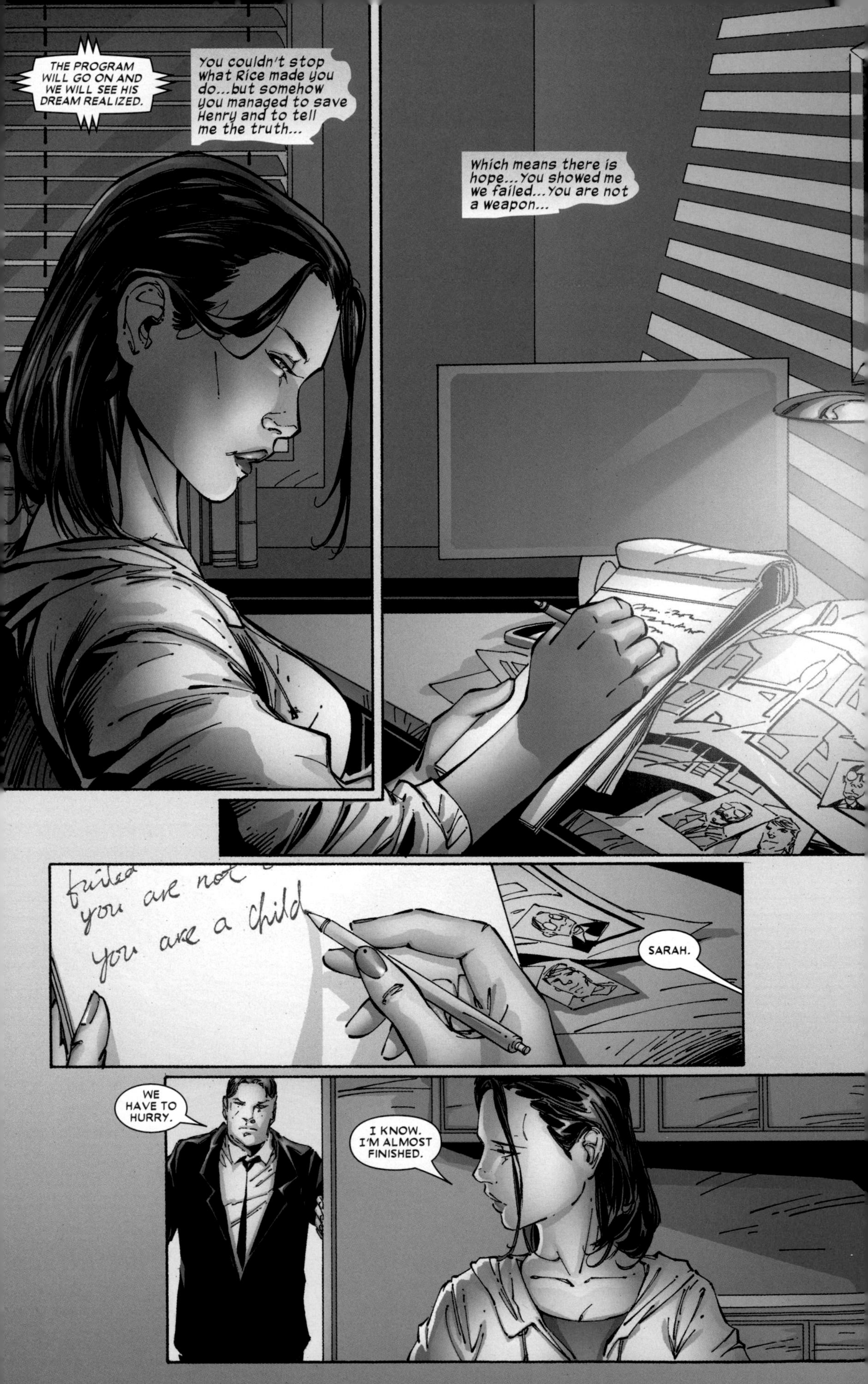
THE PROGRAM WILL GO ON AND WE WILL SEE HIS DREAM REALIZED.
You couldn't stop what Rice made you do...but somehow you managed to save Henry and to tell me the truth...
Which means there is hope...You showed me we failed...You are not a weapon...
failed
you are not
you are a child
SARAH.
WE HAVE TO HURRY.
I KNOW. I'M ALMOST FINISHED.

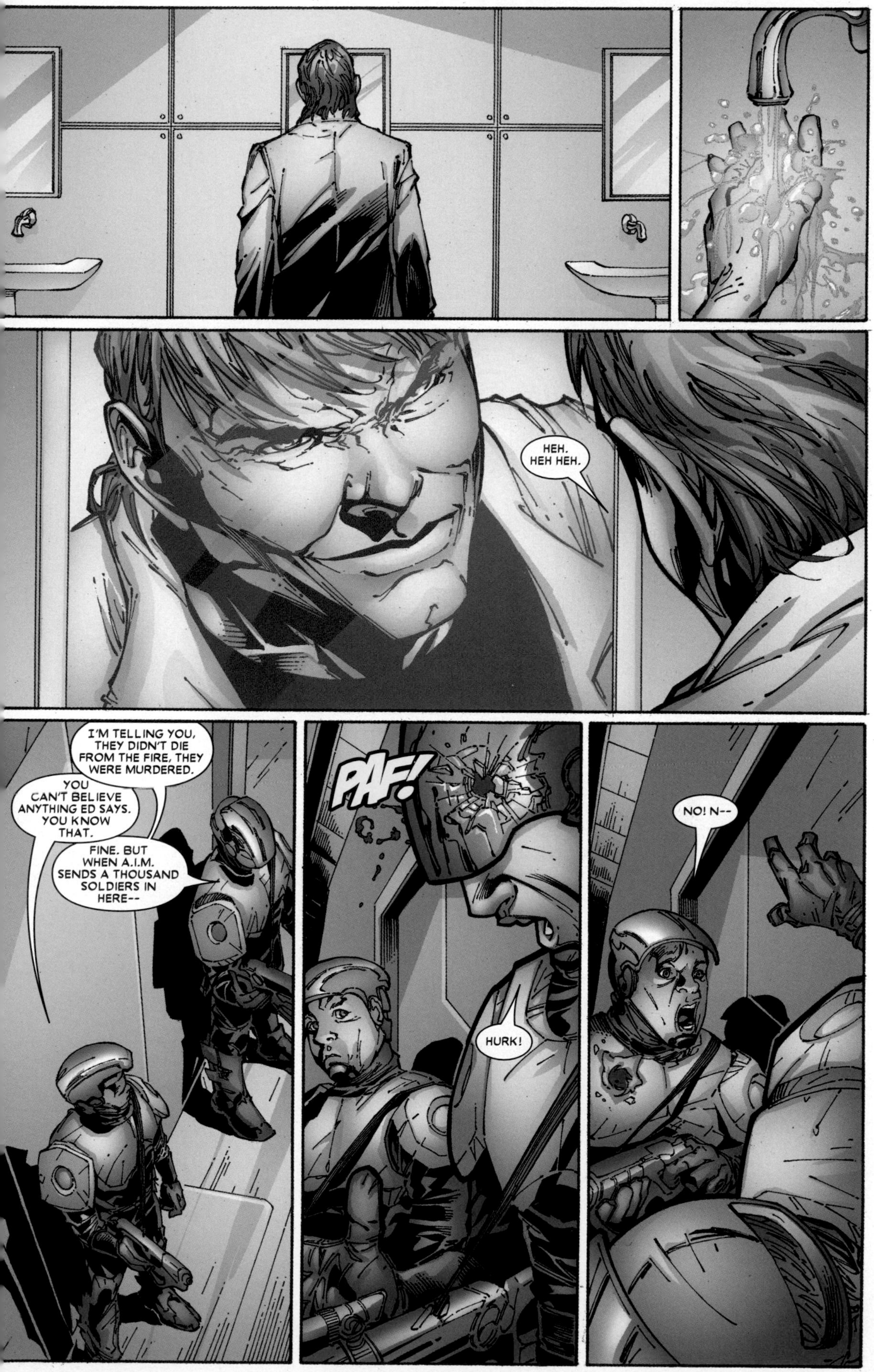
HEH.
HEH HEH.
I'M TELLING YOU, THEY DIDN'T DIE FROM THE FIRE, THEY WERE MURDERED.
YOU CAN'T BELIEVE ANYTHING ED SAYS. YOU KNOW THAT.
FINE. BUT WHEN A.I.M. SENDS A THOUSAND SOLDIERS IN HERE--
PAF!
HURK!
NO! N--

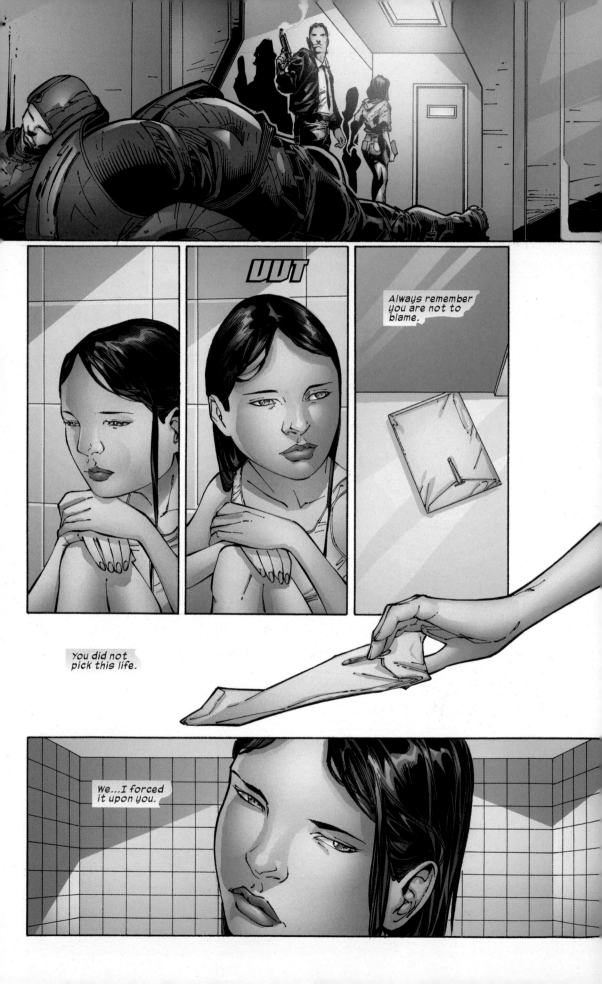

UUT

Always remember you are not to blame.

You did not pick this life.

We...I forced it upon you.

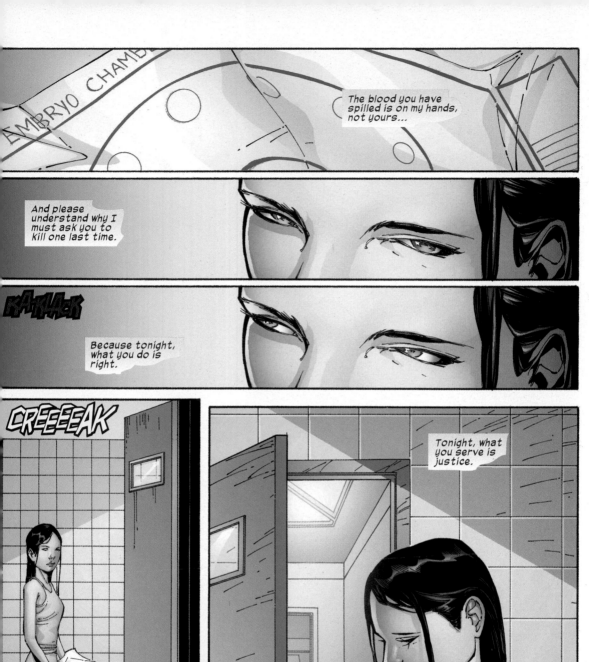

The blood you have spilled is on my hands, not yours...

And please understand why I must ask you to kill one last time.

KA-KLACK

Because tonight, what you do is right.

EMBRYO CHAMBE

CREEEEAK

Tonight, what you serve is justice.

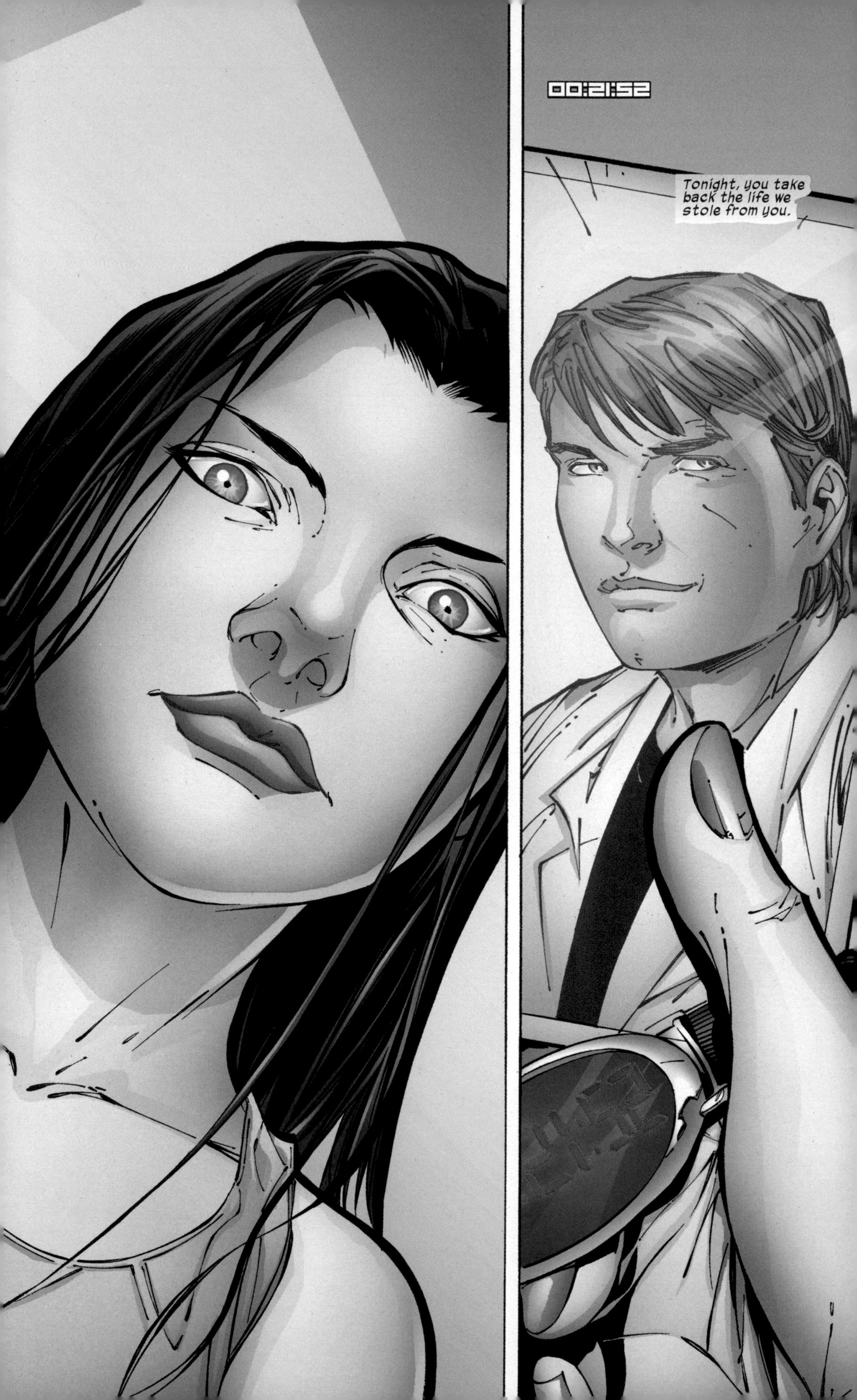
00:21:52
Tonight, you take back the life we stole from you.

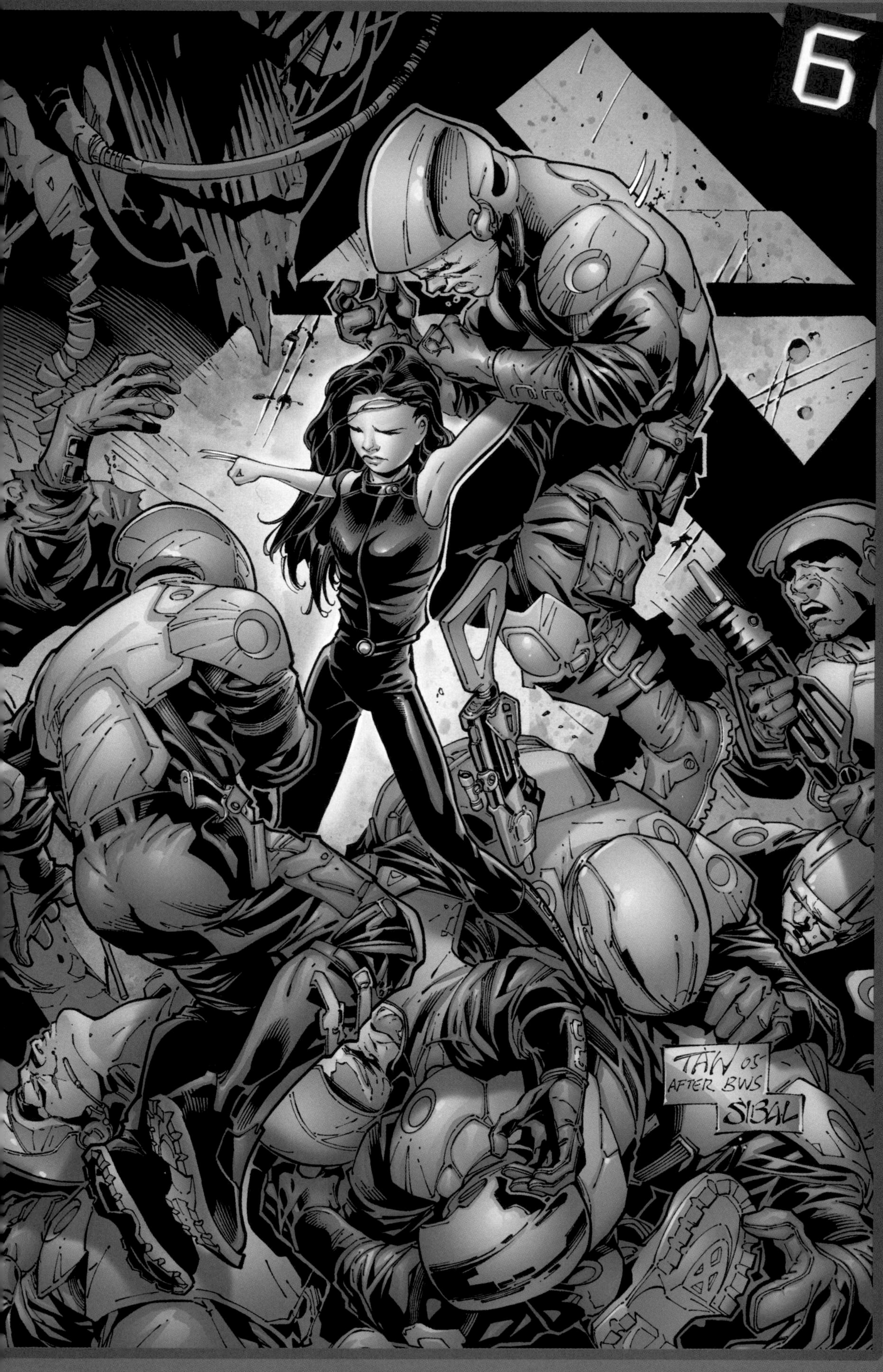

6
TAN 05
AFTER BWS
SIBAL

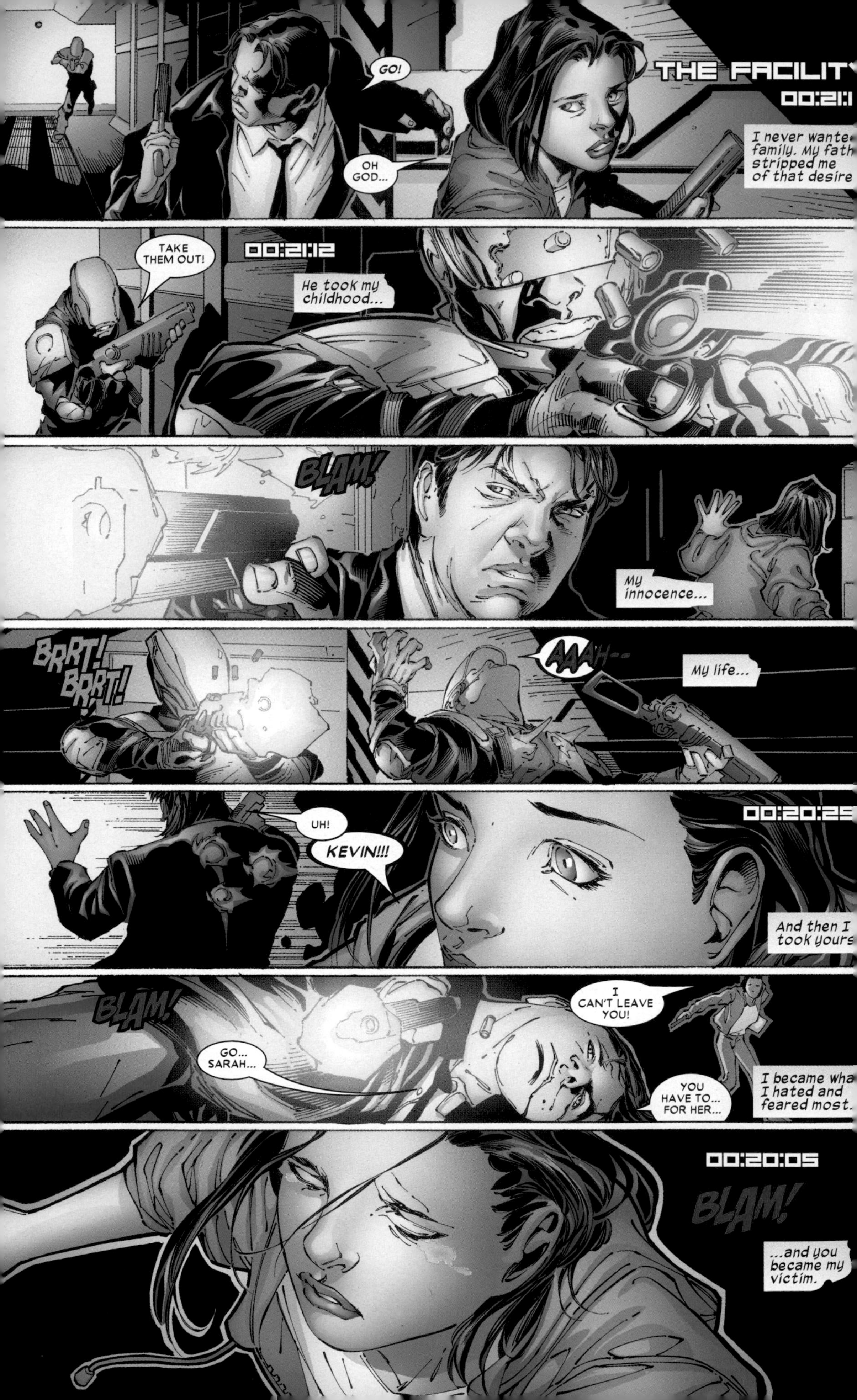
THE FACILITY
00:21:1
GO!
OH GOD...
I never wante family. My fath stripped me of that desire
TAKE THEM OUT!
00:21:12
He took my childhood...
BLAM!
My innocence...
BRRT! BRRT!
AAAH--
My life...
00:20:25
UH!
KEVIN!!!
And then I took yours
BLAM!
I CAN'T LEAVE YOU!
GO... SARAH...
YOU HAVE TO... FOR HER...
I became wha I hated and feared most.
00:20:05
BLAM!
...and you became my victim.

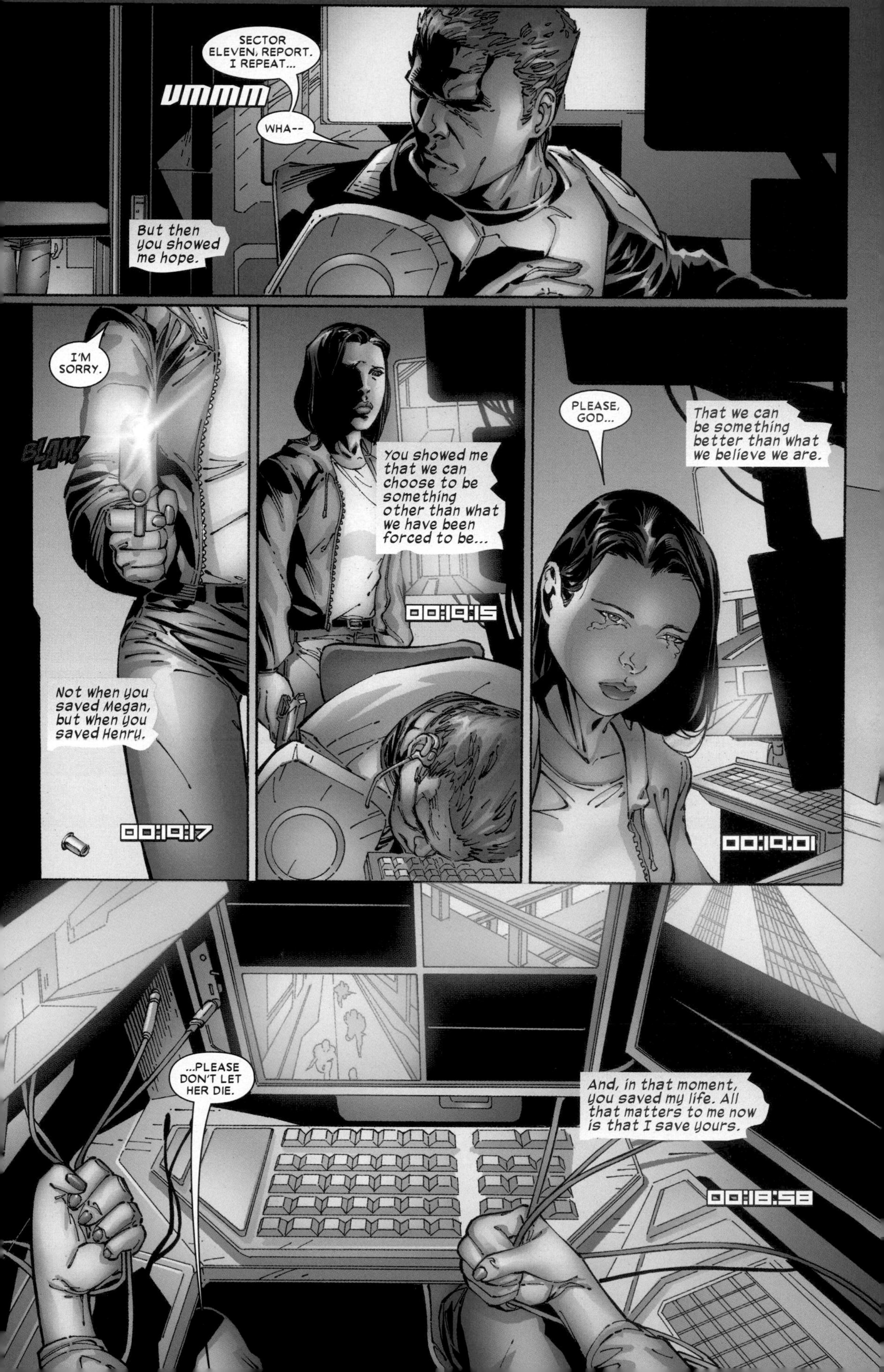
SECTOR ELEVEN, REPORT. I REPEAT...
VMMMM
WHA--
But then you showed me hope.
I'M SORRY.
BLAM!
Not when you saved Megan, but when you saved Henry.
00:19:17
You showed me that we can choose to be something other than what we have been forced to be...
00:19:15
PLEASE, GOD...
That we can be something better than what we believe we are.
00:19:01
...PLEASE DON'T LET HER DIE.
And, in that moment, you saved my life. All that matters to me now is that I save yours.
00:18:58

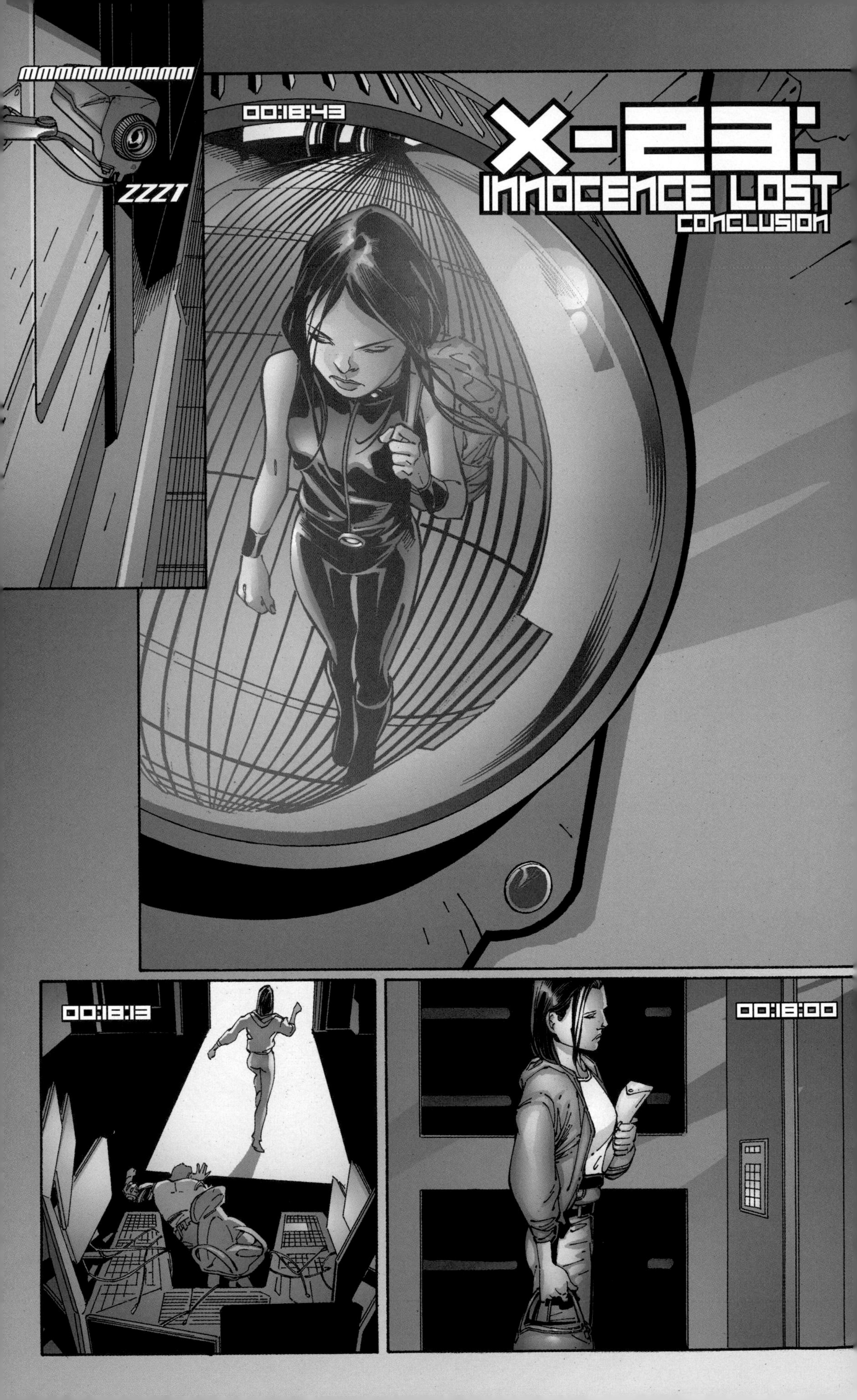
MMMMMMMMMMM
ZZZT
00:18:43
X-23:
INNOCENCE LOST
CONCLUSION
00:18:13
00:18:00

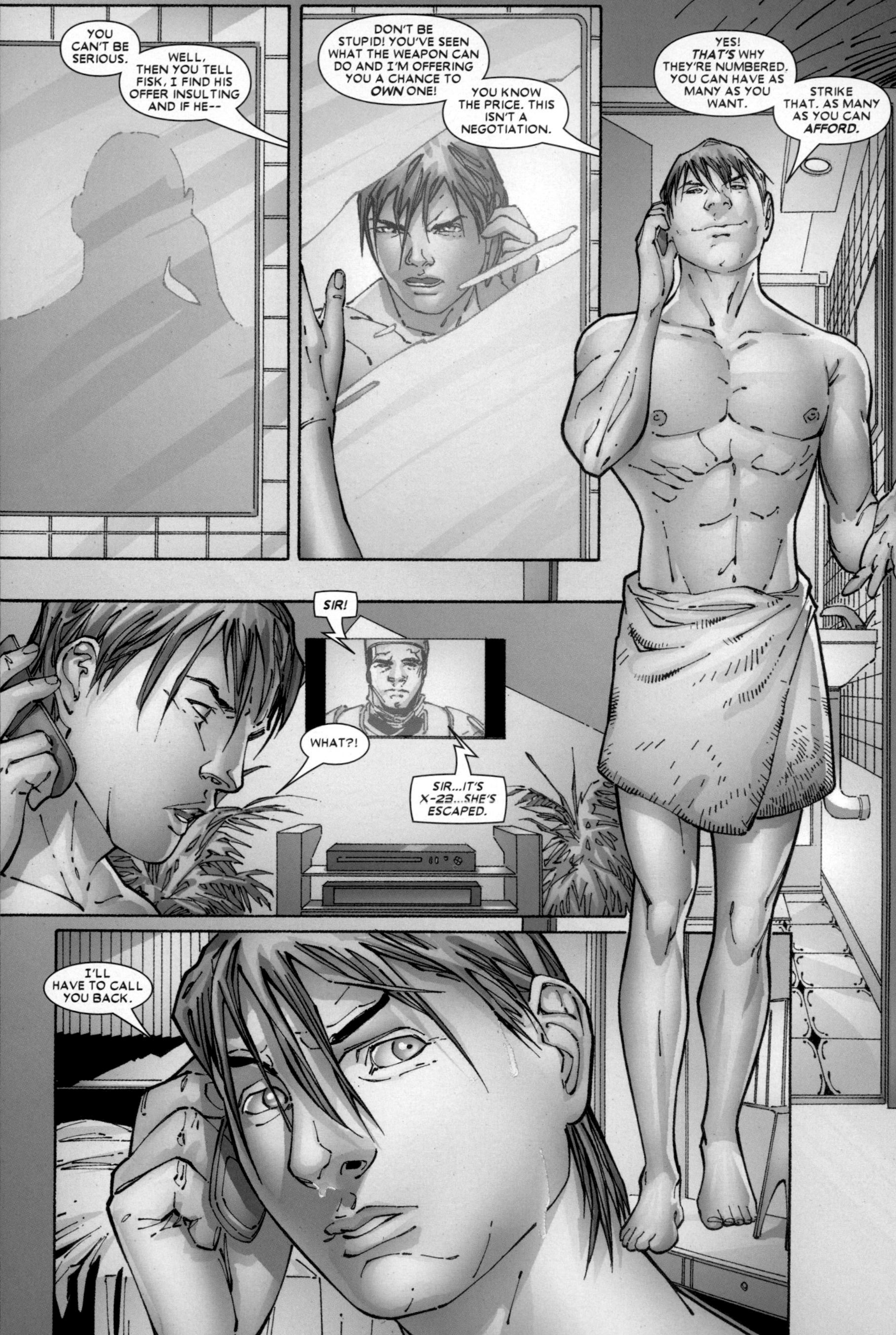
YOU CAN'T BE SERIOUS.
WELL, THEN YOU TELL FISK, I FIND HIS OFFER INSULTING AND IF HE--
DON'T BE STUPID! YOU'VE SEEN WHAT THE WEAPON CAN DO AND I'M OFFERING YOU A CHANCE TO OWN ONE!
YOU KNOW THE PRICE. THIS ISN'T A NEGOTIATION.
YES! THAT'S WHY THEY'RE NUMBERED. YOU CAN HAVE AS MANY AS YOU WANT.
STRIKE THAT. AS MANY AS YOU CAN AFFORD.
SIR!
WHAT?!
SIR...IT'S X-23...SHE'S ESCAPED.
I'LL HAVE TO CALL YOU BACK.

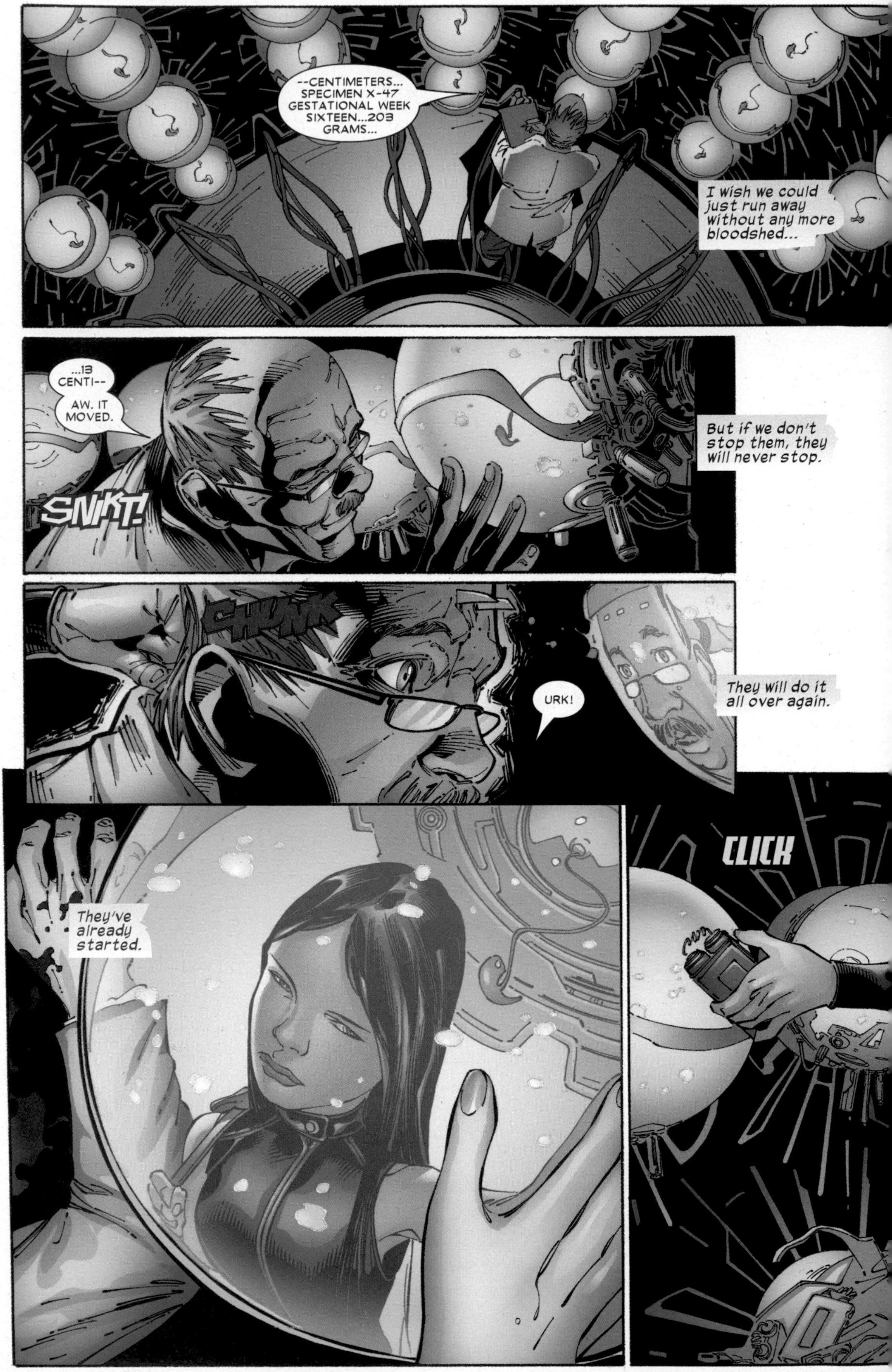
--CENTIMETERS... SPECIMEN X-47 GESTATIONAL WEEK SIXTEEN...203 GRAMS...
I wish we could just run away without any more bloodshed...
...13 CENTI--
AW. IT MOVED.
SNIKT!
But if we don't stop them, they will never stop.
CHUNK
URK!
They will do it all over again.
They've already started.
CLICK

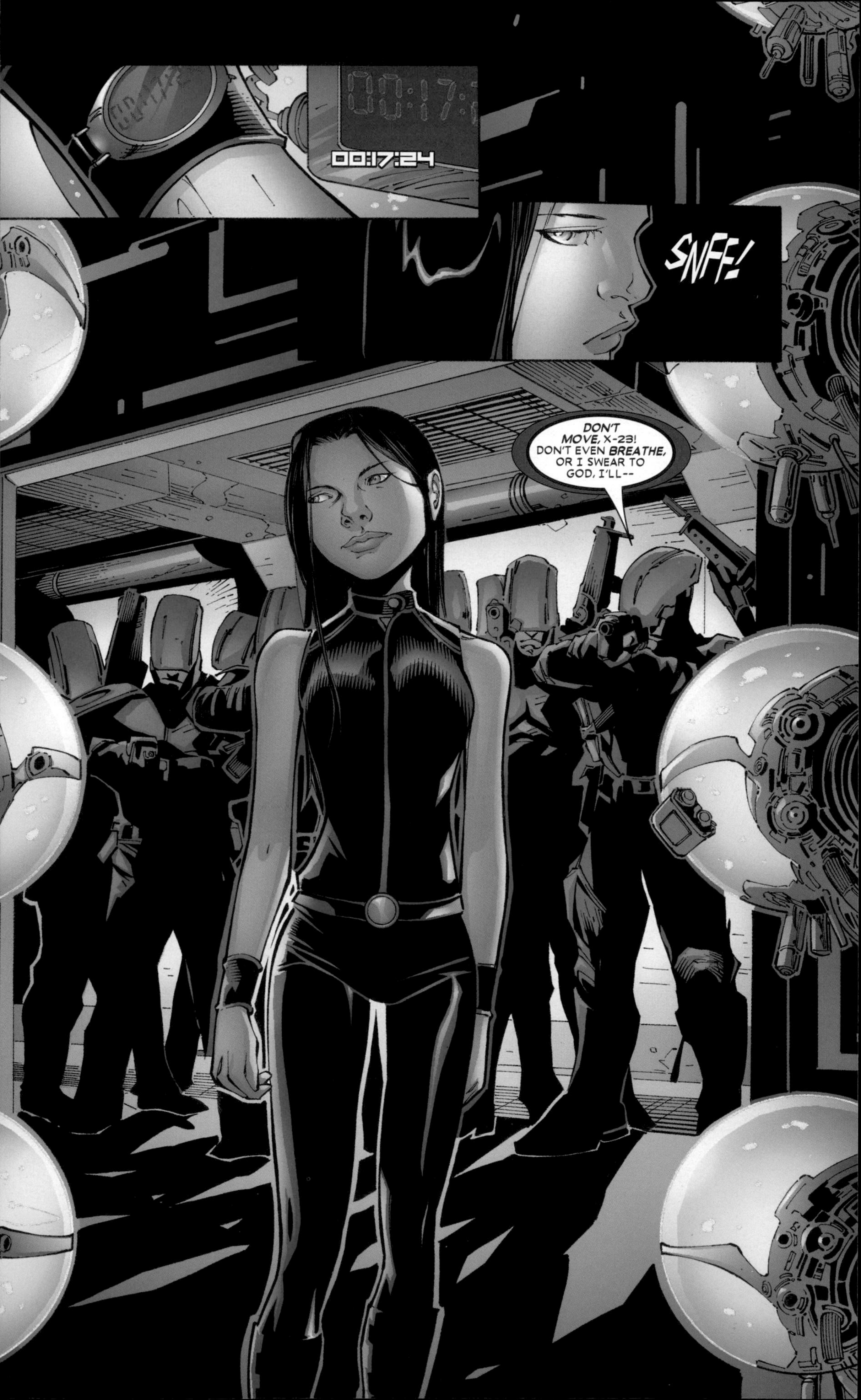
00:17:24
SNFF!
DON'T MOVE, X-23! DON'T EVEN BREATHE, OR I SWEAR TO GOD, I'LL--

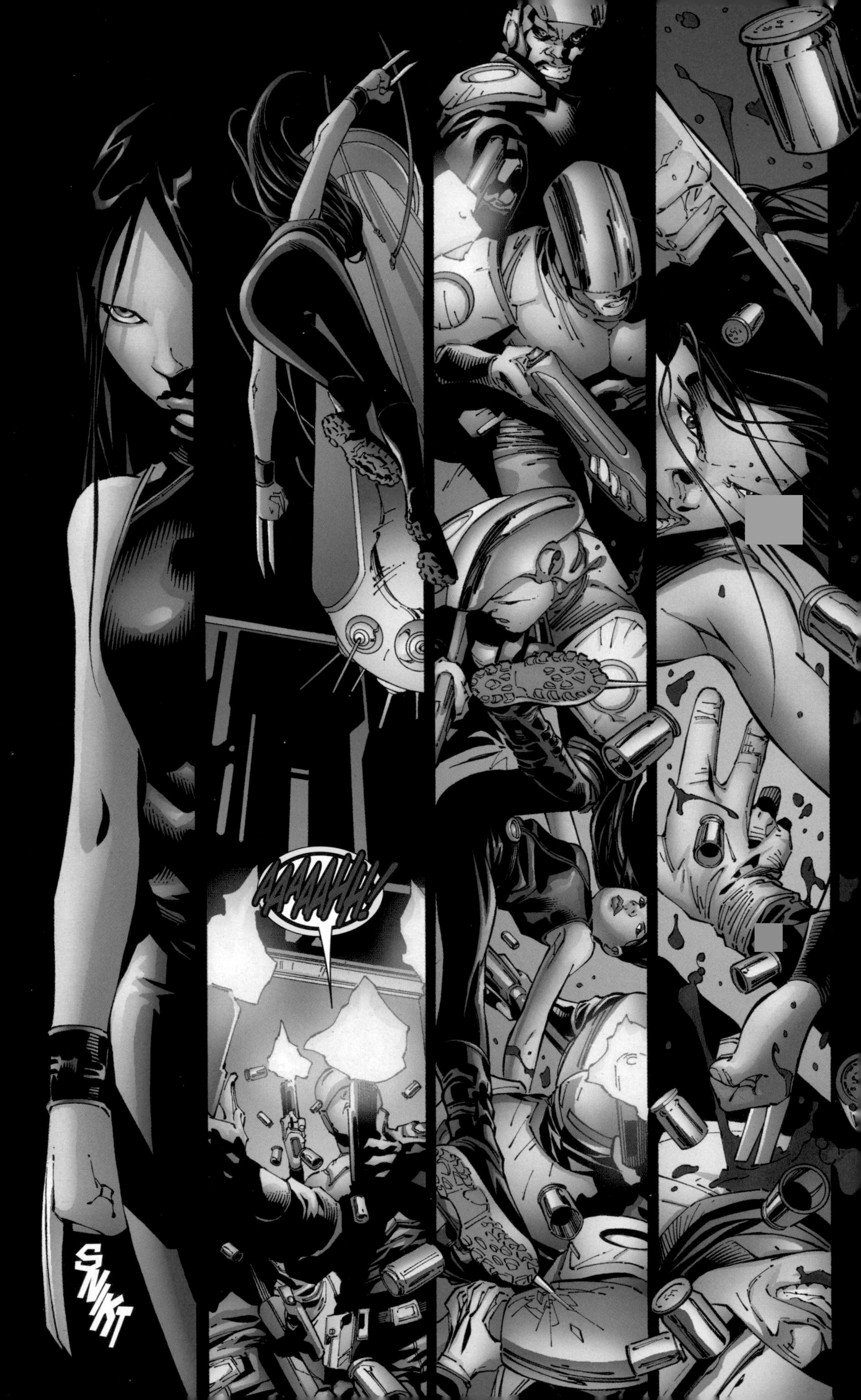
AAAAAHH!
SNIKT

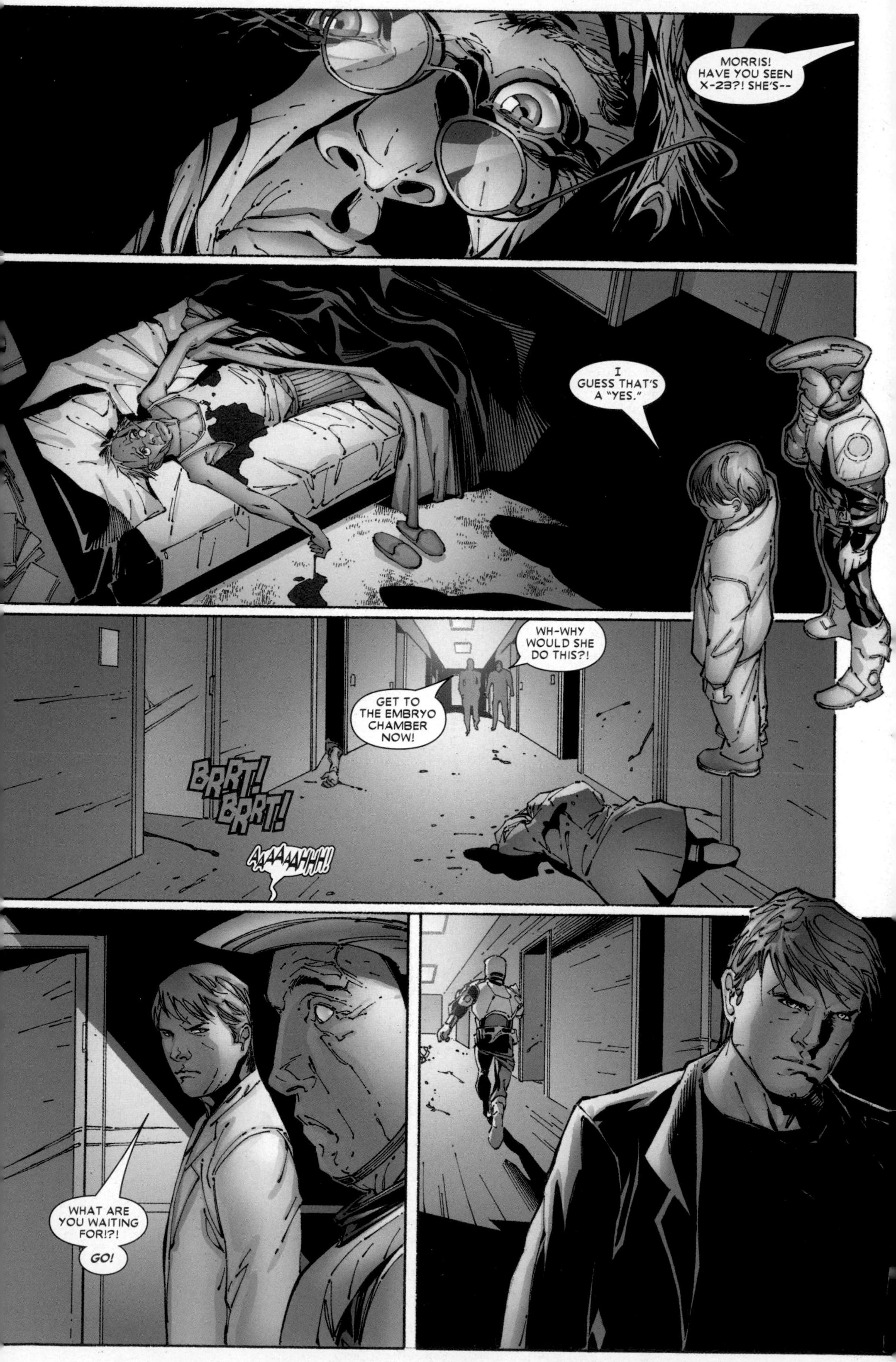
MORRIS! HAVE YOU SEEN X-23?! SHE'S--
I GUESS THAT'S A "YES."
WH-WHY WOULD SHE DO THIS?!
GET TO THE EMBRYO CHAMBER NOW!
BRRT! BRRT!
AAAAAHHH!
WHAT ARE YOU WAITING FOR!?!
GO!

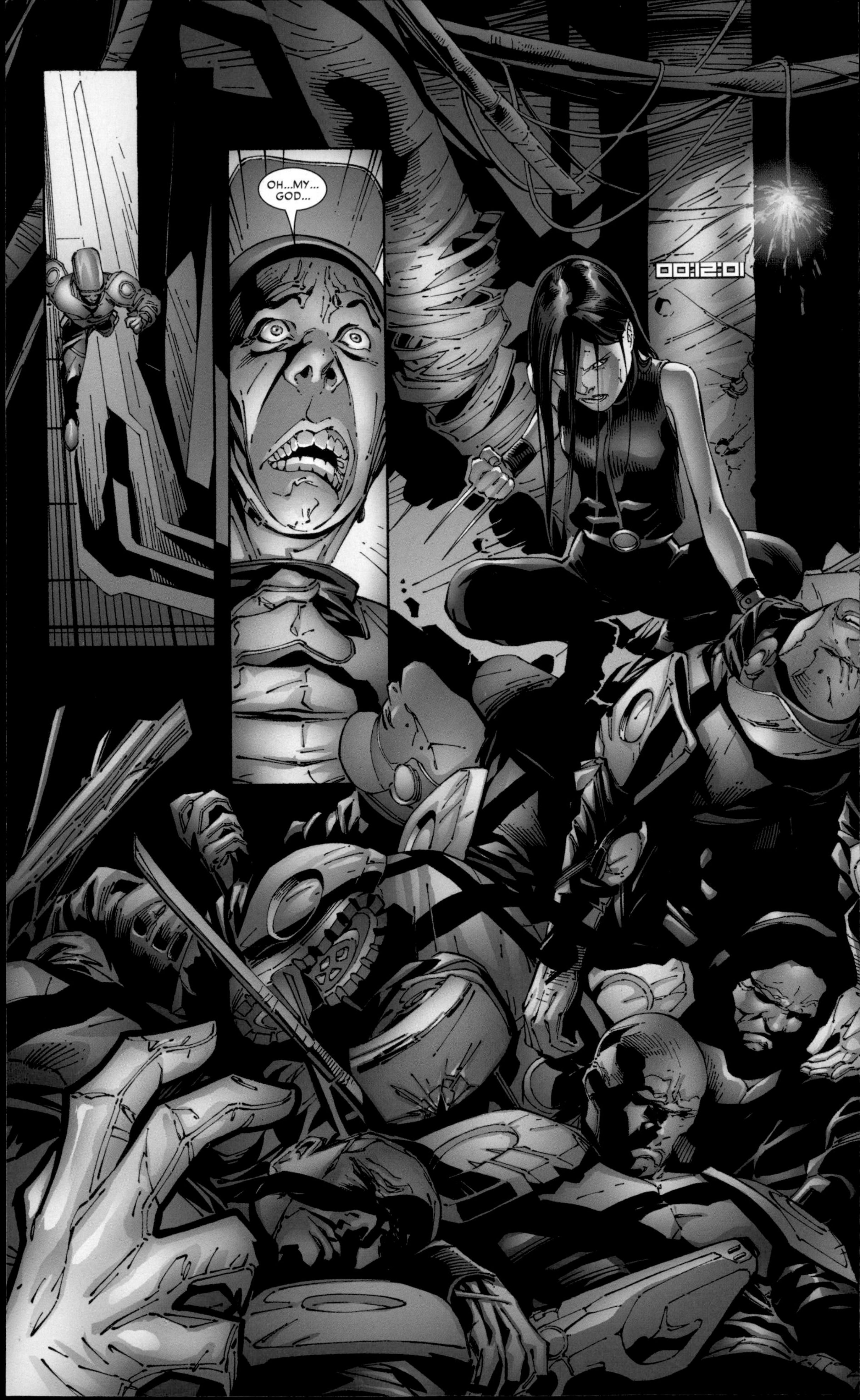
OH...MY...
GOD...
00:12:01

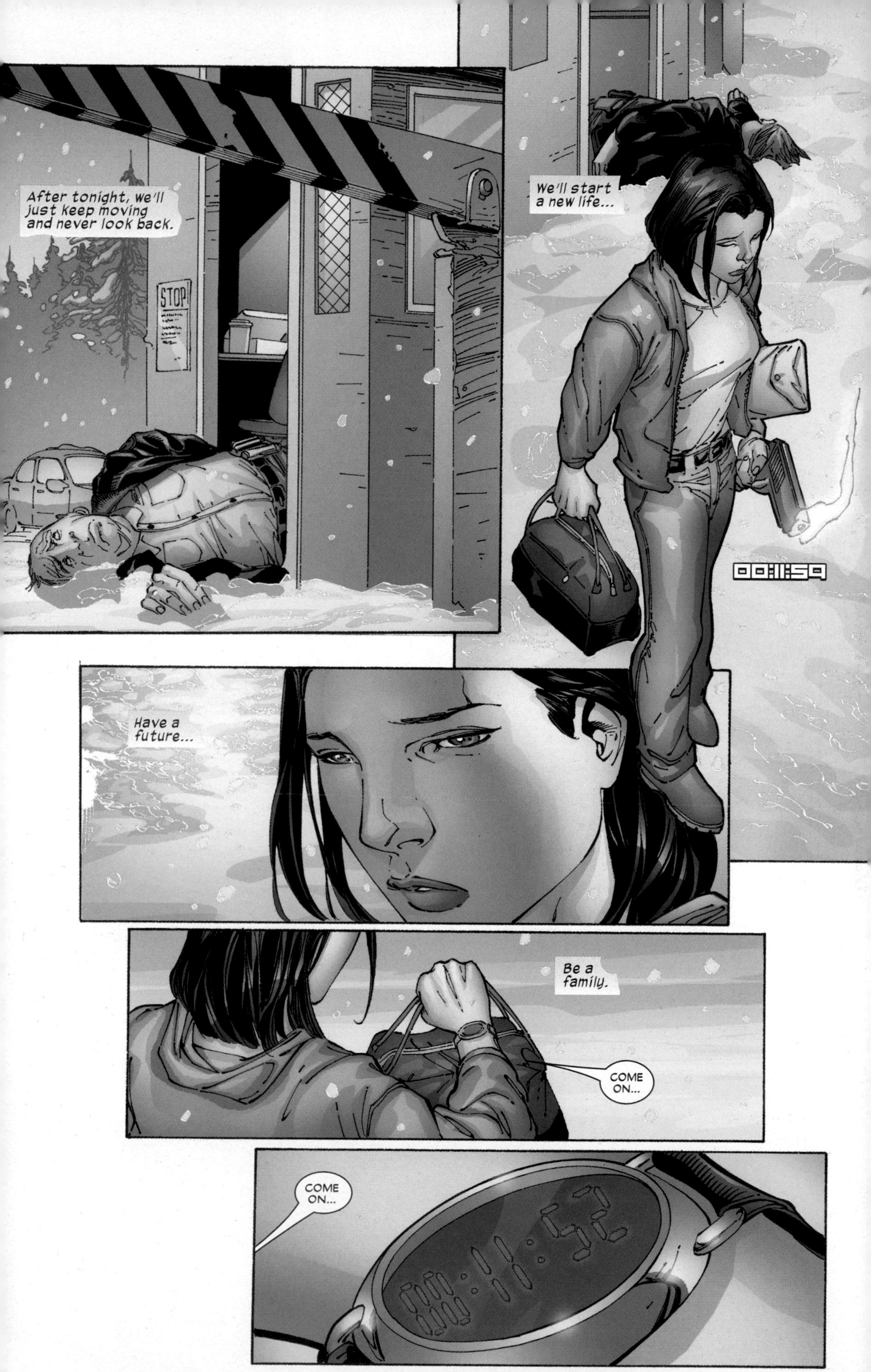
After tonight, we'll just keep moving and never look back.
STOP
We'll start a new life...
00:11:59
Have a future...
Be a family.
COME ON...
COME ON...

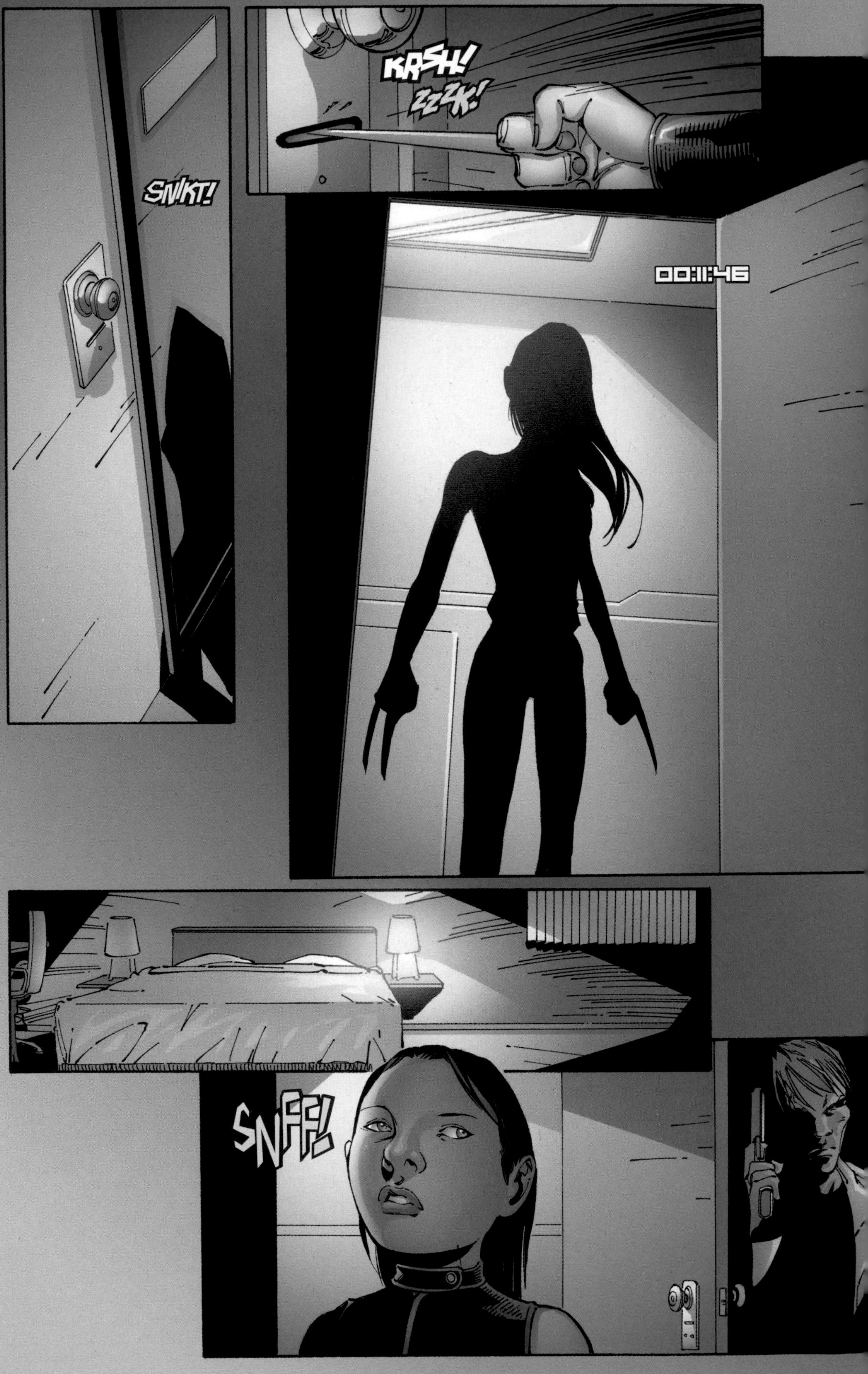

SNIKT!
KRASH!
ZZZK!
00:11:46
SNFF!

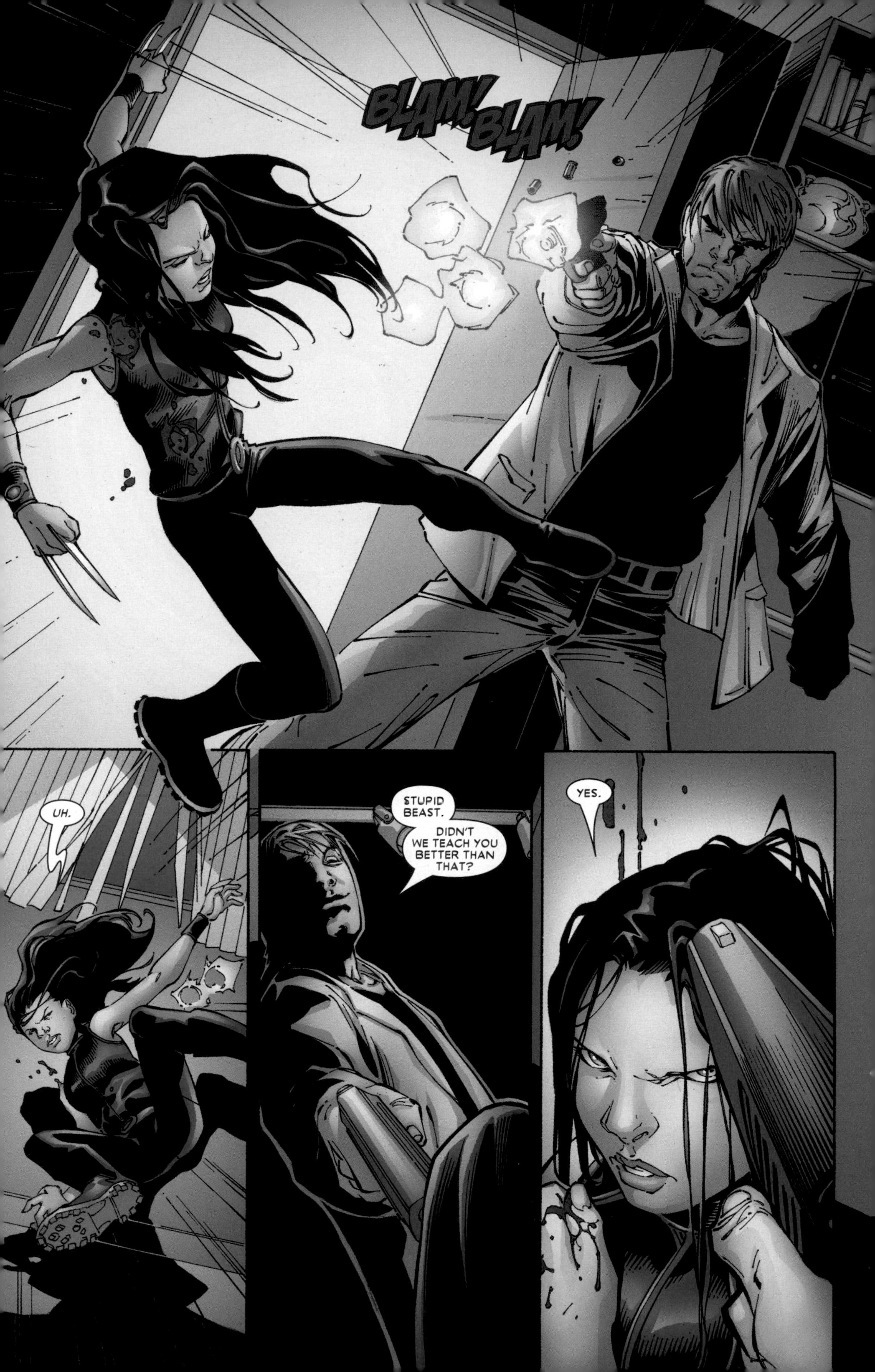
BLAM! BLAM!
UH.
STUPID BEAST.
DIDN'T WE TEACH YOU BETTER THAN THAT?
YES.

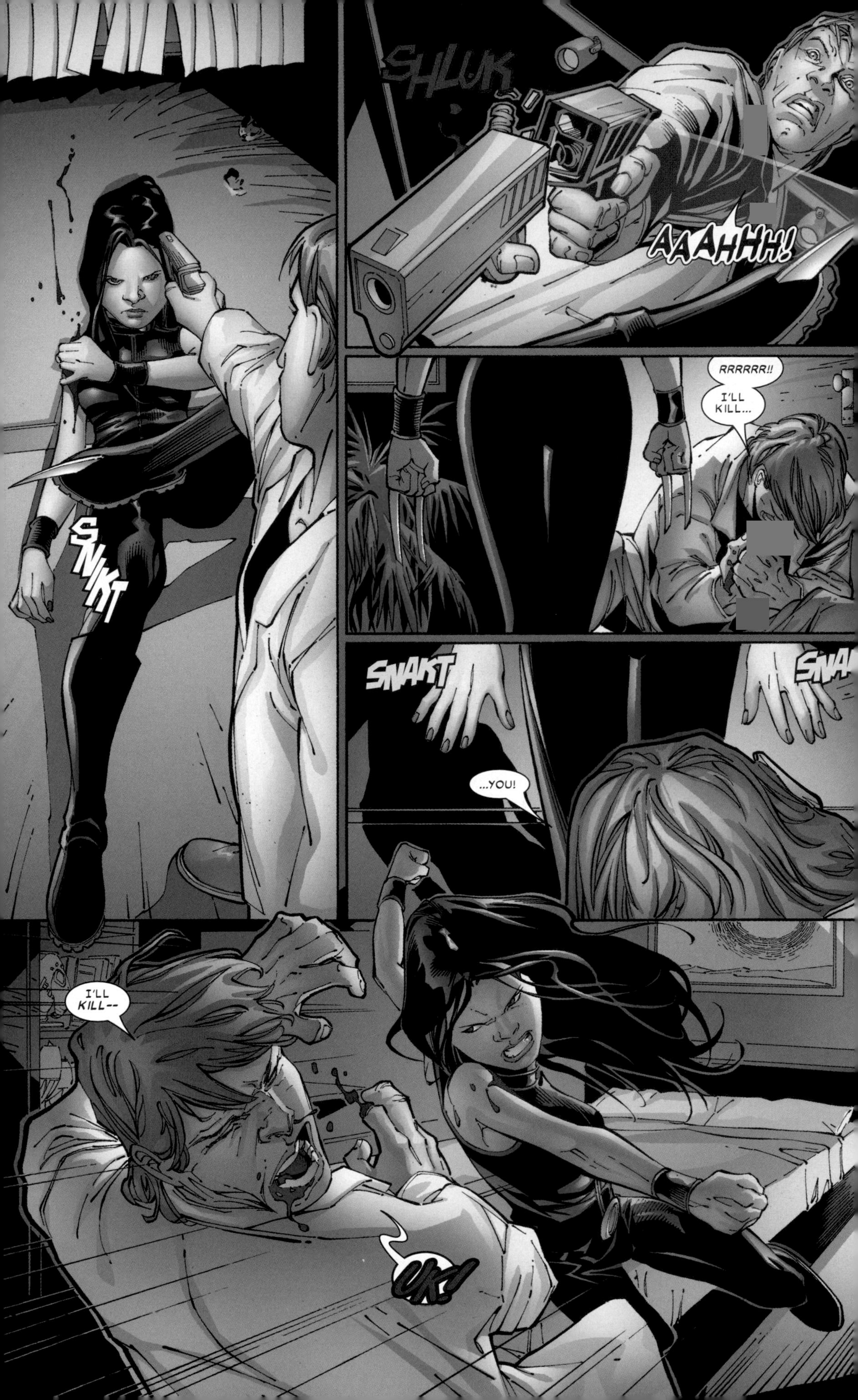
SNIKT
SHLUK
AAAHHH!
RRRRRR!!
I'LL KILL...
SNAKT
...YOU!
I'LL KILL--
UK!

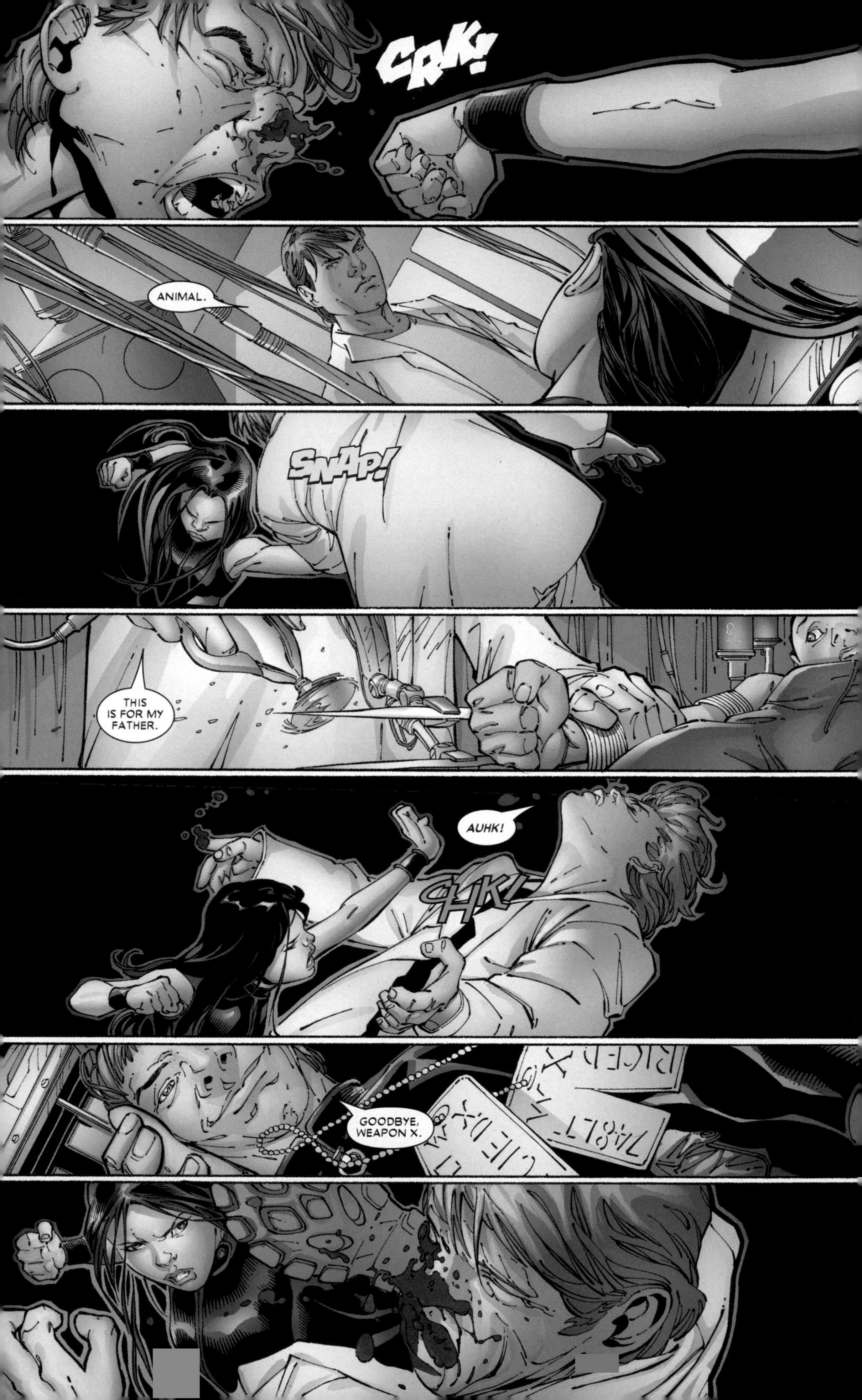
CRK!
ANIMAL.
SNAP!
THIS IS FOR MY FATHER.
AUHK!
CHK!
GOODBYE, WEAPON X.

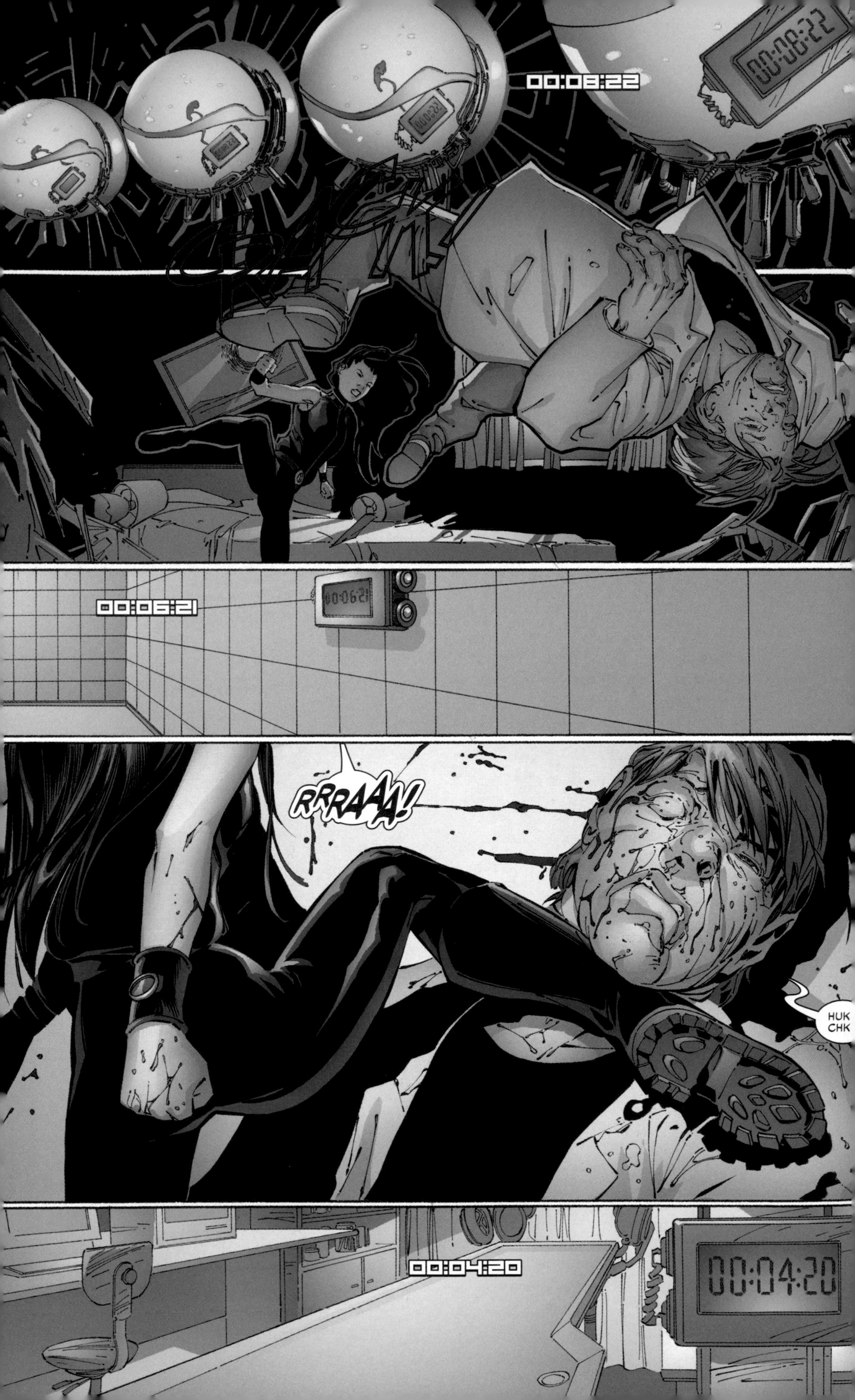

00:08:22
CRACK
00:06:21
RRRAAA!
HUK CHK
00:04:20

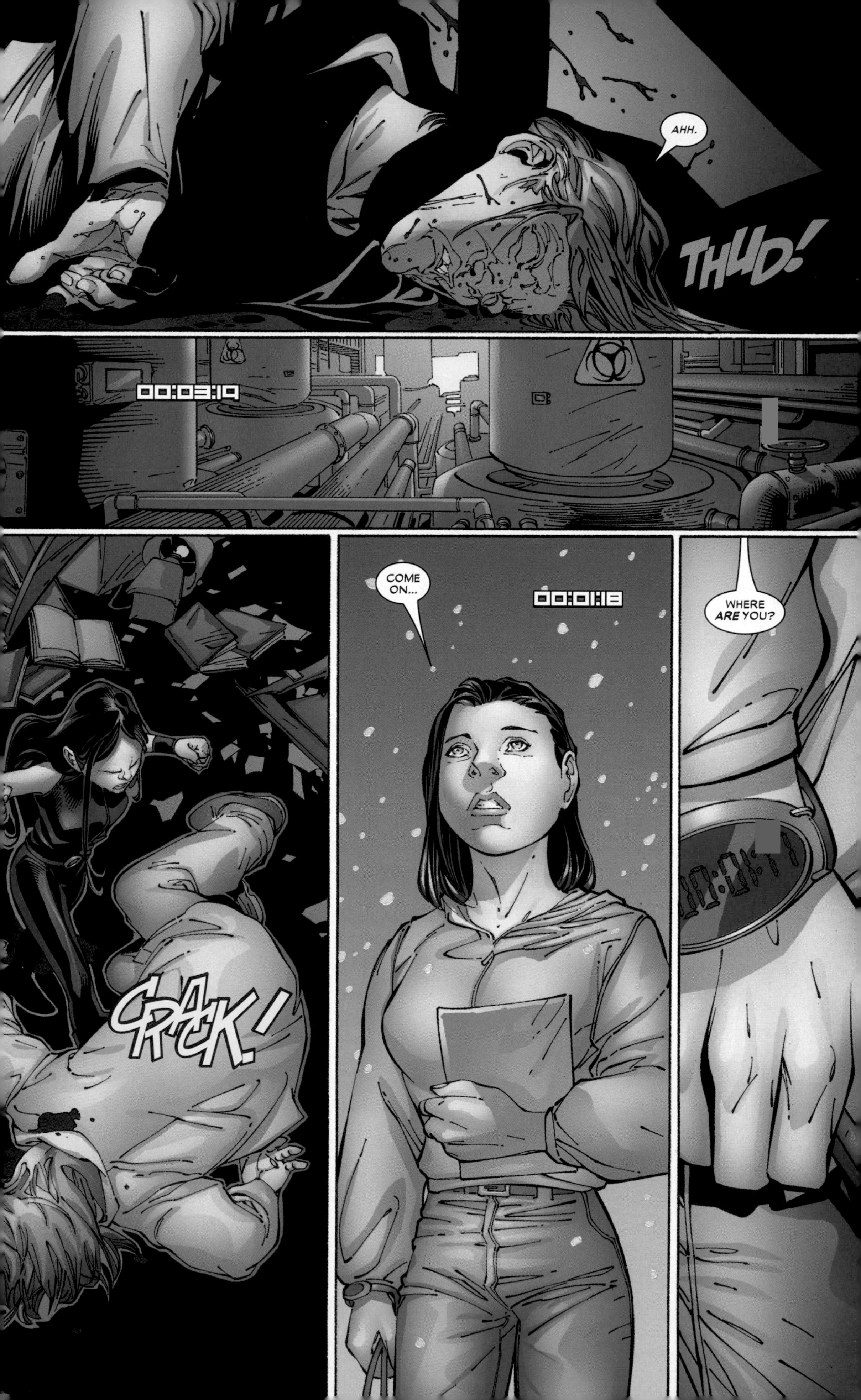
AHH.
THUD!
00:03:19
CRACK!
COME ON...
00:01:18
WHERE ARE YOU?

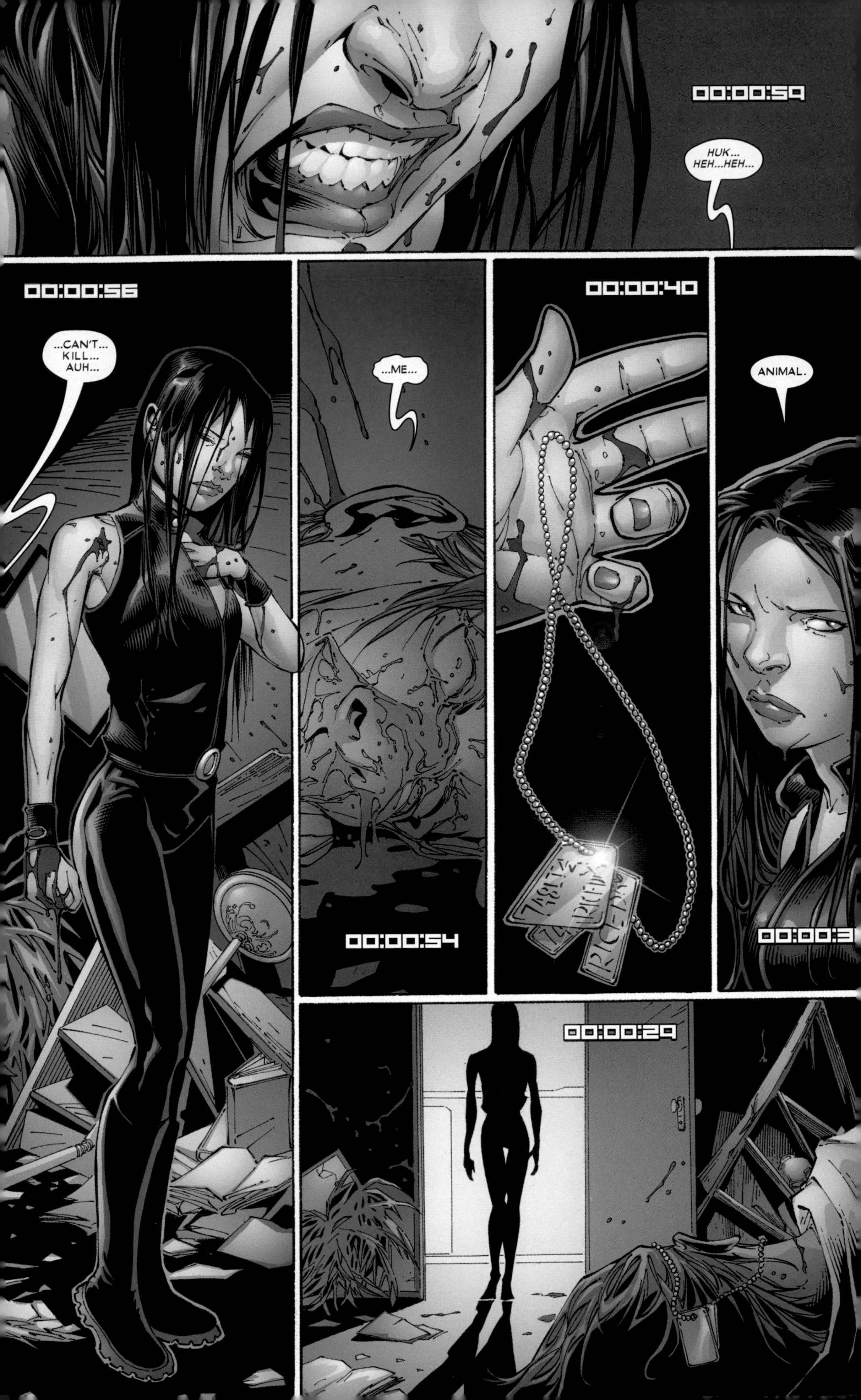
00:00:59
HUK... HEH...HEH...
00:00:56
...CAN'T... KILL... AUH...
...ME...
00:00:54
00:00:40
ANIMAL.
00:00:3
00:00:29

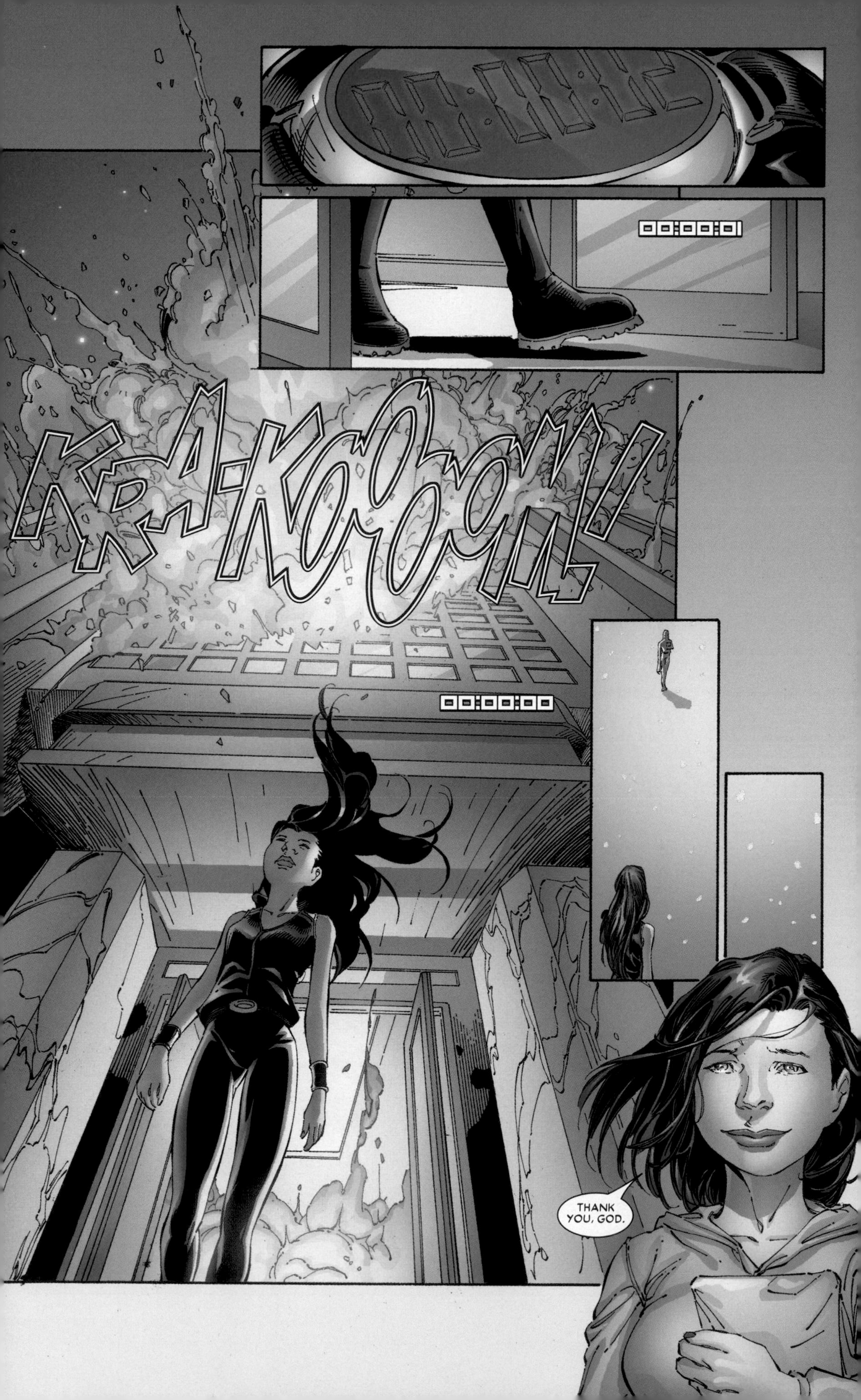
00:00:01
KRA-KOOOOM!
00:00:00
THANK YOU, GOD.

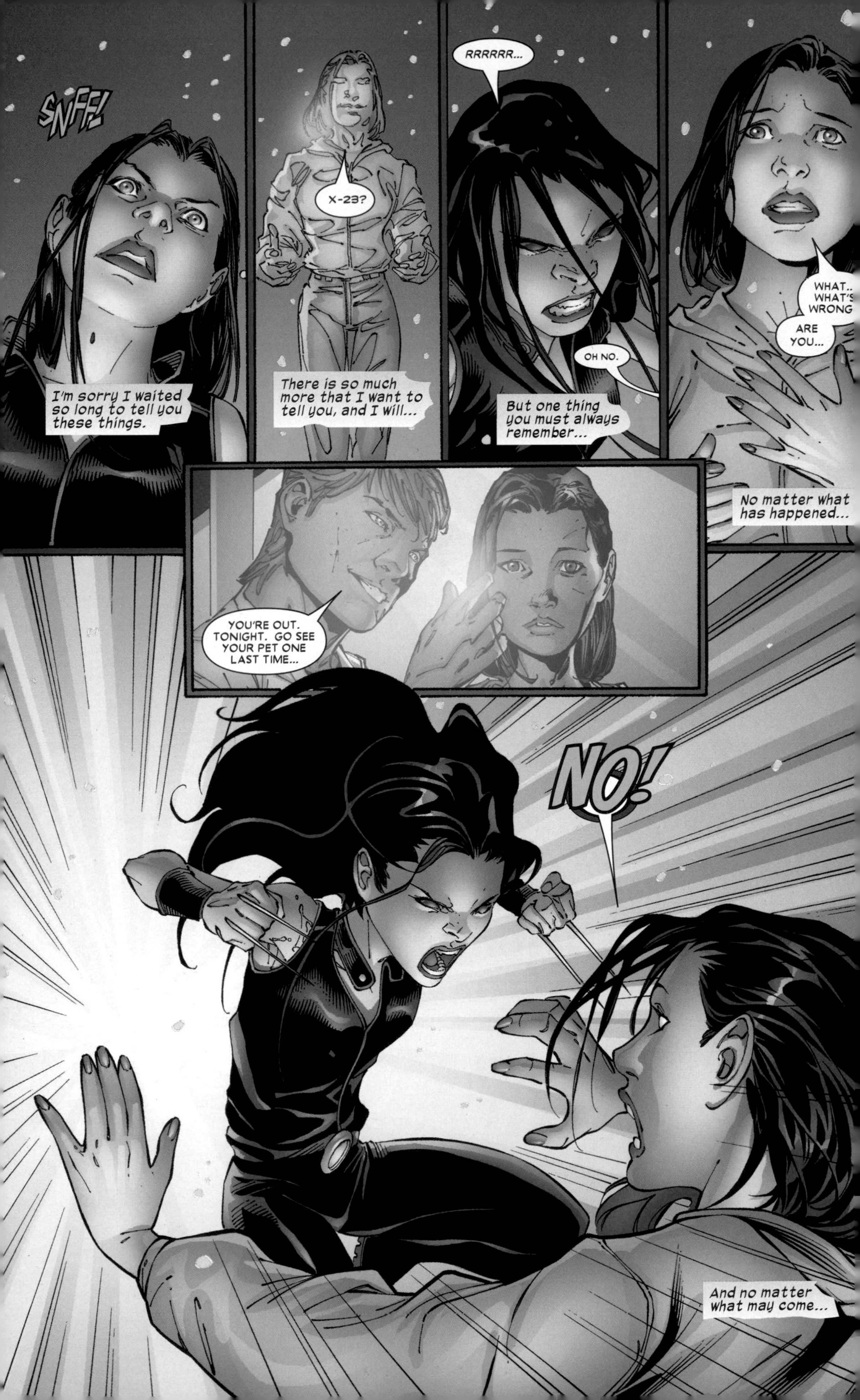
SNFF!
I'm sorry I waited so long to tell you these things.
X-23?
There is so much more that I want to tell you, and I will...
RRRRRR...
OH NO.
But one thing you must always remember...
WHAT... WHAT'S WRONG
ARE YOU...
No matter what has happened...
YOU'RE OUT. TONIGHT. GO SEE YOUR PET ONE LAST TIME...
NO!
And no matter what may come...

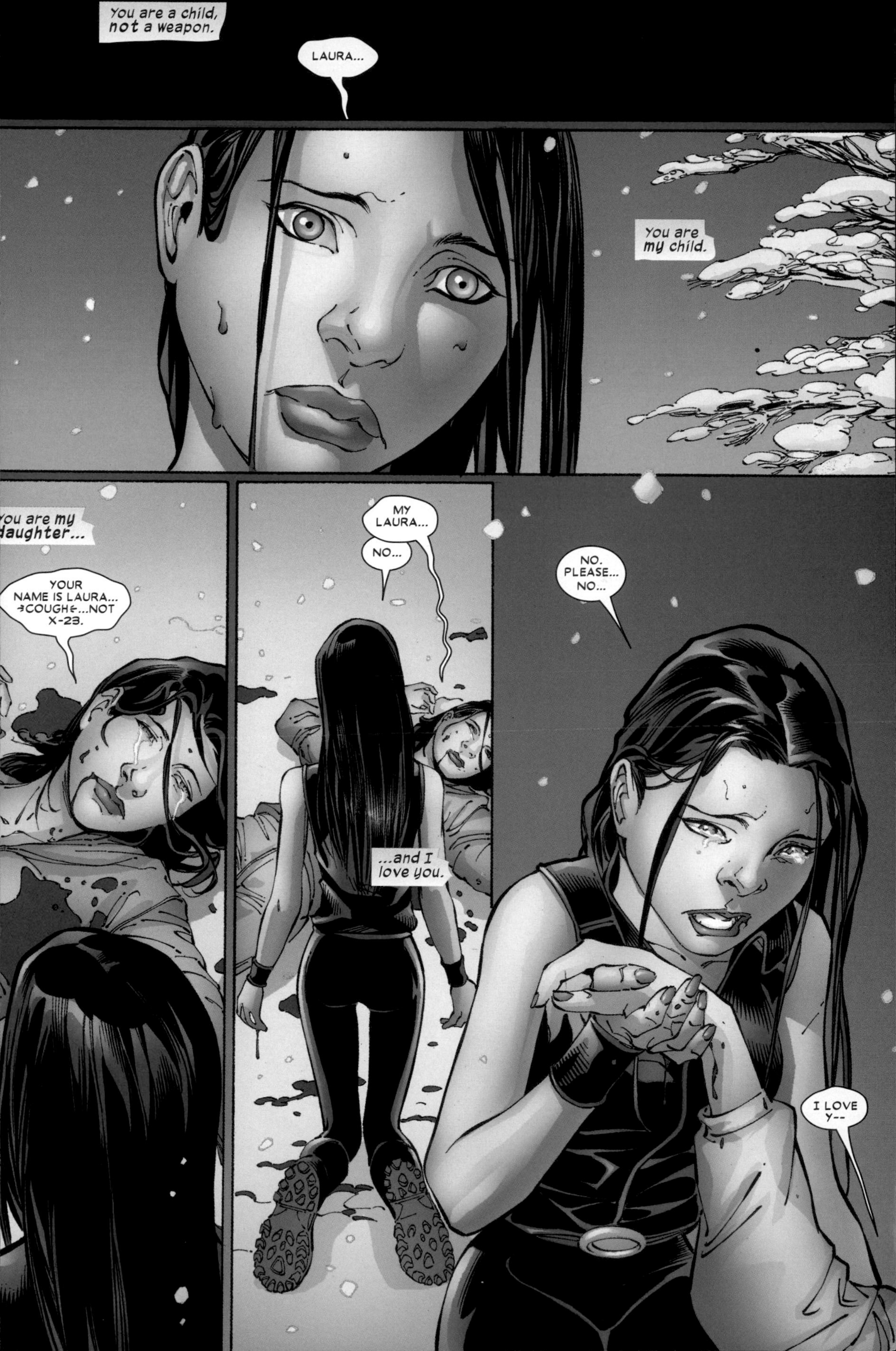

You are a child, not a weapon.
LAURA...
You are my child.
You are my daughter...
YOUR NAME IS LAURA... ⇒COUGH⇐...NOT X-23.
MY LAURA...
NO...
...and I love you.
NO. PLEASE... NO...
I LOVE Y--

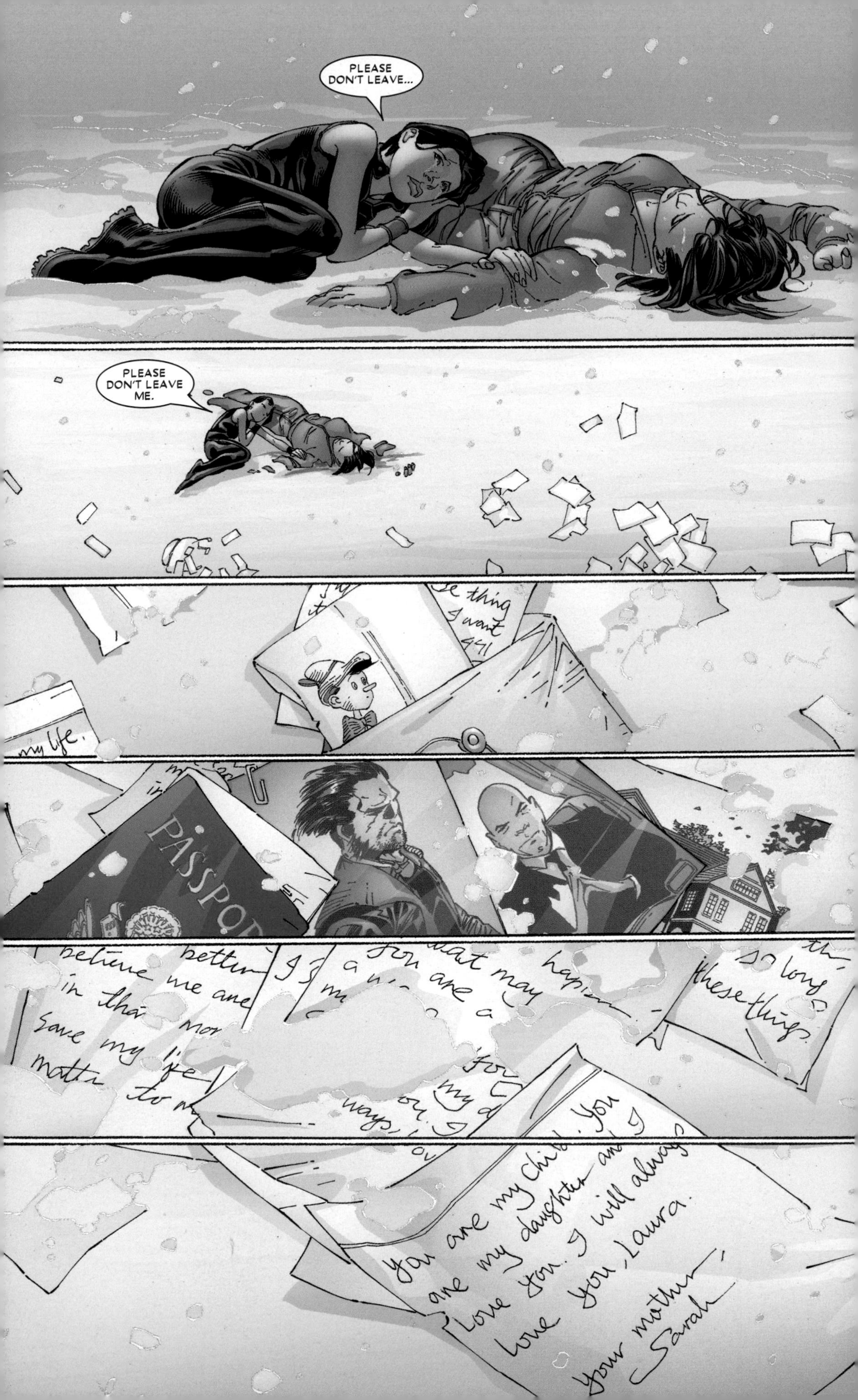
PLEASE DON'T LEAVE...
PLEASE DON'T LEAVE ME.
my life.
these things.
You are my child. You
are my daughter and I
Love you. I will always
Love you, Laura.
Your mother
Sarah

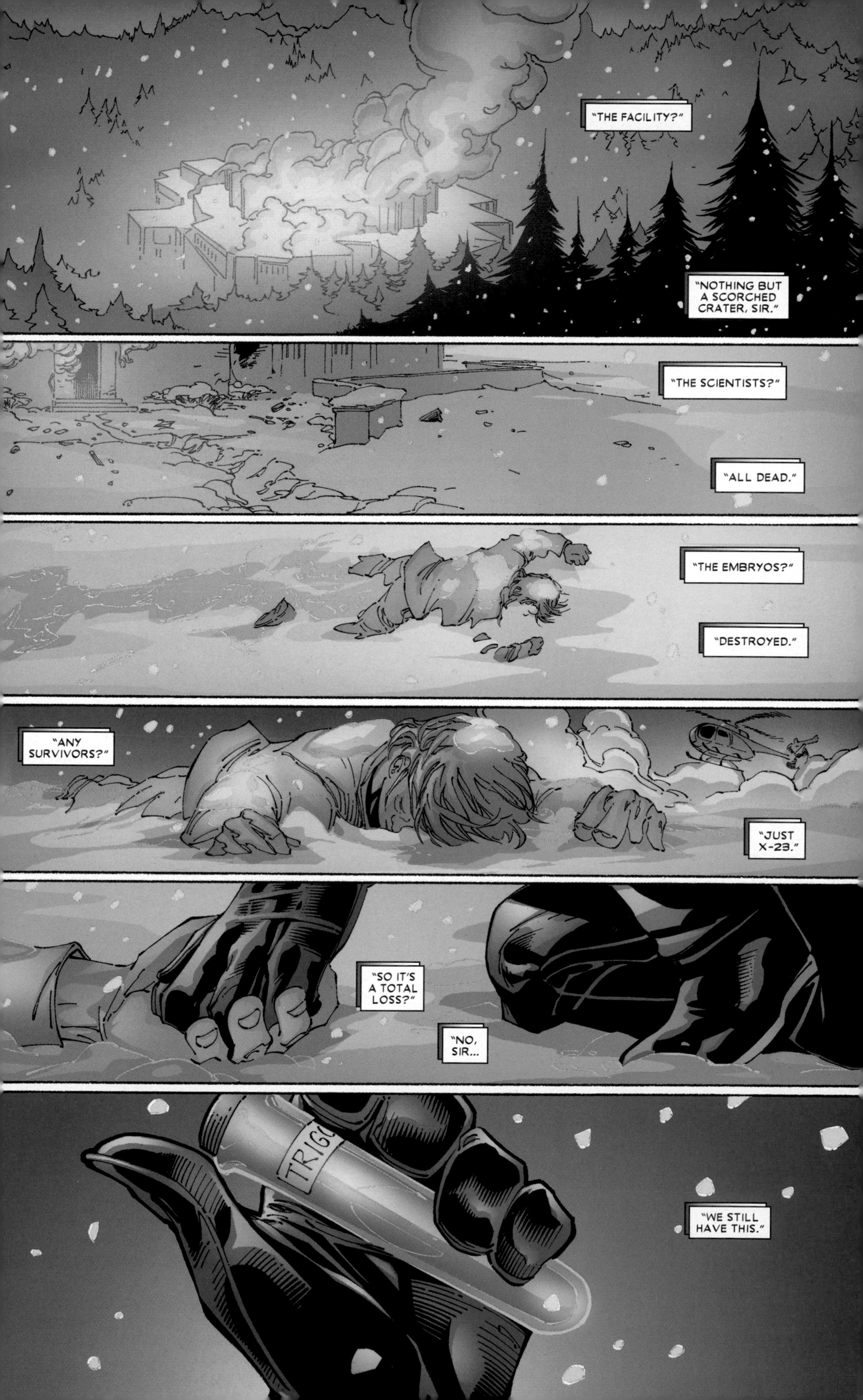
"THE FACILITY?"
"NOTHING BUT A SCORCHED CRATER, SIR."
"THE SCIENTISTS?"
"ALL DEAD."
"THE EMBRYOS?"
"DESTROYED."
"ANY SURVIVORS?"
"JUST X-23."
"SO IT'S A TOTAL LOSS?"
"NO, SIR...
"WE STILL HAVE THIS."

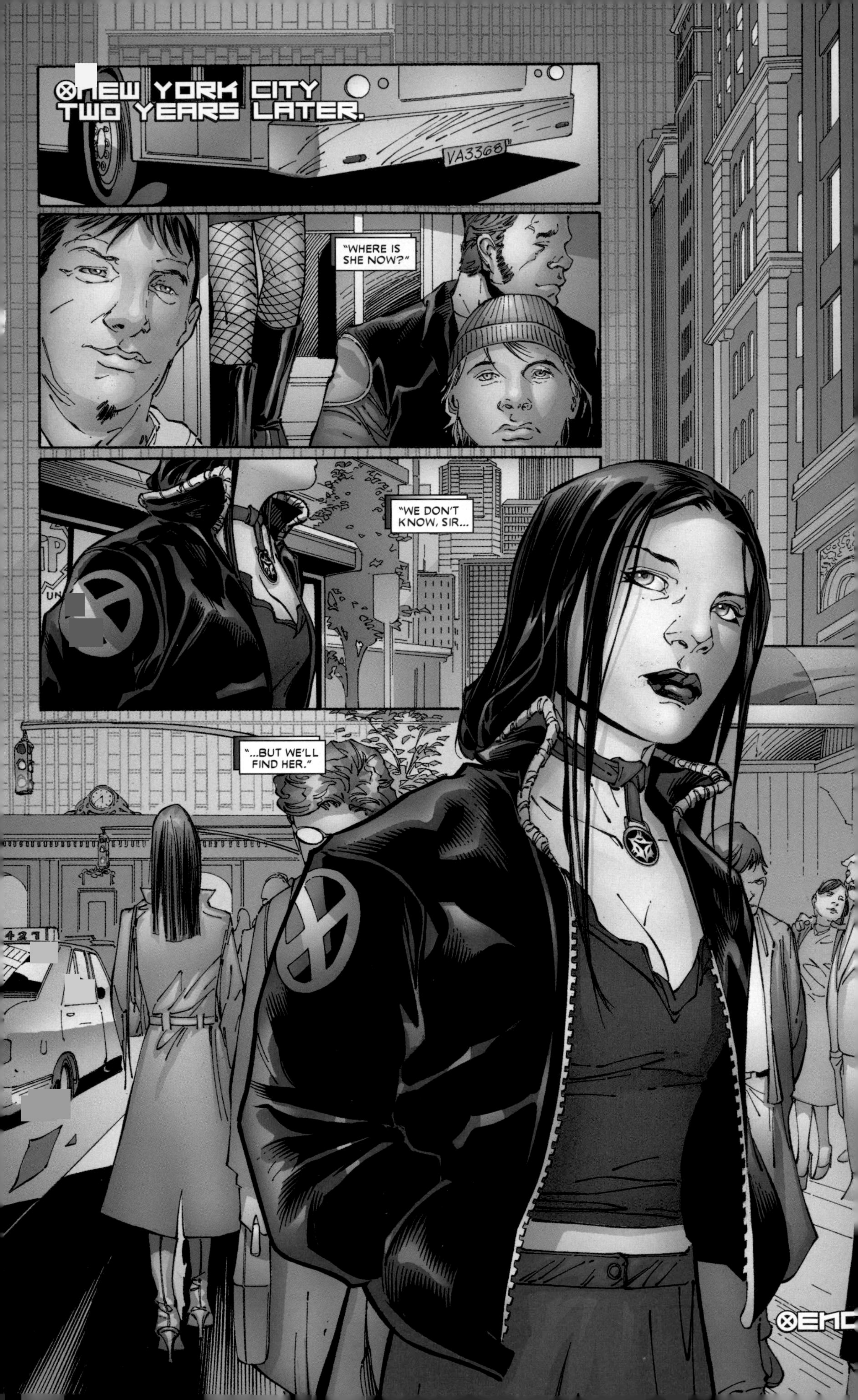
NEW YORK CITY
TWO YEARS LATER.
"WHERE IS SHE NOW?"
"WE DON'T KNOW, SIR...
"...BUT WE'LL FIND HER."
END